Kaltrina Nuredini

Altmetrics for Digital Libraries

Concepts, Applications,
Evaluation, and Recommendations

Logos Verlag Berlin

λογος

Bibliografische Information der Deutschen Nationalbibliothek

Die Deutsche Nationalbibliothek verzeichnet diese Publikation in der Deutschen Nationalbibliografie; detaillierte bibliografische Daten sind im Internet über http://dnb.d-nb.de abrufbar.

ISBN 978-3-8325-5309-8

Logos Verlag Berlin GmbH
Georg-Knorr-Str. 4, Geb. 10,
D-12681 Berlin
Germany

Tel.:   +49 (0)30 / 42 85 10 90
Fax: +49 (0)30 / 42 85 10 92
http://www.logos-verlag.de

Altmetrics for Digital Libraries: Concepts, Applications, Evaluation, and Recommendations

Dissertation

zur Erlangung des akademischen Grades
Doktor der Ingenieurwissenschaften
(Dr.-Ing.)

an der Technischen Fakultät
der Christian-Albrechts-Universität zu Kiel

Kaltrina Nuredini

Kiel

2021

folgendes stehen:

1. Gutachterin: Prof. Dr. Isabella Peters
2. Gutachter: Prof. Dr. Klaus Tochtermann
Datum der mündlichen Prüfung: 26.03.2021

Zum Druck genehmigt: 06.06.2021

Dedication

In loving memory of my beloved younger brother Vigan Nuredini, who always believed in me.

Acknowledgments

I would like to express my sincere gratitude to my supervisor Prof. Dr. Isabella Peters for supporting me during these past 6 years and for providing me guidance, encouragement, and kind advice throughout my research. She has been a key inspirational role model within my journey.

I would also like to sincerely thank Prof. Dr. Klaus Tochtermann and Dr. Tamara Pianos for allowing me to work and research in such an excellent environment at ZBW (Leibniz Information Centre for Economic). Moreover, a special thanks to my ZBW colleagues, especially Dr. Nicholas Fraser and Steffen Lemke, for their useful and inspiring feedback on my PhD. Thank you to Dr. Guido Scherp and Dr. Atif Latif for their generous feedback that helped me throughout the way. I would also like to thank Bernd Schlünsen for his collaboration and support with integrating altmetrics data in some articles of EconBiz, which I used for my survey.

In addition, I would also appreciate Thomas Arpe from the University of Kiel (CAU) for helping me with any server-related issues that were encountered when hosting and accessing my research data.

Likewise, I owe thanks to Altmetric.com and Mendeley for offering me the opportunity to access and use the altmetric data for this research.

To my wonderful husband, Nico Wichmann, I thank you not only for dealing with the challenges of PhD life but also for supporting me during hard times and while writing this thesis.

Last but not least, I would like to thank my parents, who, in their worse days, showed support and motivated me to continue to study and research. Finally, I would like to thank my lovely sister, who was always there for me when I needed her most.

Abstract

The volume of scientific literature is rapidly increasing, which has led to researchers becoming overloaded by the number of articles that they have available for reading and difficulties in estimating their quality and relevance (e.g., based on their research interests). Library portals, in these circumstances, are increasingly getting more relevant by using quality indicators that can help researchers during their research discovery process. Several evaluation methods (e.g., citations, Journal Impact Factor, and peer-reviews) have been used and suggested by library portals to help researchers filter out the relevant articles (e.g., articles that have received high citations) for their needs. However, in some cases, these methods have been criticized, and a number of weaknesses have been identified and discussed. For example, citations usually take a long time to appear, and some articles that are important can remain uncited.

With the growing presence of social media today, new alternative indicators, known as "altmetrics," have been encountered and proposed as complementary indicators to traditional measures (i.e., bibliometrics). They can help to identify the online attention received by articles, which might act as a further indicator for research assessment. One often mentioned advantage of these alternative indicators is, for example, that they appear much faster compared to citations. A large number of studies have explored altmetrics for different disciplines, but few studies have reported about altmetrics in the fields of Economics and Business Studies. Furthermore, no studies can be found so far that analyzed altmetrics within these disciplines with respect to libraries and information overload.

Thus, this thesis explores opportunities for introducing altmetrics as new method for filtering relevant articles (in library portals) within the discipline of Economic and Business Studies literature. To achieve this objective, we have worked on four main aspects of investigating altmetrics and altmetrics data, respectively, of which the results can be used to fill the gap in this field of research.

(1) We first highlight to what extent altmetric information from the two altmetric providers Mendeley and Altmetric.com is present within the journals of Economics and Business Studies. Based on the coverage, we demonstrate that altmetrics data are sparse in these disciplines, and when considering altmetrics data for real-world applications (e.g., in libraries), higher aggregation levels, such as journal level, can overcome their sparsity well.

(2) We perform and discuss the correlations of citations on article and journal levels between different types and sources of altmetrics. We could show that Mendeley counts are positive and strongly correlated with citation counts on both article and journal levels, whereas other indicators such as Twitter counts and Altmetric Attention Score are significantly correlated only on journal level. With these correlations, we could suggest Mendeley counts for Economic and Business Studies journals/articles as an alternative indicator to citations.

(3) In conjunction with the findings related to altmetrics in Economics and Business Studies journals, we discuss three use cases derived from three ZBW personas in terms of altmetrics.

We investigate the use of altmetrics data for potential users with interests in new trends, social media platforms and journal rankings.

(4) We investigated the behavior of economic researchers using a survey by exploring the usefulness of different altmetrics on journal level while they make decisions for selecting one article for reading. According to the user evaluation results, we demonstrate that altmetrics are not well known and understood by the economic community. However, this does not mean that these indicators are not helpful at all to economists. Instead, it brings forward the problem of how to introduce altmetrics to the economic community in the right way using which characteristics (e.g., as visible numbers attached at library records or behind the library's relevance ranking system).

Considering the aforementioned findings of this thesis, we can suggest several forms of presenting altmetric information in library portals, using EconBiz as the proof-of-concept, with the intention to assist both researchers and libraries to identify relevant journals or articles (e.g., highly mentioned online and recently published) for their need and to cope with the information overload.

Abstrakt

Das Volumen der wissenschaftlichen Literatur nimmt rasch zu, was dazu geführt hat, dass Forscher durch die Anzahl der Artikel, die sie zum Lesen zur Verfügung haben, und durch Schwierigkeiten bei der Einschätzung ihrer Qualität und Relevanz (z. B. basierend auf ihren Forschungsinteressen) überlastet werden. Unter diesen Umständen sind Bibliotheksportale zunehmend daran interessiert, Qualitätsindikatoren zu verwenden, die Forschern bei ihrer Suche nach geeigneter Literatur helfen können. Verschiedene Bewertungsmethoden (z. B. Zitationen, Journal Impact Factor, Peer-Reviews usw.) wurden von Bibliotheksportalen verwendet und vorgeschlagen, um Forschern dabei zu helfen, die relevanten Artikel (z. B. Artikel, die viele Zitationen erhalten haben) für ihre Bedürfnisse herauszufiltern. In einigen Fällen wurden diese Methoden jedoch kritisiert und eine Reihe von Schwachstellen identifiziert und diskutiert. Zum Beispiel dauert es normalerweise lange, bis Zitate erscheinen, und einige wichtige Artikel bleiben ohne Zitationen.

Mit der zunehmenden Präsenz von sozialen Medien wurden neue alternative Indikatoren bekannt als „Altmetrics" entwickelt und als ergänzende Indikatoren zu traditionellen Maßnahmen (d. h. bibliometrische Indikatoren) vorgeschlagen. Sie können als weiterer Indikator für die Bewertung der Forschung dienen, indem sie dazu beitragen, die Online-Aufmerksamkeit von Artikeln zu identifizieren. Ein häufig genannter Vorteil dieser alternativen Indikatoren ist beispielsweise, dass sie im Vergleich zu Zitationen viel schneller erscheinen. Eine große Anzahl von Studien hat Altmetrics für verschiedene Disziplinen untersucht, aber nur wenige Studien haben über Altmetrics in den Bereichen der Volks- und Betriebswirtschaftslehre berichtet. Darüber hinaus können bisher keine Studien gefunden werden, die Altmetrics innerhalb dieser Disziplinen in Bezug auf Bibliotheken und Informationsüberflutung analysieren.

In dieser Arbeit werden daher Möglichkeiten untersucht, Altmetrics als neue Methode zum Filtern relevanter Artikel (in Bibliotheksportalen) innerhalb der Disziplinen der wirtschaftswissenschaftlichen Literatur einzuführen. Um dieses Ziel zu erreichen, haben wir an vier Hauptaspekten der Untersuchung von Altmetrics bzw. altmetrischen Daten gearbeitet, deren Ergebnisse dazu beitragen sollen, die wissenschaftliche Lücke in diesem Bereich zu schließen.

(1) Zunächst untersuchen wir, inwieweit altmetrische Daten zu den Fachzeitschriften für Wirtschaftswissenschaften bei den beiden Altmetric-Anbietern Mendeley und Altmetric.com vorhanden sind. Basierend darauf zeigen wir, dass altmetrische Daten in diesen Disziplinen nur spärlich vorhanden sind und für reale Anwendungen (z. B. in Bibliotheken) höhere Aggregationsebenen, wie z. B. die Zeitschriftenebene, den Mangel an altmetrischen Daten gut überwinden können.

(2) Wir berechnen und diskutieren die Korrelationen von verschiedenen Arten von altmetrischen Daten mit Zitaten auf Artikel- und Zeitschriftenebene und zeigen, dass die Mendeley Reader Counts sowohl auf Artikel-, als auch auf Zeitschriftenebene stark positiv mit den Zitationszahlen korreliert sind, während andere Indikatoren wie Twitter Counts, Altmetric

Attention Score und mehr nur auf Journalebene signifikant korreliert sind. Basierend auf diesen Korrelationen könnten wir Mendeley Reader Counts für volks- und betriebswirtschafts-wissenschaftliche Zeitschriften / Artikel als alternativen Indikator zu Zitaten vorschlagen.

(3) Aufbauend auf den gewonnenen Erkenntnissen über die Eigenschaften von altmetrischen Daten für wirtschaftswissenschaftliche Zeitschriften diskutieren wir drei Anwendungsfälle, welche durch drei ZBW-Personas und deren Bezug zu Altmetrics hergeleitet wurden. Wir untersuchen hierbei die Verwendung von altmetrischen Daten für potentielle Nutzer mit Interesse in neuen Trends, Sozialen Medien und klassischen Zeitschriftenrankings.

(4) Mit Hilfe einer Umfrage haben wir das Verhalten von Wirtschaftswissenschaftlern in Bezug die Nutzung von altmetrischen Daten auf Zeitschriftenebene beim Aussuchen eines Artikels untersucht. Die Ergebnisse der Umfrage zeigen, dass Altmetrics in der Wirtschafts-gemeinschaft bisher nicht gut bekannt und verstanden sind. Dies bedeutet jedoch nicht, dass diese Indikatoren für Wirtschaftswissenschaftler nicht hilfreich sein können. Stattdessen wird das Problem aufgeworfen, wie Altmetrics auf die richtige Art und Weise in die Wirtschafts-gemeinschaft eingeführt werden können (z. B. angehängt als sichtbare Zahlen oder „versteckt" hinter dem Relevanzrankingsystem der Bibliothek).

In Anbetracht der oben genannten Ergebnisse dieser Arbeit können wir verschiedene Formen der Darstellung altmetrischer Informationen in Bibliotheksportalen vorschlagen, wobei EconBiz als proof-of-concept verwendet wird, um Forschern und Bibliotheken dabei zu helfen, relevante Zeitschriften oder Artikel (z. B. online häufig erwähnt und kürzlich veröffentlicht) für ihre Bedürfnisse zu identifizieren und eine Überlastung durch zu viele Informationen zu verhindern.

Contents

List of Figures

List of Tables

Chapter 1

Introduction

"It's Not Information Overload. It's Filter Failure."

Clay Shirky

The continuing adoption of technology (i.e., computers, cell phones, and information systems) and the associated large-scale growth of information have led to the "big data" movement (Diebold, 2012; Mayer-Schönberger & Cukier, 2013), where "big data" refers to the large volume of information that no longer fits in the memory that modern computers use for processing (Mayer-Schönberger & Cukier, 2013). According to Boyd and Crawford (2012), the definition of "big data" is composed of *technology* that includes maximum computation power and accurate algorithms. This technology can help to *analyze different large datasets* to figure out patterns for better social, technological, and legal statements. And finally, there is *a belief that* with the large datasets, new knowledge and insights will be generated.

However, according to literature, there are different definitions and interpretations of the term "big data" because big data is not only about the size of the data but also about the change that is present with the digital reality (Kaufmann, 2019). Big data, first, has been characterized based on the three Vs dimension model: "Volume", which depicts the size of the data; "Velocity", which considers the speed of the data; and "Variety", which includes various data types. Nevertheless, with the continuous development and the change of digital information, other dimensions were added to the big data movement: first, the "Value", which is related to the process of pulling out valuable information, or also known as "Big Data Analytics"; and second, "Veracity", which considers data governance and privacy concerns (Blazquez & Domenech, 2018).

The information growth comes from the utilization of digital devices, networks, web, social media platforms, and more (Blazquez & Domenech, 2018), for example, the use of digital cameras that provide high-resolution photos and require more storage capacity. This digital information is stored, shared, and replicated. Additionally, people place online orders, share their opinions about the products, make contacts, and more. These actions leave traces online, which, first, can lead to a massive growth of data and, second, can be further analyzed to help track economic, industrial, and social behaviors (Blazquez & Domenech, 2018). As reported by the International Data Corporation (IDC)[1], which is owned by the world's leading company for technology data—International Data Group (IDG)[2], the size of digital information has grown faster than expected; IDC research expects the global amount of data, which in 2018 was 33 zettabytes, to grow by an average of 61% each year, resulting in 175 zettabytes of data by 2025 (Patrizio, 2018).

---

[1] IDC: https://www.idc.com/
[2] IDG: https://www.idg.com/

For the first time, astronomy and genomics experienced digital data explosion, and then afterward, big data affected businesses, education, health, science, government, and every other field in the general public (Mayer-Schönberger & Cukier, 2013). Generally, the stored information increases four times faster than the world economy, and this information overload causes people to feel overwhelmed and causes them difficulties, for instance, in how to narrow a massive amount of digital information to use for a specific purpose.

This issue affected academics (researchers) because online publishing and dissemination became easier with the use of digital archives and the volume of scientific output exploded, meaning that researchers are no longer able to read all content that is relevant for them (Mayer-Schönberger & Cukier, 2013). Scientific output is shared by researchers in different formats (e.g., journal articles and conference proceedings) with the intention to communicate scientific knowledge (Borgman, 1989). Several studies analyzed the growth of scientific output over the last centuries (Price, 1963; Bornmann & Mutz, 2015; White, 2019). The first study that made an alarming prediction about the increase in scientific output is from Price (1963) with the well-known figure of journal distribution year-wise (Figure 1.1). Price observed that the number of journals increased exponentially from the year 1665 and predicted a 10-fold increase in journals every 50 years (~4.7% per year). His prediction suggested that in the year 2000, the number of journals will reach 1 million.

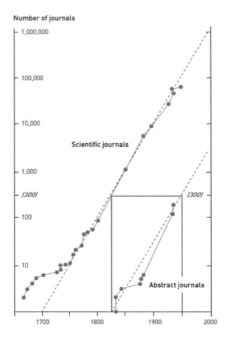

Figure 1.1: Graphic illustration by Price (1963) of the exponential growth of journals over the years. Source: The figure is a remake taken from Leydesdorff (2008) for better illustrative reasons.

As of 2016, Scopus [3] (a journal indexing database) recorded 23,000 scientific journals originating from 1823 onwards (Sugimoto & Larivière, 2018), confirming that Price's prediction did not happen; however, a constant increase has been spotted for journal articles instead (Haustein, 2012).

The study of Bornmann and Mutz (2015) discusses the exponential growth of scientific literature (see Figure 1.2) for different disciplines (e.g., natural sciences, social sciences, medical and health) indexed in Web of Science (WoS) published from 1980 to 2012. The study shows three growth phases of scientific literature; the first phase is identified with less than 1% growth in the middle of 18th century, the second phase is identified with 2–3% between the two world wars, and the last phase is identified with 9% growth in 2012.

Another study presents the growth of scientific publications (e.g., journals and books), related to "Science and Engineering," confirming a global increase at an average rate of 4% per year between 2007 and 2017 (White, 2019).

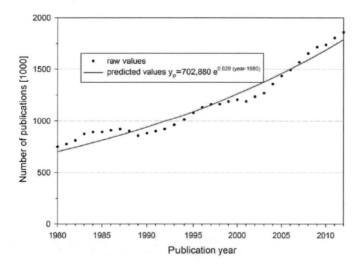

Figure 1.2: Exponential growth of WoS articles by year across all disciplines. Source: Bornmann and Mutz (2015, Fig. 1).

The aforementioned findings, together with a number of similar studies (Lawrence et al., 1999; Odlyzko, 2002; Van Noorden, 2014), confirm the prominent growth of scientific output which now exceeds the ability of researchers to filter and identify relevant articles for their needs (Mayer-Schönberger & Cukier, 2013). In a study by Shirky (2008), he mentioned that the

---

[3] Scopus: https://www.scopus.com/

problem does not rely on information overload that we currently face but is related to the filter failure.

Shirky also claimed that: "…when you feel yourself getting too much information, it's not to say to yourself what's happen to the information, but rather what filter just broke?"

Based on the above question from Shirky (2008), there is a need to design suitable filters for modern information flow to help sift for the information that we need. Nevertheless, the information overload problem and the need for filters were evident even in 1991, with Richard Dougherty stating "It seems that we need to develop better information filtering systems" to manage the explosion of information, respectively, scientific output (Dougherty, 1991, p. 339 as cited in Hopkins, 1995, p. 308). Given this long-term problem of scientific growth, several techniques (e.g., searching library databases and using indicators to evaluate the impact of articles) have been suggested to researchers to help cope with information overload and to filter literature with or without the use of technology.

The ongoing growth of literature has especially affected libraries, which are central information providers for high-quality scientific content for research and teaching communities (Borgman, 1999). Today, libraries are no longer places with card files; they have welcomed new technology and are fueled by digital revolution, research, and practice (Borgman, 1999; Li et al., 2019). With the presence of technology, libraries considerably invested in digital content and made them available through library services, mostly known as library web portals—a "doorway" to provide one access point of information to users (Zhou, 2003). These libraries need storage and retrieval systems to be able to hold digital data of different kind such as text, graphics, audio, and video (Borgman, 1999). With the use of technology, many researchers and practitioners from diverse disciplines are working on different research-related library issues. For example, researchers in computer science are concerned on exploring different algorithms and technologies of access and retrieval of digital content. On the contrary, librarians and information professionals focus on the collection and organization of such libraries (Borgman, 1999; Li et al., 2019).

1.1. Motivation

In the presence of information overload, it is easy to find a large number of articles that are of readers' interest; nevertheless, it is much too difficult and time-consuming to sift for the most important articles related to the problem at hand (Hopkins, 1995). Libraries, especially, are challenged by the information overload because their role is not only to show as many quality articles as possible to their users based on their subject of need but also to provide some strategies to narrow the volume of literature to their users and help them to make decisions and select what they need (Hopkins, 1995; Dobreva et al., 2018).

Over the years, librarians have suggested several strategies to assist library users in overcoming the information overload, of which most still continue to be effective (Blummer & Kenton, 2014). First, initiatives have been focused on recommending how information in libraries should be presented (e.g., organization, selection, and format) and offer instructions for information literacy (Rudd & Rudd, 1986). However, strategies are mostly related to exploring different software technologies that can assist in narrowing literature (Lossau, 2004). Lossau (2004) suggested that libraries should explore different database search techniques and filters to restrict searches, for example, on publication date or language to enhance the relevancy of results, with the intention to reduce the amount of unwanted information, thus helping to decrease the information overload.

Another important technique that plays an essential role in narrowing down the number of scientific articles is quality filtering, which considers citation frequency as an indicator of value or a proxy to identify "relevant" or "important" journal articles, suggested by Pao. Quality filtering attempts to reduce the quantity of scientific journals of a particular subject to some articles that can be recommended as "relevant" based on the users' needs (Pao, 1975). According to Pao, the proposed method may be used for medical literature to identify the highly relevant articles (articles that are mostly cited are judged as most important; Pao, 1975). The strategies mentioned here as well as other related strategies that exist in the literature contain best practices for reducing users' information overload in libraries and assist libraries in overcoming this problem. Even though some libraries have adopted ranking strategies for their portals using quality filtering methods, not all academic and special libraries that provide literature for a specific field of research are able to offer such solutions due to the high costs or personnel requirements needed for implementation (Hopkins, 1995).

Despite the fact that citations are seen as helpful indicators in disseminating scientific literature and possible solution as a useful strategy for libraries as well, citation-based indicators are criticized for several reasons in literature, also highlighted specifically, 10 years ago, in a public declaration (manifesto)[4]. The authors of the manifesto, which considered the rapid increase of scientific output, and the growing number of researchers who incorporate web tools into their work claimed that the three primary existing traditional filters for scientific outputs, namely, peer-review, citation counts, and Journal Impact Factor (JIF), are failing (Priem et al., 2010). JIF was developed from the Science Citation Index (SCI) and is used for assessing the performance of journals based on citations (Garfield, 1972). SCI was established by Eugene Garfield and is the world's oldest database of articles and citations (Garfield, 1972), now maintained from Clarivate Analytics[5]. For example, JIF considers citations accumulated for articles published in a journal over a 2-year period (Seglen, 1997). This 2-year citation window only encapsulates the short-term impact of scientific articles and is suggested as problematic because it benefits mostly disciplines that gather citations faster than others (DORA [6] declaration; Seglen, 1997; Larivière & Sugimoto, 2019). Citation counts used for individual articles instead can help to improve the assessment of scientific literature, can help to find relationships between articles, and can be used to discover research trends by finding out how often articles are cited (Lawrence et al., 1999). But, for a certain fraction of articles, a large percentage of articles will take at least 2 years or more (depending on the discipline) to receive the first citations (Brody et al., 2006), and many influential articles might remain uncited (MacRoberts & MacRoberts, 1989). Peer-review, known as the mechanism for quality control, is identified as an essential process in science because it allows a research article to be read and

---

[4] Altmetrics: a manifesto: http://altmetrics.org/manifesto/
[5] Clarivate Analytics: https://clarivate.com/
[6] DORA declaration: https://sfdora.org/read/

scrutinized by experts of the field. This process might be useful to improve the quality of the article as well as to detect errors and fraud (Smith, 2006). However, peer-review is also identified as flawed because of its defects, such as it takes a very long time for an article to be reviewed, is very expensive, is highly subjective, and creates bias against authors (Smith, 2006). Moreover, reviewers' judgments are suggested to be biased because these judgments are not only based on the scientific merit of the article but also influenced by the authors' qualities (Bornmann, 2011).

The authors of the manifesto considered the evident problems of traditional filters and introduced altmetrics as complements of citation-based indicators, which are used for filtering literature and are seen as indicators that can assess the online impact of scientific literature (Priem et al., 2010; Thelwall et al., 2013; Costas et al., 2015; Trueger et al., 2015; Nuredini & Peters, 2016; Bornmann et al., 2019). Specifically, altmetrics as new measures derived from online and social media sources, such as Facebook, News, Blogs, Wikipedia, and Policy Documents, are suggested as indicators that can quantify the online impact of scholarly literature on social media users (Bornmann et al., 2019). A number of studies have found that altmetrics are the complements of traditional indicators for research evaluation (Bar-Ilan et al., 2012; Priem et al., 2012), suggesting that altmetrics reflect a different type of impact (Loach and Evans, 2015) and that they can be used side by side with citations.

Various tools are developed that can track the online attention from social media sources for scientific outputs. Peters et al. (2014) identified four altmetric tools (i.e., Altmetric.com[7], ImpactStory[8], Plum Analytics[9], and Webometric Analyst[10]) and compared them with each other. The findings show that different altmetric providers gather altmetric data from various social media sources with variable coverage; for example, Altmetric.com has better coverage of articles mentioned on Twitter, whereas Plum Analytics tracks better Facebook posts. Another altmetric tool that is not directly covered in the article of Peters et al. (2014) but used extensively for exploring scientific articles for altmetric information, or specifically readership information, is Mendeley[11]. Mendeley is a social reference management system (sometimes also referred to as the academic social network) that allows users to search for articles, adds them to their libraries along with their metadata, and organizes them in folders for better retrieval (Mohammadi & Thelwall, 2014). A more detailed description of Mendeley is found in Chapter 3 of this thesis. Several studies have explored the uptake and usage of research articles in Mendeley (Haustein & Larivière, 2014; Zahedi et al., 2014b, 2017), to understand the meaning of Mendeley readership information. Zahedi et al. (2017) suggested that Mendeley readership information compared to citation counts could be used as an early indicator to identify highly cited articles and reflect scientific and other alternative impacts (Zahedi et al., 2015).

A great number of empirical studies have investigated the presence of altmetrics in different disciplines (e.g., health, biomedical research, and social science) considering different altmetric providers. The studies revealed disciplinary differences based on the coverages of articles and

---

[7] Altmetric.com: https://www.altmetric.com
[8] Impact Story: https://impactstory.org/
[9] Plum Analytics: https://plumanalytics.com/
[10] Webometric Analyst: http://lexiurl.wlv.ac.uk/
[11] Mendeley: https://www.mendeley.com/

6

correlations with citation counts and altmetric sources represented in altmetric providers (Mohammadi & Thelwall, 2014). The Journal of the Association for Information Science and Technology (JASIST) articles published between 2001 and 2011 are found with 97% of Mendeley readers (Bar-Ilan, 2012). Haustein and Larivière (2014) explored research articles in "biomedical research," "clinical medicine," and "health and psychology" where they found that "psychology" articles have the highest Mendeley shares (81%). Mohammadi and Thelwall (2014) investigated "social sciences" and "humanities" articles for the publication year 2008, and they found coverage of 54% of articles in Mendeley. Costas et al. (2015), which explored altmetrics from Altmetric.com in different disciplines, found that "social sciences" and "humanities" articles are covered with 22%; "life and earth sciences" articles are covered with 20%; and "natural sciences," "engineering," and "mathematics and computer science" articles are covered with less than 10%. Ortega (2018a) highlighted disciplinary differences based on the impact of altmetrics derived from Altmetric.com, PlumX, and Crossref Eventdata[12]. The author, for example, found that "social science" articles are mostly downloaded and viewed, whereas "health sciences" articles show low Mendeley shares. Htoo and Na (2017) revealed disciplinary differences between correlation counts for "social science" disciplines. Significant but weak correlation has been found between altmetrics (e.g., Facebook counts) and citation counts in "political science" and "information science," whereas no correlations between altmetrics and citation counts, except Mendeley, are found in "business finance" and "law".

By investigating altmetric indicators, several benefits have been identified when using altmetrics in impact measurement that are ignored by most of the traditional indicators. Bornmann (2014a; 2015a,b) highlighted four of them. First, altmetrics can identify an online impact for the scientific output from a wider audience. Altmetrics consider other types of readers, such as mainstream media editors and other stakeholders, while citations are usually used only by scientific authors. Second, altmetrics do not only allow the evaluation of scientific articles but can also be applied to a diversity of research products, such as presentation slides, algorithms, and software applications. Third, altmetrics can speed up impact evaluations of articles by showing online attraction within a significantly shorter time scale than citations, while citations need approximately 3 years after the publication of articles to show an impact. Lastly, altmetrics can be retrieved from different altmetric providers (e.g., Altmetric.com and Mendeley) that allow crawling of their web Application Programming Interface (APIs). APIs enable programmatic access to altmetric information connected to articles[13] where some provide free access to altmetric data (e.g., Mendeley API).

Given the benefits of altmetric indicators for depicting the online impact of scientific output (Bornmann, 2014a,b), libraries have increasingly become interested in using altmetrics data to facilitate filtering of articles, provide context information to articles, and help patrons—as well as library staff—in assessing the relevance of publications (Nuredini & Peters, 2016). Moreover, publishing houses and aggregators of altmetric data provide social media indicators by attaching them to their products and promoting those articles or other research outputs (Konkiel et al., 2015). Moreover, digital libraries are engaged in performing research in specialized areas, since many new challenges (e.g., the use of social media, the changing

---

[12] Crossref Eventdata: https://www.crossref.org/services/event-data/
[13] Example API of Altmetric.com: https://www.altmetric.com/products/altmetric-api/

behavior of users, and new privacy legislation) have emerged, which require discussion and further investigation (Dobreva et al., 2018). Nowadays, research articles are often shared in social media platforms, for example, in Twitter, tweets can be used as indicators of impact. The study of Raamkumar et al., (2018) investigated whether the sentiments of the tweets for particular computer science articles can inform about the performance of these articles (i.e., the quality of articles—citations). The authors suggested that articles with all sentiments do perform better than those with neutral sentiments.

By now, the perceived popularity of altmetrics and its usage as a scientometric tool frequently is sold as easy to understand and easy to implement (e.g., by bookmarklets[14]). The use of Altmetric.com bookmarklet enables researchers or users of libraries to find out the online attention of scientific articles using the DOIs they locate on the library portals. Moreover, altmetric information for a specific DOI can be accessed without any additional account or log in, by only using the bookmarklet instead (Trueger et al., 2015). Additionally, several case studies confirm the benefits of implementing altmetric badges into their library portals. For example, the Biodiversity Heritage Library (BHL)[15], which is the world's largest open access digital library for biodiversity literature and archives, adopted altmetric badges[16] within their records with the intention to help their readers see where the research content within that discipline is communicated online (Altmetric Engineering, 2017).

The altmetric badges (i.e., donuts) are implemented within the library portal visualized as a donut, which represents the online influence of that particular scientific product (e.g., article) from different sources that Altmetric.com tracks (see Chapter 3 for more detailed information about the altmetric donut). BHL confirmed that with the use of altmetrics, they identified which books are, in particular, popular and which, for their goal, altmetric information is valuable since they are aware of their successful contents.

On the contrary, the use of altmetrics was also adopted by ScienceOpen[17], which is a platform that allows researchers to do an advanced search based on various criteria (i.e., citations and Altmetric Attention Score) and find scientific content as straightforward as possible. This platform has implemented the Altmetric Attention Score from Altmetric.com at the "Sort By" function, allowing users of this platform to sort articles based on the Altmetric Attention Score (see Figure 1.3). Altmetric Attention Score[18] (see Chapter 3 for more details) is a counting number that shows the total amount of the attention research outputs (i.e., articles) have already received online from social media sources.

---

[14] Bookmarklets from Altmetric.com: https://www.altmetric.com/products/free-tools/bookmarklet
[15] Biodiversity Heritage Library: https://www.biodiversitylibrary.org/
[16] Altmetric badges: https://www.altmetric.com/products/altmetric-badges/
[17] ScienceOpen: https://about.scienceopen.com/
[18] How is the Altmetric Attention Score calculated:
     https://help.altmetric.com/support/solutions/articles/6000060969-how-is-the-altmetric-attention-score-calculated-

Figure 1.3: A screenshot of ScienceOpen and the use of the Altmetric Attention Score for sorting purposes.

So far several strategies (some highlighted above) have been taken into account for implementing altmetric information of different forms (e.g., the implementation of badges), especially from Altmetric.com, in digital libraries, which are reported as easy to implement and as useful tools that can promote the impact of articles within the library.

Even though altmetric data have been integrated into library portals based on the build-in tools offered commercially, have been investigated extensively for their coverage in different disciplines, have been highlighted as early indicators for impact, and have been suggested to digital libraries (Thelwall et al., 2013), there is paucity literature that discusses the scientific methodologies on how library portals can present altmetrics. Given the fact that there are disciplinary differences between the coverage and correlation of altmetrics data, interested parties (e.g., libraries) should not ignore these differences because the interpretation of altmetrics can be misleading. Moreover, Thelwall (2020, p. 5) claimed that "tweet counts for cancer-related research are likely to be much higher than for pure (basic) mathematics research. Thus, it would not be fair to compare aggregate tweet counts between sets of documents that were not from the same field." These cases should be kept into account when using the right presentation of altmetrics for libraries.

In addition, the Leiden Manifesto presented several principles that are mainly discussed from Coombs and Peters (2017) with respect to libraries by highlighting several practical recommendations about the development and provision of metrics services in libraries. Several principles of a high priority, for example, "Quantitative evaluation should support qualitative", "Keep data collection and analytical processes open, transparent and simple," and "Allow those evaluated to verify data and analysis," can contribute to make careful integration of various metrics (e.g., altmetrics) in library portals. For example, according to these principles, libraries are strongly encouraged to collaborate with researchers with respect to defining concepts and methods regarding scholarly data, their quality, openness, and the need for updates.

Therefore, considering several principles that should be utilized in libraries, research methods, and results retrieved from scientific studies, other possible strategies can be taken into account, which can precisely aid in the integration of altmetrics in library systems, for example, which aggregation levels of altmetrics make sense to use (because altmetrics are still sparse) or which social media sources are preferable where the articles in that particular discipline are found with the most online attention.

Even though altmetrics have been investigated broadly, only a couple of studies focused specifically on Economic and Business Studies journal articles and investigated altmetric information and their coverage for these disciplines (Nuredini & Peters, 2015, 2016; De Filippo & Sanz-Casado, 2018; Drongstrup et al., 2019); however, these studies do not provide an extensive investigation of altmetrics information for a large scale of journals in these disciplines, give no possible suggestions on methods that could be used to analyze altmetrics with respect to libraries, and do not suggest how to integrate altmetrics within the library systems with an Economic focus. Therefore, this thesis will try to close this gap and shed light on this characteristic.

1.2. Dissertation scope

Motivated by the new presented indicators known as altmetrics, the possibility to collect and process these data, and the open issues of bibliometrics (e.g., JIF and citation counts), the main aim of this research is to explore altmetric information for libraries as a strategy for reducing information overload by providing novel insights for filtering the information needed. This research is performed within the environment of "Social Media Analytics"[19], which is a new research field emerged in business informatics, with the intention to develop new information systems or build new knowledge in regard to social media data (Stieglitz et al., 2014).

The focus of this thesis is based on investigating and suggesting altmetric information for special libraries with an emphasis on the disciplines of economics (or in German "Volkswirtschaftslehre") and business studies ("Betriebswirtschaftslehre") literature. Economics (E)[20] and business studies (BS) are subdisciplines of economics (or in German "Wirtschaftswissenschaften"), which belongs generally to social sciences.

E and BS disciplines were chosen for two main reasons:

1) This research at hand was possible to be performed within the environment of ZBW— Leibniz Information Centre for Economics[21], which is the world's largest library specialized for economic literature. ZBW offers two important library services: EconBiz[22] and Econstor[23]. EconBiz is an online library portal that covers different types of economic literature (i.e., journal articles and conference articles) and provides a literature search function and access to

---

[19] Social Media Analytics: https://www.enzyklopaedie-der-wirtschaftsinformatik.de/wi-enzyklopaedie/lexikon/daten-wissen/Wissensmanagement/Soziales-Netzwerk/Social-Media/index.html?searchterm=social+media

[20] In this thesis, the acronyms E for economics and BS for business studies journals are used interchangeably.

[21] ZBW: https://www.zbw.eu/

[22] EconBiz: https://www.econbiz.de/

[23] Econstor: https://www.econstor.eu/

free and licensed texts. Econstor is a non-commercial publication server that indexes economic scientific literature, mostly working papers (i.e., preprints), that are freely accessible based on the open access principle (Weiland, 2011). ZBW has more than 4 million books and articles[24], is a member of the Leibniz Association[25] research organization, and is allied with Kiel University[26].

Besides the fact that ZBW covers a large number of E and BS journals (as of 2018, ZBW indexed 26,671 journal subscriptions; ZBW, 2018), it is also strongly engaged with Science 2.0 technologies by looking at how social media will impact all phases of research (e.g., publication process). ZBW is also supporting the Open Science movement toward open research that enables different research outputs to be free to use by anyone (Peters et al., 2014). ZBW's primary goal is to provide new approaches to disseminate literature and especially to help its library users to find relevant articles for reading according to different strategies that will address the information overload problem (Peters et al., 2015). To meet this criterion, ZBW contains a research group in computer science and information science and operates a high-tech information infrastructure for allowing researchers to conduct research and improve its services such as EconBiz and Econstor (Peters et al., 2014). Specifically, in ZBW, the Web Science approach is explored by studying economists and their interaction with web and different social media platforms to better understand how economists use these platforms for research purposes. Second, ZBW intends to provide researchers tools for conducting better and more efficient research work, which is done under the Knowledge Discovery approach, focusing on the investigation of different machine learning techniques. For example, the study of Hajra and Tochtermann (2017) helps to boost the visibility of articles that are found in other repositories, so that the reader can find more literature related to the closed article for which they are searching for a short time period.

2) The main findings of the previous studies from Nuredini and Peters (2015, 2016) that explored Mendeley and Altmetric.com for the top 30 journals from economics and business studies are seen as potential findings, which should be further extended and therefore helpful because the insights can contribute to what libraries with economic focus should know in advance when incorporating altmetric information on their digital portals. Based on previous research results, the authors found a good coverage of the top 30 journals and their articles within these disciplines, with 77.5% of articles found in Mendeley and 38% in Altmetric.com. However, these studies explored only a small set of journals (top 30) from both BS and E, upon which their results are based on. Thus, by increasing the number of journals for investigation, it is interesting to see first to what extent these journals are found with metadata (e.g., the title of the article and authors) from crawling Crossref[27] for articles digital object identifier (DOIs). Crossref is a data service platform that is used to retrieve all articles and its metadata published in journals. Second, when considering a larger amount of journals with retrieved metadata, it is interesting to investigate whether the same patterns of altmetric information from the two providers are found. Third, and most importantly, with the use of a large dataset in economic

---

[24] Facts and figures about ZBW: http://www.zbw.eu/en/about-us/profile/facts-figures/
[25] Leinbniz gemeinschaft: https://www.leibniz-gemeinschaft.de/en/home/
[26] Kiel University: https://www.uni-kiel.de/de/
[27] Crossref: https://www.crossref.org/

and business studies, one can determine whether, for all journals included in the investigation, altmetric information is present. According to the result, one can suggest possible ways, such as filter methods, that can be suitable for enriching an economic library portal with altmetrics. Nuredini and Peters (2015) revealed that Mendeley readership information might be important for economists since they can determine the appropriate journal for them based on the Mendeley's target group of users (e.g., based on academic status or discipline). Besides, they found that JIF and Altmetric Attention Score on a journal level are positively but weakly correlated, and they suggest altmetrics as a complementary source of information to traditional indicators. Since the studies of Nuredini and Peters (2015, 2016) investigated the top 30 journals that belong to the most important A+ class journals, according to Handelsblatt ranking[28], covering around 2% of the entire list of journals, see Table 1.1, they do not highlight the altmetric behavior for lower-ranked journals. Handelsblatt ranking sorts journals according to academic importance: highly cited journals are depicted as A+ and A and are ranked higher than other journals (see Appendix I and II about the journal and their classes). The remaining journals are listed below and are ranked under classes B, C, D, E, and F (Krapf, 2010).

Therefore, the scope of this dissertation is to consider a larger scale sample of journals in E and BS, which will extend the knowledge of altmetric information gained from the two previous studies. Specifically, one objective is to consider journals below class A+ by investigating whether journals listed within classes A, B, C, D, E, and F also receive any online attention to make more precise conclusions about the use of altmetrics in these disciplines. The coverage of a large number of journals and their articles is important in this research because, based on the number of journals/articles found with altmetric information, we can discuss the presentation of altmetric information for different ranked journals.

Table 1.1: Handelsblatt ranking journals in E and BS and their coverages in each class.

	Economic journals in Handelsblatt ranking						
Classes	A+	A	B	C	D	E	F
No. of journals	10	15	26	76	128	256	1,297
% of journals in classes	0.55%	0.83%	1.44%	4.20%	7.08%	14.16%	71.74%
	Business studies journals in Handelsblatt ranking						
Classes	A+	A	B	C	D	E	F
No. of journals	23	52	76	227	378	759	341
% of journals in classes	1.24%	2.80%	4.09%	12.23%	20.37%	40.89%	18.37%

Moreover, by expanding the knowledge, we can, for example, suggest that altmetrics are present also for journals that are not ranked within the top 30 from Handelsblatt ranking. These journals and their articles might have received online attention within social media platforms, and this information is available for implementation in digital libraries, which can ensure that

---

[28] Handelsblatt ranking: https://www.handelsblatt.com/politik/deutschland/journal-ranking/9665428.html?ticket=ST-3244048-addR2Cf3Wpi4OMXCY0fm-ap5

the coverage of altmetrics is present also for journals that are not highly ranked according to particular rankings. The presence of altmetric information for a large number of journals can assist in suggesting implementation concepts of altmetrics in libraries. In this way, economists, while searching for literature in the portal, for many articles, can find altmetrics attached to them, undependable if the journals are highly ranked or not, which might consider these indicators as useful filters (e.g., based on the online attention the respective research product have received) when selecting a journal or article for reading or publishing. Furthermore, we can suggest which levels of altmetrics (i.e., article level or journal level) make sense to show and attach to library records and why such information would make a better presentation. Additionally, we will investigate whether highly ranked journals in E and BS are popular on social media platforms, which will help suggest altmetrics as complementary indicators to rankings that usually include citation counts for evaluating journals.

With reference to the aforementioned reasons, this research will shed light on two important characteristics, first, will explore the presence of altmetrics for a large scale of journal articles (in this case for E and BS disciplines) and, second, will understand the user behavior when applying altmetrics to decide what to read.

The first characteristic will present an analytical approach that will explore altmetrics for a large scale of E and BS journals/articles. It will provide a detailed methodology for retrieving altmetric information, especially for scientific outputs such as journals and articles, considering the ISSNs and DOIs. It will present data issues that one can identify during the data selection and retrieval processes. It will highlight the methodology that will be used to retrieve altmetrics, especially for journal articles in E and BS. Afterwards, this research will analyze altmetrics presence in E and BS disciplines, identify which readership information and Altmetric Attention Sources are present more for these types of articles, and will present the correlation between citations and altmetrics.

The second characteristic will present a user evaluation, which will understand economists' behavior and needs when selecting an article for reading by introducing altmetric information. Both characteristics that will be covered here can be further generalized into other disciplines as well. Specifically, all findings of this research will provide insights regarding altmetric data that will be used as a proof-of-concept for library portals, with an economic focus, such as EconBiz, with the intention to help their users, for example, filter articles or journals based on the online attention the journal or articles have received. Although the focus of this thesis is very specific, based on the methodologies provided within this research, other library portals with a different focus can benefit according to the above-mentioned characteristics.

1.3. Proof-of-concept

In order to address different possible applications and integration of altmetrics, especially with an economic focus, a library portal (in this case, EconBiz) will be taken into consideration. Using EconBiz (see Section 1.4 for more details), this thesis will be able to suggest possible forms of integrating altmetrics using the following characteristics:

13

- Dependently of the technology of the digital portal (e.g., ranking algorithms)
- User requirements to improve EconBiz (e.g., ZBW personas)
- The coverage, correlations, and characteristics of altmetric information available for this discipline
- The economists' behavior evaluation about the use of altmetric data

With the available data retrieved from altmetric providers and the survey results, the concept at the end will show several forms (e.g., which altmetric indicators are useful as filters of articles with the most online attention) of presenting altmetric information for journal articles. The representation forms of altmetrics will be based on the results retrieved from the scientific investigation that will take place based on the formulated research questions.

This proof-of-concept can be further generalized by different library portals using the same methodologies on different data sets.

1.4. EconBiz portal

EconBiz is a ZBW service and an online library portal with a special focus on economic and business studies literature. The EconBiz database, known as ECONIS, started to index documents with publication dates from 1919 onwards. As of 2017, the EconBiz portal covered more than 10 million publications from different databases such as books, journal articles, and working papers (Pianos & Klemenz, 2017) with 1.5 million of those documents being freely available (Pianos & Siegfried, 2019). EconBiz also allows searching of additional databases with an economics literature focus, such as Econstor and RePEc[29], an open bibliographic database for economics literature, as well as searchable for University Library of Cologne (USB), which includes the business studies and social science section and BASE (Bielefeld Academic Search Engine), the open access database for economics and business.

EconBiz enables users to create their own accounts, manage their favorite list of articles, export article results into different reference management systems (e.g., Zotero and Mendeley), and provide a help function "Did you mean" for users search typing errors (ZBW, 2012). It further integrates the controlled vocabulary "Thesaurus for Economics" (STW), which is a valuable support to improve the search results and retrieval of literature (ZBW, 2013).

EconBiz migrated from a virtual library to a portal with search engine functionality in 2010, which runs under the VuFind[30] technology (Lucene/SoIR; ZBW, 2018). It offers search functionality (see Figure 1.4) with a page of retrieved results (i.e., indexed articles) as well as single pages of articles and their metadata (known as article detail page). EconBiz searches are mostly conducted based on the Known-Item-Search, which is a method used by users in libraries for information seeking and retrieval processes (Linhart, 2015).

The Known-Item-Search is used in cases when the user a) is looking for a specific article, b) does not have to know that the article exists in the portal, and c) has some bibliographic data for the search but not all. In EconBiz, the most used activity of Known-Item-Search is the search

---

[29] RePEc: http://repec.org
[30] VuFind: https://vufind.org/vufind/

of the full title of the article, which users afterward happen to reformulate by shortening it (Linhart, 2015).

Although most of the searches are done based on the article's title, Pianos and Klemenz (2017) observed that since the number of articles and journals indexed in EconBiz increases, the use of quality indicators for filtering scientific articles would be an essential plan for EconBiz future advances. Pianos (2010), who analyzed the extraction of users' requirements of the EconBiz portal, found that users of EconBiz want to find the literature relevant for them. Pianos (2010) also suggested that complex searches and different search filters can improve the service and support users optimize their searches, which will lead to better information retrieval and better search results of user significance.

Figure 1.4: Screenshot of the EconBiz portal start page.

According to ZBW's annual reports, from 2012 until 2016, the number of unique EconBiz users increased from 900,000 to roughly 2,500,000 users per year (ZBW, 2012, 2016). Based on data from the annual reports, the number of digital journals indexed in Econbiz has also increased, reaching 20,303 digital indexed journals in 2018 (ZBW, 2018; Figure 1.5).

Since the EconBiz portal adopted the search engine functionality in 2010[31], several relevance ranking strategies have been tested and some are implemented (Linhart, 2015). Currently, the relevance ranking methodology in EconBiz is based on matches in the title, author, abstract, and the position and frequency of the search term in the article (EconBiz, 2012). This relevance ranking can also be influenced by factors such as the openness and the recently published date of articles. However, a project known as LibRank[32], which is being developed within the EconBiz environment and data and funded by the German Research Foundation (DFG), started to investigate other relevance ranking methods for better performance in EconBiz. One of the experiments that LibRank considered is to rank search results based on popularity factors (i.e., citations; Plassmeier et al., 2015).

---

[31] Suchmaschine für Wirtschaftswissenschaften www.econbiz.de jetzt mit neuem Gesicht: https://www.inetbib.de/listenarchiv/msg43181.html
[32] LibRank: http://www.librank.info/

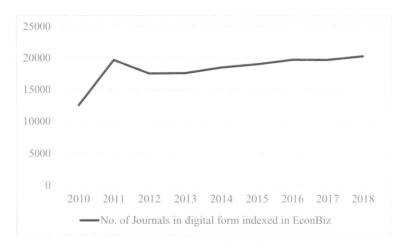

Figure 1.5: Year-wise journal indexing in ZBW.

Plassmeier et al. (2015) studied the relevance of search results based on non-textual factors or popularity-based factors that focus on citation counts of articles, author metrics, and usage data rather than text statistics (e.g., the position and the frequency of the search term in the article or publication dates). The authors used the Characteristic Score and Scales (CSS) method to correct the citation data and usage data biases and to classify articles into "poorly cited," "fairly cited," "remarkably cited," and "outstandingly cited" groups. This method is confirmed as highly promising by producing valuable benefits to the users' needs (Plassmeier et al., 2015). However, the CSS worked well for normalizing citation data but not for usage data, suggesting that future studies are needed to explore other normalization methods for the better performance of the relevance model.

A comparison study about the scholarly search methods conducted between EconBiz and Google Scholar[33] suggested that Google Scholar is "not enough" for literature search (Krueger, 2017). Google Scholar is a free search engine that indexes full text or metadata of academic literature, which allows the internet community (i.e., researchers) to perform searches and find literature for their needs (Jacsó, 2005). Google Scholar offers a great opportunity to search for academic literature based on the titles of articles; however, it provides fewer filters (e.g., filter articles based on publication date) to specify the search. But EconBiz offers many ways to filter search results (e.g., based on subject, year of publication, language, and type of publication, i.e., article, book, and more). The ranking of search results in Google Scholar is not fully transparent on how it is calculated; however, according to the sources published, Google Scholar considers citation counts in their ranking mechanism, in which the results often return older articles first, since they had time to gather high citation counts compared to newly published articles (Krueger, 2017).

---

[33] Google Scholar: https://scholar.google.com/

1.5. ZBW personas

This thesis additionally considers some characteristics of fictional personas created by ZBW as sources for discussing altmetric information, which, therefore, act as helpful use cases for suggesting application scenarios of altmetric information to library portals with a special focus (e.g., EconBiz). These application scenarios, in this case, could be used as strategies to help reduce information overload and to help users of EconBiz to find relevant articles based on their needs. At this point, relevant articles can be those that are retrieved based on the researchers' interests. For example, a researcher is interested to see all articles that have accumulated the highest Altmetric Scores but published recently.

ZBW has created six fictional personas with individual features, names, and pictures to support users by having an excellent experience while using ZBW services (e.g., EconBiz and Econstor). These personas are prototypical people whose characteristics have emerged from surveys and interviews related to their research process, conducted at ZBW. The personas data are based on socio-demographic, behavioral, and psychographic variables, which are continually adapted and developed by ZBW (Siegfried, 2015). A description of the ZBW personas can be found under https://www.zbw.eu/fileadmin/pdf/veranstaltungen/2017-bibtag-siegfried-personas.pdf

Generally, ZBW personas are constructed based on four dimensions. The first dimension includes the personal specification of fictional personas, for example, name, age, background, salary, academic qualification, and job. The second dimension highlights the content that these personas are using for their research and the possible ways in which they find the content for reading. The third dimension is related to the tools that personas use during their research and to their motivations to succeed. The fourth dimension consists of personas' online activities during their research process (e.g., the use of social media tools). Our study is focused on analyzing the second dimension (i.e., finding research content) and the fourth dimension of the personas.

Within this thesis, the ZBW personas are first analyzed in terms of the second and fourth dimension, and according to their specified needs for finding research content, use cases are created and further enhanced by introducing altmetric information. For example, the persona Dr. Dorothee Wiese wrote that she is interested in journal rankings for publishing her work. We therefore built a new use case by suggesting journal level information according to the data from Mendeley and Altmetric.com, which might serve for her journal selection process. The new use cases presented in this section will be further discussed in Chapters 3 and 5.

ZBW's original personas include two professors who work at a University and a University of Applied Sciences, two researchers, and two students, of which one is a Post Doc researcher, one is a PhD student, and two are master students, all with economic and business studies background. We chose three example use cases that are related and helpful for this research. These use cases are further enhanced from the original ZBW personas based on our research focus and are presented below.

1) **Persona 1**: Dr. Dorothee Wiese, a Post Doc researcher at the university, **use case: journal rankings** – Dr. Wiese in her persona presents that she uses VHB [34] (Der Verband der Hochschullehrer für Betriebswirtschaft) journal ranking (based on surveying the members of VHB to judge the quality of journals) when she selects journals to publish her work in (for more information about economics journal ranking see Chapter 2). Since she is interested in journal rankings, we enhance her use case for this research using altmetric information. In this case, we suggest the use of journal level information according to Mendeley and Altmetric.com data, which might assist her by providing alternative information to select a journal for publishing in. The study of Loach and Evans (2015) suggested a new journal ranking based on altmetric information, and they compared this journal ranking with the traditional citation-based ranking Journal Impact Factor. The authors suggest that journal rankings based on altmetrics show some similarities with JIF, especially when considering blog counts. Articles published to journals with high JIF seem to be mentioned in blog posts as well. In this case, Dorothee will select journals, for example, based on journal articles mentioned in blogs. In Chapters 3 and 5, we will discuss to what extent journal level altmetric information is useful for economic authors when selecting a journal for publishing their works in. The need for this use case is also highlighted within the research work of Janßen (2018) performed in ZBW, which explores different journal level indicators (e.g., journal output, ranking, and metrics) by increasing awareness why a "Journal Map" is needed and is important for libraries to support its users to select a journal based on their needs. "Journal Map" was suggested as a tool for future implementation, which, based on the multidimensionality view of different metric representations, can compare journals with each other.

2) **Persona 2**: Anngret Weihmann, professor at the University of Applied Sciences, **use case: new trends** – Prof. Weihmann, in her persona, is interested in finding new trendy topics or articles within a specific subject. She does not mention explicitly what kind of tools can help her find new topic trends. For this thesis, based on research conducted so far from altmetric community, we assume that altmetric information can play an important role here. As we are already aware that citations accrue slowly than altmetrics, altmetric information can appear earlier than citations, and therefore, they can speed up impact evaluations of articles by showing online attraction significantly within a shorter time scale than citations (Bornmann, 2015a,b; Holmberg, 2015). According to this use case, altmetric information will be discussed in this thesis in the following ways: 1) altmetric information will be used as a source to filter trendy topics in Chapter 3 based on the existing literature and 2) altmetric information will be used and presented as a proof of concept to identify trendy topics for E and BS journals in Chapter 5.

3) **Persona 3:** Luisa Müller and Lukas Schneider, master students in economics, **use case: use of social media sources**. Luisa and Lukas are two master students whose personas indicate that Facebook groups play a useful role in their research activities because they get informed about new literature from their colleagues within these groups. Using this use case, we will discuss the use of social media sources in academia and the distinction of these tools for different disciplines and different target research groups (Chapter 3). In literature (e.g., in Mehrazar et al. 2018), it has been discussed that there is a distinction of how social media tools are used

---

[34] VHB journal ranking : https://www.vhbonline.org/vhb4you/vhb-jourqual/vhb-jourqual-3/gesamtliste

between different types of researchers. Experienced researchers use social media platforms (i.e., Twitter and LinkedIn) to share their research output with the public. In contrast, young researchers often use social media channels that provide questioning and answering features (e.g., StackExchange, StackOverflow, and GitHub). Based on Chapter 5, we will identify social media sources in which economics literature is mostly found. Given this insight, we can suggest specific social media channels, mostly intended for economics literature, as tools to help researchers of different types (e.g., authors and students) find literature.

1.6. Research questions

In this section, the research questions that are explored for this thesis are listed. Some of the research questions have sub-questions for specifications. The presented research questions below are helpful to understand first, to what extent altmetric information are present for journal articles in E and BS, and second, whether altmetrics data are useful for economic researchers. With the findings of the research questions and the fact that libraries are interested in adopting altmetrics, we can make valuable decisions, what libraries with economic focus should know, for example, where sufficient data is available for valid analyses, which altmetric aggregator should be used for the goals set and which aspects of altmetrics can be implemented in a reasonable way and therefore be useful as filter features. The answers to these research questions are mostly shown in Chapters 5 and 6, and each of the answers will help to draw valuable conclusions (see Chapter 7), for example, about the appropriate ways of using altmetrics in economic libraries (e.g., use as filters).

RQ 1: *To what extent are readership information from Mendeley and Altmetric Attention Sources from Altmetric.com present for E and BS journals?*

This research question is divided into two parts. The first part explores altmetric readership information from Mendeley for E and BS journals, and the second part similarly presents Altmetric Attention Sources found from Altmetric.com for E and BS journals. The investigation of these research questions can be found in Chapter 5. Detailed information and functionalities about Almetric providers are shown in Chapter 3.

1.1. Which category of readership information from Mendeley (i.e., academic status, country, and discipline) is mostly used for economic and business studies literature?

Mendeley presents three types of user demographics (readership information): academic status, country, and discipline (see Chapter 3 for more information). Within this study, we show which of these categories is mostly presented by the readers of Mendeley and therefore represents a higher number of articles in E and BS. With the findings of this research question (Chapter 5), we can reveal the reading behavior of different types of users and can suggest the proper use of readership information from Mendeley for libraries, especially with an E and BS focus (see Chapter 7). Given the findings, we can suggest which readership information can be useful to filter out the articles in E and BS based on the reading behavior of the users in Mendeley.

1.2. Concerning Altmetric Attention Sources provided by Altmetric.com, for example, Twitter, Facebook, and blogs, which sources have higher coverages of economic and business studies journals/articles?

Since Altmetric.com tracks 19 different attention sources for journal articles (see Chapter 3 for more details), within this study, all the given sources are explored for journal articles in economics and business studies, and the top five sources with the highest scores are presented (Chapter 5). We assume that the top Altmetric Attention Sources are those sources where more economic articles are shared in comparison with sources where fewer articles are found. Given the findings of this question, the most significant sources will be suggested for use in library portals, which will help users filter out the most socially influential journal articles.

RQ 2: *Are journal level information useful for authors of scientific articles to help them decide which journal to send their work to and therefore useful indicators for libraries as well?*

Journal level altmetric information as an indicator and the different reasons behind the use of this indicator will be discussed in Chapter 3. We will address whether this indicator can complement, for example, journal ranking for journal selection purposes. The results of this question are based on the investigation presented in Chapter 5. We show the correlation between different altmetrics and citations and we can make valuable decisions whether journal level altmetrics can be useful sources for economists to filter out the journals they want to publish their articles. Additionally, we can find out whether altmetrics on journal level can be useful sources to libraries and for what purpose.

RQ 3: *What Altmetric Attention Sources from Altmetric.com are mostly used by which groups of economists (based on Mendeley readership information)?*

Since different Altmetric Attention Sources (e.g., Twitter) are used for different purposes and in various disciplines, with this research question, we can provide insights about the use of such sources by different groups of economists. Given the findings of this part of the research, we will highlight different types of academic statuses from Mendeley users who read articles that have been mentioned in attention sources from Altmetric.com (Chapter 5).

RQ 4: *Do altmetric information on a journal level (as new filters) generally help economists to select the most interesting article to read first?*

This research question is based on the analysis of survey responses regarding economists' use of journal information (i.e., altmetrics) during their article selection process and the relevance of this information. Given the responses from the survey, we will understand which altmetric sources and Mendeley readership information were most helpful to economists for article selection. Moreover, if the academic status and age of economists play an important role in selecting an article, we can suggest different forms of altmetrics based on demographic data. The answers to these questions will be discussed in Chapter 6.

1.7. Scientific contribution

The scientific contributions of this PhD thesis are divided into three main parts (visualized in the Figure 1.6) and are summarized below.

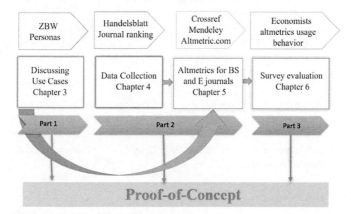

Figure 1.6: A graphical representation of this research.

• We first highlight to what extent altmetric information from two altmetric providers Mendeley and Altmetric.com is present within the journals of economics and business studies. Based on the coverage, we demonstrate that altmetrics data are sparse in these disciplines, and when considering altmetrics data for real-world applications (e.g., in libraries), higher aggregation levels, such as journal level, can overcome their sparsity well. By doing so, it will be ensured that for every record, altmetric information could be displayed, which lowers, or even avoids, user frustration.

• Second, we perform and discuss the correlations of citations on article and journal levels between different types of altmetrics (e.g., Twitter). We could show that Mendeley counts are positive and strongly correlated with citation counts on both article and journal levels, whereas other indicators such as Twitter counts and Altmetric Score are significantly correlated only on journal level. With these correlations, we could suggest Mendeley counts for economic and business studies journals/articles as alternative indicators to citations.

• Third, in conjunction with the findings related to the altmetrics in economics and business studies journals, we discuss three use cases derived from three ZBW personas in terms of altmetrics:

    o For the first persona that is interested on journal ranking information to select a journal for publishing his/her work, we identified that altmetrics on journal level can additionally be used within this use case, since these indicators show high and positive correlation values with citation counts and can appear within a shorter time than citations do.

    o For the second persona, which is interested in identifying new trends in research, we presented a proof of concept for identifying the trends within E and BS journal articles. Topics for recently published articles are retrieved using Latent Dirichlet Allocation

(LDA), and we compared the average values of altmetric indicators (e.g., AAS) per each topic.

   o For the third persona, which is interested in social media platforms for finding literature, we revealed the top Altmetric Sources where economic and business studies literature is found with most online attention and recommended tracking these sources, especially for finding literature.

- Fourth, we investigated the behavior of economic researchers using a survey by exploring the usefulness of different altmetrics on journal level while they make decisions for selecting one article for reading. According to the user evaluation results, we demonstrated altmetrics are not well known and understood by the economic community.

Therefore considering the aforementioned scientific contribution of this thesis, we can suggest several forms of presenting altmetric information as a proof of concept in library portals, especially in EconBiz with the intention to assist both researchers and libraries identify relevant articles (e.g., highly mentioned online and recently published) or journals for their need and cope with the information overload.

1.8. Published work

The building blocks presented in this thesis have been published in international conferences and a workshop; the other works are published in a book chapter and in a journal. The corresponding publications for this thesis are listed below:

Nuredini, K. & Peters, I. (2015). Economic and business studies journals and readership information from Mendeley. In F. Pehar, C. Schlögl, & C. Wolff, Re: inventing Information Science in the Networked Society, *Proceedings of the 14th International Symposium on Information Science (ISI 2015)*, Zadar, Croatia, pp. 380–392. Glückstadt: Verlag Werner Hülsbusch.

Abstract:
We present Mendeley readership information for 30 journals from the German Handelsblatt ranking for economics and business studies from 2010 to 2012. We use readership data to characterize both fields by journals with over 20 years of publication activity. The analysis focusses on journal output, reader counts, scientific disciplines, academic status, and the geographic origin of readers. The results show that Mendeley provides relatively good coverage of research articles for both disciplines. The majority of readers are Ph.D. students in business administration from the United States and Germany. Moderate correlations are found between journals' reader numbers and impact factors. The results suggest that Mendeley's readership data on journal level add useful information to research evaluation and journal rankings and help economists to publish in the best journal according to the intended target groups.

Author contribution:
Nuredini, K., designed the study, coded the scripts to retrieve Crossref and Mendeley data for readership information, added the data to a MySQL database, and analyzed the retrieved data. Nuredini, K., wrote the first draft of the article and presented the data. Peters, I., contributed to the article revision and supervised the findings of this work.

Nuredini, K. & Peters, I. (2016). Enriching the knowledge of altmetrics studies by exploring social media metrics for economic and business studies journals suggested. *Proceedings of the 21st International Conference on Science and Technology Indicators (STI Conference 2016), València, Spain, September* 14–16.

Abstract:
We present a case study of articles published in 30 journals from economics and business studies (EBS) using social media metrics from Altmetric.com. Our results confirm that altmetric information is significantly better present for recent articles. The top 3 most used altmetric sources in EBS journals are Mendeley, Twitter, and News. Low but positive correlations ($r = 0.2991$) are identified between citation counts and Altmetric Scores on article level but they increase on journal level ($r = 0.614$). However, articles from highly cited journals do neither receive high online attention nor are they better represented on social media.

Author contribution:
Nuredini, K., contributed to the conception and design of the study. Nuredini, K., downloaded the Altmetric.com data from the Altmetric Explorer, coded the script to send the data to a MySQL database for further analysis, and presented the data. Nuredini, K., provided the correlation with citations and altmetrics scores. Nuredini, K., wrote the first draft of the article. Peters, I., helped supervise the article.

Nuredini, K., Latif, A., & Peters, I. (2017). Case study on open access journals in economic and business studies and their engagement on the web. The 2017 Altmetrics Workshop, Toronto, Canada, September 26.

Abstract:
We studied the top 4 journals of open access (OA) and closed access from EBS to see their coverage on the social web. The first result showed that OA journals are not well covered in Altmetric.com because we found only 4 out of 10 with altmetric data. However, the found journals statistics show that OA journals have a higher coverage with 65% of papers as compared to closed journals (44%). Both OA and closed journals have Mendeley and Twitter as their top sources and are distinct at the third source. OA journals are mostly found in Mendeley and Facebook environments, whereas closed journals are available in Twitter and in Stories. However, Mendeley values might be underestimated because of the Altmetric.com data selection process. Altmetrics for closed journals/articles span over more social media sources and their altmetric counts are higher than those of OA journal/articles. For closed journals, the known moderate and positive correlation between citations and altmetrics is confirmed. For OA journals, however, we see a weak indication for a negative relation between altmetrics and citations which means that the more the journal is cited, the less altmetrics the journal gets or

the more altmetrics it gets, the fewer it is cited. Based on the case study, the openness of journals doesn't lead to a more online attention.

Author contribution:
Nuredini, K., contributed to the conception and design of the study. The author coded the script for querying Crossref and downloaded the Altmetric.com data from the Altmetric Explorer. The author coded the script to send the data to a MySQL database for further analysis. Nuredini, K., wrote the first draft of the article. Latif, A., assisted with data analysis, and Peters, I., helped supervise this research work.

Nuredini, K., & Peters, I. (2019). The presence and issues of altmetrics and citation data from Crossref for working papers with different identifiers from Econstor and RePEc in the discipline of economic and business studies. *Proceedings of the 17th International Conference on Scientometrics and Informetrics (ISSI 2019), Rome, Italy.*

Abstract:
We explore altmetric information from Altmetric.com for working papers from Econstor repository and its major contributor RePEc, in the discipline of economics and business studies. Our results show that altmetric information is differently present for different working paper identifiers. This study focuses in three identifiers: handles, DOIs, and URLs. In this case, handles from Econstor are not well covered in Altmetric.com (0, 2%) where a better coverage is for working papers with DOIs (7%). Econstor URLs are less found in Altmetric.com with a coverage of 0, 3%. The top most used altmetric source for working papers in economic and business studies is Twitter for handles and DOIs and for URLs is Policy Posts. Mendeley counts are well present for working papers with DOIs but not for handles. A negative correlation ($r = -0.0157$) is identified between citation counts from Crossref and Altmetric Scores. Cited working papers do not receive online attention and vice versa.

Author contribution:
Nuredini, K., examined the technical details related to collecting different identifiers for working papers and downloading altmetric data for related identifiers, as well as adding the retrieved data to a MySQL database for further analysis. Nuredini, K., wrote the first draft of the article. Peters, I., contributed to the article revision and approved the article.

Nuredini, K., Lemke, S., & Peters, I. (2020). Social media and altmetrics. In R. Ball (Ed.), Handbook Bibliometrics. Berlin: De Gruyter.

Abstract:
This chapter describes the relationship between social media and altmetrics. It briefly discusses how social media platforms' features can create altmetrics and why this is in line with the concept of "affordances." Since altmetrics are build on the data that are derived from user activities on social media platforms, the affordances of these platforms are important for the development of altmetrics. Affordances produce meaning and control the behavior of users that interact with such platforms. Although social media platforms are not necessarily targeted to researchers, the features of these platforms often support the research enterprise. Therefore, this chapter also explains researchers' social media engagement, for example, for what reasons

which researchers use social media platforms on their daily basis. It also provides three classification approaches that aid the interpretation of altmetrics. Last but not least, it discusses the issues that influence the general adoption of altmetrics by focusing on the challenges social media platforms present to altmetrics.

Author contribution:
Nuredini, K., contributed to several sections of this book chapter. Nuredini, K., wrote the manuscript with support from Peters, I, and Lemke, S. Peters, I., designed the chapter and suggested the conceptual ideas. Peters, I., also wrote some sections of this book chapter. All authors contributed to the final manuscript.

Nuredini, K. (2021). Investigating altmetric information for the top 1,000 journals from Handelsblatt ranking in economic and business studies. *Journal of Economic Surveys.*

Abstract:
In this study, we explore the top 1,000 journals in economics (E) and business studies (BS) as an extension of the two previous studies from Nuredini and Peters (2015, 2016). Moderate shares (43.8%) are found for articles published during 2011–2018 in Altmetric.com, whereas Mendeley covers a more prominent share with 47% of journal articles in economics and business studies. The results of this study show that altmetric information is significantly better present for articles published between 2016 and 2017. The top 5 most used altmetric sources for economic and business studies journals are Twitter, News, Facebook, Blogs, and Policy Documents. Low but positive correlations ($\rho = 0.143$ for BS and $\rho = 0.160$ for E) are identified between citation counts and Altmetric Scores on article level, but they increase on journal level ($\rho = 0.733$ for BS and $\rho = 0.813$ for E journals). Furthermore, highly cited journals do receive great online attention, especially from social media platforms such as Twitter and Mendeley.

Author contribution:
Nuredini, K., designed and developed the theory of this research. Nuredini, K., researched all the technical details, designed the tables, performed the analysis, and interpreted the results. The author wrote the manuscript in consultation with Peters, I.

1.9. Structure of the thesis

This thesis is outlined below by briefly describing each chapter.

Part I: Introduction, background, and literature review

Chapter 1: Introduction. This chapter will introduce the problem of information overload, especially in academia, and the fact that scientific output is increasing and researchers feel overwhelmed from all that content. The need for new filters (i.e., altmetrics) will be covered, which goes beyond citations and presents altmetrics as complementary indicators for narrowing information overload. Particular attention will be paid to introducing the EconBiz library portal, its features, and the need for presenting altmetric information within EconBiz to help its users find relevant articles for their needs. Additionally, three use cases will be shown based on the fictional personas created by ZBW on behalf of EconBiz portal and will be further used and enhanced for exploring different aspects of altmetrics in libraries. Furthermore, this chapter will highlight the research questions, structure of the thesis as well as the published work.

Chapter 2: Journals and traditional impact filters with focus on economics. This chapter is wholly dedicated to journals, what they are, who uses them, and for what purpose. Next, different traditional impact indicators (i.e., citations, Impact Factor, and journal ranking) will be introduced and discussed mainly as sources of filtering the right journals or articles for reading, with a focus on economics. Moreover, it will consider the citations as sources for determining the impact of articles and journals and for identifying "trendy topics."

Chapter 3: Altmetrics as new filters. This chapter discusses the introduction of altmetrics in detail and, in particular, the substantial studies made in altmetrics. Also, in this chapter, we provide general information about the most investigated and relevant altmetric providers (i.e., Mendeley and Altmetric.com). After that, we will discuss three essential use cases derived from the ZBW personas based on current studies as sources of altmetrics.

Part II: Altmetric studies for economic and business studies journals

Chapter 4: Methodology: data and technical approaches. This chapter will present the journal selection process based on the Handelsblatt ranking, and the selected journal list will then be used as sources for retrieving altmetric information from two altmetric providers: Mendeley and Altmetric.com. What follows are the technical approaches that can be used to gather altmetric data from two altmetric data providers. Next, we will present the workflow, technological issues, challenges, and limitations during the data collection. Additionally, we show how the data are saved in a MySQL database, queried, and calculated.

Chapter 5: Top 1,000 economic and business studies journals and their altmetric information. This chapter will present the highlights of analyzing Mendeley and Altmetric.com data for journals in E and BS. The content of this chapter will be divided into two parts. The first one focuses on the data retrieved from Mendeley, specifically the coverage of journals and articles and their readership information. The second part will present the data found from Altmetric.com, such as the coverage of E and BS journals, and identify the top most used Altmetric Attention Sources for the related disciplines. It will explore the correlation of citation counts and altmetrics for different altmetric sources (i.e., Twitter and Blogs) and will discuss the "trendy topics" (topics assigned using LDA) of E and BS articles.

Part III: Survey for user evaluation based on altmetric information

Chapter 6: Does the filtering of journal articles work using altmetrics? The last part of this research will evaluate economists' behavior using a survey to investigate their article selection processes, based on different metrics for article evaluation; however, the focus of metrics will be mainly on altmetric data. The participants of the survey will be asked to evaluate four different articles based on the given journal information (i.e., altmetrics). This chapter will highlight whether economic researchers are familiar with altmetrics in general and whether altmetrics are seen as useful indicators for their article selection.

Chapter 7: Discussion, conclusion, and future work. In this chapter, we will discuss the insights gathered from the proceeding chapters of this thesis. We will address several implications of the findings (as proof of concept), especially that would be useful for libraries with an economic focus, and the generalized possibilities that emerged from this research and, therefore, applicable for other libraries. And in the last part of this chapter, we will discuss the future work.

Chapter 2

Journals and traditional impact filters

Given the large increase of scientific literature (e.g., journals) first captured from Price (1963) and later confirmed from different studies (Ware & Mabe, 2012; Bornmann & Mutz, 2015), researchers were and still are affected by this growth, feeling overwhelmed when deciding what to read and where to publish. This chapter focuses on journals as scientific output and different bibliometric methods implemented as measures for determining the impact of journals and the ability to filter the relevant journals from the rest. Several bibliometric (i.e., citations) methods will be described and discussed as sources used by two prominent figures: researchers and libraries.

In this chapter, first, journals as scientific output are described, starting from the infancy stage until now. Then, several data sources for indexing journals are mentioned, of which the most dominant data sources for economic and business studies journals will be addressed. Next, citations as sources for determining the impact of articles and journals especially used for information retrieval and for identifying "trendy topics" will be covered. Lastly, various important journal indicators as relevance filters for journal impact will be mentioned, followed by their limitations. Additionally, these indicators will be examined in terms of the usage for economics literature by economists.

2.1. Journals

Scholarly communication is a process where researchers share, disseminate, and publish their research results globally in academic communities (Abelson, 1980). Abelson (1980, p. 60) emphasizes that "without communication, there would be no science," and the use of scientific journals already established one of the forms depicted as the written form of communicating science. Borgman (1989) set a more detailed definition of scholarly communication:

> "By *scholarly communication,* we mean the study of how scholars in any field (e.g., physical, biological, social, and behavioral sciences, humanities, technology) use and disseminate information through formal and informal channels. The study of scholarly communication includes the growth of scholarly information, the relationships among research areas and disciplines, the information needs and uses of individual user groups, and the relationships among formal and informal methods of communication." (Borgman, 1989, p. 586).

Scientific journals are the heart of scholarly communication (Tomajko & Drake, 1985). They distinct from popular magazines and newspapers because they publish technical and research content (Haustein, 2012). This content is analyzed using qualitative methods such as peer-reviews adopted from the scientific editorial board that contributes to decisions and evaluations of such research results (Frey & Rost, 2010) as well as quantitative methods using citation counts (see Section 2.2).

Around 80% of scientific output from different disciplines (e.g., physics, clinical medicine, and mathematics) is published in journals (Haustein, 2012). By using scientific journals, one can benefit from sharing and disseminating scientific knowledge and help to rank scientific works and aid promotions (Hall, 2011). In the literature, journals have different terms that are used interchangeably, such as periodicals, academic journals, scholarly journals, or serials (Haustein, 2012).

Before journals emerged, the communication between researchers was done by writing letters to each other. This process was not relevant because the letters were restricted to one person at a time and with a very limited number of copies (Tomajko & Drake, 1985). But then, scientific societies (at first from European countries) increased and got developed, which lead to the rise of journals. The first scientific journals appeared in 1665. The three oldest scientific journals are listed in Table 2.1, where *Journal des Sçavans* is considered as the first scientific journal and was focused on church history and legal reports (Tomajko & Drake, 1985; UNESCO, 2015). Afterward, during the 17th and beginning of the 18th century, many journals were unsuccessful because they were not able to produce significant scientific output, missed sponsoring, and had communication problems. First, journals were not accepted as a definitive form of publication and researchers rather used books for their contributions (Kronick, 1976). But in the middle of the 18th century, journals were accepted as a channel for sharing scientific knowledge and started to evolve, so that new journals for different disciplines were produced. In the year 1900, around the world, 10,000 scientific journals were recorded (Tomajko & Drake, 1985). From then onwards, scientific journals started to increase steadily. Price (1963) was the first that noticed this increase by suggesting that journals will increase exponentially. During the 20th century, the exponential growth of scientific output (i.e., journal articles) was confirmed because the number of researchers increased along with their published articles and fundings. With the rapid growth of journal publication, different problems appeared, such as publication delays, restrictions of the article length, referee missing that lead to access problems (Tomajko & Drake, 1985), as well as the main challenge, how to select the appropriate sources from all that output.

Table 2.1: Oldest scientific journals around the world. Source: UNESCO (2015).

Oldest journals	ISSN	Year
The Journal des Sçavans	0021-8103	1665
The Philosophical Transaction of the Royal Society	1364-503X	1665
The American Journal of Science	0002-9599	1818

Later in the 20th century, electronic archives were introduced that allowed researchers to communicate their research results by granting access to their files from remote computers (Borgman, 2000; Swan, 2006). From the 1990s, electronic journals were launched but first they were questionable for both librarians and the research community. Librarians were concerned whether this type of periodicals will be permanently accessible and researchers were not sure if their studies published in electronic journals would count in their careers (Swan, 2006). However, the attraction of using electronic journals got increased by the advantage of accessing them from everywhere anytime (Swan, 2006). With the use of online journals, readers can access journal articles at any time of their production stage without waiting for journal issues. According to Cope and Phillips (2014), online journals help researchers to cite recent articles.

Electronic publishing led to the development of the Open Access (OA) movement that made publishing freely available (Shen & Björk, 2015). The application of the OA movement leads to an increase in articles' impact (i.e., citation advantage; Eysenbach, 2006) and is highly used in the field of economics with 65% coverage of OA articles (Norris et al., 2008).

2.1.1. The history of journals in economics and business studies

The first published research works of economists happened in the United Kingdom with two initial journals: one known as a semiprofessional journal, *Journal of the Royal Statistical Society*, started in 1838 and the other known as a first full professional journal (because it addressed mainly economists) *The Royal Economic Journal* (Diamond, 1989). In the United States, the first economic journal was published in 1886, known as *Quarterly Journal of Economics*, which published work of its faculty members (Harvard University) and its former students. In 1986, journals were seen as more file-oriented rather than the older journals, which published more general research. Economic literature, however, was believed, in the early years of research, to be very technical. Therefore, it was recommended to also consider the non-technical levels of research by creating a new journal in 1987, *Journal of Economic Perspectives* (Diamond, 1989). In 1885, the American Economic Association (AEA) was developed with the purpose to encourage and support economists to publish research works with a focus on historical and statistical studies of industrial life (Coats, 1960). As of 1995, the AEA offered two important journals, the *Journal of Economic Literature* and *Journal of Economic Perspectives,* which gave economists the opportunity to publish their findings.

Goldschmidt and Szmrecsanyi (2007) studied the economic academic discourse over the years for several economic journals and found that economists have their own academic writing genre. Economic authors seem to imitate the same writing style of argumentation based on the writing style of the journals they want to publish their work in. The research work of economists and in which journals they publish lead to the evaluation of the economists' performance, which is being used as indicators for hiring, promotion, and tenure (Ritzberger, 2008). Moreover, for that reason, economists started to rank journals with the intention to show objective information on journal quality and measure the value of researchers' intellectual contributions (Ritzberger, 2008). The rankings use different methods (e.g., citation counts, Impact Factors); however, each of these methods was and is still criticized by the research community (Seglen, 1998; Bollen et al., 2009).

For example, the top 27 economic journals (see Table 2.2) indexed in ISI in 1986 are listed in the work of Diamond (1989). Citation counts are used as selection criteria provided by ISI for ranking the top journals.

Table 2.2: The top economic journals indexed by ISI in 1986 provided by Diamond (1989). The table is a remake from Diamond (1989) for better illustrative reasons, including only the journal names and the year of development.

Journal name	Begun	Journal name	Begun
American Economic Review	1911	Journal of Financial Economics	1974
Brookings Papers on Economic Activity	1970	Journal of International Economics	1971
Canadian Journals of Economics	1968	Journal of Labor Economics	1983
Econometrica	1933	Journal of Law and Economics	1958
Economic Inquiry	1962	Journal of Mathematical Economics	1974
Economic Journal	1891	Journal of Monetary Economics	1975
Economica	1921	Journal of Political Economy	1892
Economics Letters	1978	Journal of Public Economics	1972
European Economic Review	1972	Oxford Economic Papers	1938
International Economic Review	1960	Quarterly Journals of Economics	1970
Journal of Development Economics	1974	Rand Journal of Economics	1970
Journal of Econometrics	1973	Review of Economic Studies	1933
Journal of Economic Literature	1963	Review of Economics and Statistics	1976
Journal of Economic Theory	1969		

Journal rankings, however, do not only contribute to evaluating researchers' performance but also show benefits to libraries for selecting appropriate journals to index in their collection and therefore provide quality sources to its users. Journal rankings are also seen as strategies used by researchers with the intention to minimize the number of journals where they want to pay attention to (Garfield, 1972).

In the following sections, this thesis will discuss different journal level indicators and ranking methods suggested and used from the economic community, which are developed from traditional indicators. These indicators will be addressed as sources for filtering journals and are, therefore, important for researchers during their journal selection process.

2.1.2. Indexing data sources for scientific journals

Three well-known indexing data sources for scientific journals are Web of Science (WoS)[35], Scopus, and Google Scholar[36], which are generally used for searching and retrieving scientific articles for different disciplines as well as obtaining article citations for research evaluation purposes. Citations present the connection between scholarly articles by listing bibliographic references of studied articles at the end of the document (Borgman & Furner, 2002; Frey & Rost, 2010). The use of citations can help researchers find thematically related articles and determine which articles are the most influential ones by looking at their citation counts (Borgman, 1989). More detailed information about citations and different related indicators is described in Section 2.2.

WoS maintained by Clarivate Analytics is the contemporary version of the Science Citation Index (SCI), which was established by Eugene Garfield in 1964, and is the world's oldest database of articles and citations (Birkle, 2020). In 1964, the first year of SCI, 700 journals were indexed in the database, focused entirely on the natural and medical sciences. Later on, the database expended for social science with the Social Science Citation Index (SSCI) and after that with Art and Humanities Citation Index (AHCI). Eugene Garfield emphasizes that his primary goal for developing the SCI was not to evaluate research but rather to index the core journals based on the citations they received so that SCI can work as an information retrieval tool. Moreover, SCI can link similar articles using references so that researchers can find other works that share similar context and might be relevant for them (Price, 1965; Garfield, 2006). As of 2016, WoS indexed 12,700 journals, 160,000 conference proceedings, and 68,000 books (Sugimoto & Larivière, 2018).

Scopus was launched in 2004 from Elsevier[37]—the world's largest scholarly publisher. Scopus indexes a larger number of journals (23,000 journals in 2016) covering more international and open access journals compared to WoS (Bakkalbasi et al., 2006; Sugimoto & Larivière, 2018).

Google Scholar, which was released in 2004, is available for the entire internet community to perform searches and find academic literature based on their needs. It is assumed that it covers articles retrieved from institutional repositories and most important journal archives (Jacsó, 2005). One year after its release, Google Scholar adopted bibliometric information where the algorithms regarding the citations, the search, and the coverage of articles are not well-publicized (Sugimoto & Larivière, 2018). It is assumed that Google Scholar offers 160 million articles, however, with counts on non-journal articles such as PowerPoint presentations or book chapters. The coverage of E and BS journals in Google Scholar was examined from the study of Clemont and Dyckhoff (2012; see Figure 2.1), depicting three types of journal coverages. Coverages that at least have 80%, 90%, and 100% of articles in E and BS journals are found in Google Scholar.

Several studies compared the differences between these three data services, highlighting that they supplement each other. For example, Scopus has greater article coverage compared to WoS. WoS and Scopus are the best for covering citations from 1996 onwards, and both Scopus

---

[35] Web of Science: https://mjl.clarivate.com/
[36] Google Scholar: https://scholar.google.com/
[37] Elsevier: https://www.elsevier.com/

and Google Scholar can be used to identify more citations that were not found in WoS (Visser & Moed, 2008; Bar-Ilan, 2010).

Besides WoS, Scopus, and Google Scholar, which index journals from different scientific disciplines, RePEc and EconBiz are data sources that index journals with a specific focus on economic and business studies. RePEc[38] indexes journals and other scientific outputs (i.e., working papers) and, as of March 2020, covers a total of 3,500 journals. RePEc is also aimed to collect citations for scientific articles in E and BS disciplines and to provide journal rankings (Bornmann et al., 2018). Citations in this database are automatically extracted from open access articles, or the references are sent to RePEc from other stakeholders. EconBiz is an **online library portal that indexes journals in E and BS** (for more information on EconBiz, see Chapter 1) and is suggested as a leading database in terms of journal coverage for economic literature compared to Google Scholar, WoS, and Scopus.

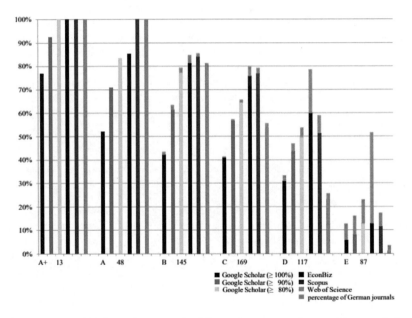

Figure 2.1: E and BS journal coverage in different data sources. Source: Clermont & Dyckhoff (2012, p.5).

In the study of Clermont and Dyckhoff (2012), journal and article coverage for E and BS literature from different data sources is explored. Google Scholar, WoS, Scopus, and EconBiz are searched for 579 journals based on **JOURQUAL2** ranking (indicating the impact of the journals). The study identifies EconBiz as the data source that generally covers more journals, especially when it comes to ones in the German language (depicted as orange bars in the graph),

---

[38] RePEc: http://repec.org/

compared to the other data sources (see Figure 2.1). Journals represented as A+ are ranked as highly important according to JOURQUAL2, and all of them are covered by EconBiz, Scopus, and Web Science. EconBiz, however, does not collect or provide citation indexes to the journal articles but explores citation counts (derived from CitEc[39] a RePEc service for bibliometrics) as sources for retrieval purposes, that is, a better ranking of search results (Plassmeier et al., 2015).

2.2. Citation analysis

Bibliometrics are first used and examined in the study of Wyndham Hulme in 1923, which primarily captured the impact of scientific literature by introducing citation analysis, which is today's most common technique (Pritchard, 1969; Borgman, 1989). Citation analysis represents the link between scientific articles and how they are related to one another (Price, 1965). Bibliometrics as a field and citation analysis were officially initiated in 1960 by Eugene Garfield at the Institute for Scientific Information (ISI) with SCI as the first database that indexed citation counts for scientific journal articles.

Moreover, a citation is a reference that points to a published article, of which its findings are used as arguments either for improving the current research, building on it, or criticizing it (Baird & Oppenheim, 1994). Citations and references, however, are two different concepts. A reference is a list of books, journal articles, conference papers, and more used when writing the new article and is shown at the end of the article study (Sugimoto & Larivière, 2018). Citations, nevertheless, are present in the body of the text by mentioning the authors and the publication year. All articles contain references, but not all articles are cited. "References are always made to past literature and are static; that is, the reference list will never grow or change over time. Citations, on the other hand, come from documents written in the future. Therefore citations are dynamic" (Sugimoto & Larivière, 2018, p. 67).

Citation count depicts the number of articles citing another article and has been applied as a measure for scientific impact; references nevertheless are less used, but they also show important insights. For example, references can be useful indicators to libraries to determine their collection based on the articles their faculty members cited (Sugimoto & Larivière, 2018). There are assumptions that citation counts are a quality indicator, which means that there is a high positive correlation between the number of citations and the quality of an article (Smith, 1981). Citations are also suggested as a measure to show the influence of an article, department, university, country, etc., as well as to indicate the link between articles and how they relate to one another (Price, 1965; Farin, 1976).

Citations, however, do come with its limitations that are listed by several studies as awareness, which should be considered for different reasons (Smith, 1981). First, it is suggested that citations should not be used as comparison measures for different disciplines since they do depend on the discipline. For example, disciplines that publish and cite more are likely to have more citation counts compared to the disciplines that publish less and receive fewer citations (e.g., art and humanities; Sugimoto & Larivière, 2018). Citations cannot be comparable based on time since citations for some disciplines (e.g., medical sciences) are present 1 year after the

---

[39] CitEc: http://citec.repec.org/s/2018/gamjpubli.html

article's publication. For other disciplines, fewer citations are shown within that year (e.g., art and humanities; MacRoberts & MacRoberts, 1989). Citation counts suffer from citation type, so it's difficult to distinguish which citations are affirmative and which citations are negative, but still, negative citations are at very low range (MacRoberts & MacRoberts, 1989).

Frey & Rost (2010) stated that citation analysis doesn't tell us whether the article that has been cited has also been read. There are cases when the authors copy the reference list that appeared in other articles end not reading them. Furthermore, citation counts may lead to biases because many researchers follow the influence of other researchers by citing the same group of researchers and neglecting others. Therefore, many influential articles might remain uncited in academia (MacRoberts & MacRoberts, 2010). For this reason, citations are seen as very skewed, since only a small number of articles accumulate large citation counts (Sugimoto & Larivière, 2018). Despite the above-mentioned and other existing limitations that citations carry, an article with high citation counts means it is still seen as potentially of high-quality research (Baird & Oppenheim, 1994).

2.2.1. Citation indexes as sources for information retrieval (IR)

Manning et al. (2008, p. 1) defined information retrieval as a task to find material (usually documents) of an unstructured nature (usually text) that satisfies an information need from within large collections (usually stored on computers). Years ago, the time needed for information retrieval was significantly higher than today, because information searches in libraries were conducted mostly via human intermediaries. Modern libraries adopted search engine functionalities with online access and retrieval processes much faster and relevant for the users' needs (Onaifo & Rasmussen, 2013).

During the last decade, different information retrieval and ranking strategies for library portals were suggested, developed, and validated to rapidly show relevant articles throughout the users' search process and therefore minimize the display of irrelevant articles (Plassmeier et al., 2015; Bian et al., 2017; Damarell et al., 2019).

Relevance is a part of the information retrieval process that answers the question of whether search/retrieved results (i.e., articles) deal with the same concept of the user query. Usually, the search produces a high number of results, which are then narrowed by the use of quality filters, such as citation counts, to identify the most cited articles and retrieve the most relevant articles (Bernstam et al., 2006). Strategies that usually use citation-based algorithms to narrow search results and show relevant articles are known as ranking strategies and have been found to be more effective than retrieval strategies that are developed based on a Boolean search, that is, using the combination of keywords and operators (e.g., and or not) that are often found in article abstracts (Bernstam et al., 2006; Bian et al., 2017).

The technique which uses citations and is mainly designed for information retrieval is known as citation indexing and was first proposed by Garfield. Citation indexing was suggested to help researchers spot the quality of the article, find other related articles, view the context of the citations, see what other researchers say about the article, and assist on showing research trends which can help to identify new research areas (Garfield, 1964; Lawrence et al., 1999; Yao & Yao, 2003). Moreover, citation indexes can contribute to search strategies that will enable them to retrieve other related articles based on the searched article. The study of Larsen (2002) claims that a combination of several search strategies in libraries is identified as useful for information retrieval, particularly by first searching for articles and then expanding the search results based on citation indexing, which retrieves and ranks articles that contain citations.

CiteSeer, for example, is a search engine and digital library for scientific articles within the field of computer and information science, which integrates the citation index to benefit its users in three important aspects. First, users can see the citation context of the article they searched by following what other authors have discussed in the article. Second, researchers are notified about new citations of the article they located, and third, a graphical representation of citations analysis is shown for different articles. All these features contribute to the evaluation process and are suggested to be helpful for researchers searching relevant articles for their needs (Lawrence et al., 1999; Yao & Yao, 2003).

2.2.2. Identifying "trendy topics" using citations

Research trends are depicted as "radically novel and relatively fast-growing research topic characterized by a certain degree of coherence, and a considerable scientific impact" (Wang, 2018, p. 3). Identifying research trends is, in particular, helpful to researchers who would like to find developments of promising research from an existing mass of literature (Fujita et al., 2014).

Citation counts have been applied to study the evaluation of scientific articles as well as to identify the trendy research topics. The study of He et al. (2009) explored topic evolution, which is used to understand the evolution of scientific topics, based on older archived scientific articles. The authors suggest that citation counts can reveal the inherent link between related topics, and using them for topic evolution may lead to the creation of new information retrieval and filtering tools. These tools can help researchers find new articles for citing in their works as well as objectively evaluate the scientific contribution of an article (He et al., 2009).

Bolelli et al. (2009) used citation-based topical term identification to identify the most influential topics between highly cited articles. They investigated computer science articles published between 1990 and 2004 by extracting terms from their abstracts and by considering citation counts to rank these articles.

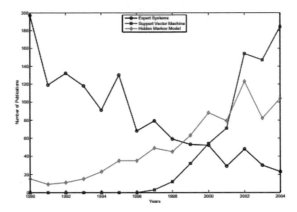

Figure 2.2: Trendy topics extracted from computer science articles published between 1990 and 2004. Source: Bolelli et al. (2009, Figure 1).

The authors visualized three trendy topics in a graphic (see Figure 2.2; i.e., Expert Systems, Support Vector Machine, and Hidden Markov Mode) and the number of times these topics were used in their dataset and found in article abstracts. The results show that the topic "Support Vector Machine" is identified as a newly emerged topic, which was not evident until 1996 and depicted as trendy in 2004. On the contrary, the topic "Expert Systems" seems to expire in 2004. The study suggests that analyzing the content of highly cited articles can help generate trendy topics, which might be of help to researchers who are interested in finding new research topics they want to engage with.

2.2.3. Citation behavior in economics

Economics as a field of research is known as "idiosyncratic" or, with other words, "unique" because economists consider their field as the most advanced and superior compared to other social science disciplines (Kapeller et al., 2017). Additionally, economics is presumed as a pragmatical field of research and is politically debatable, which leads to a particular interest in exploring the attention and citations of this research field (Kapeller et al., 2017).

Citation counts, similar to other disciplines, can play an important role in economics as well. First, citations play an important role when evaluating academics based on the quality of the articles they publish and not for their article quantity. Next, citations seem to play a decisive role in determining the salaries of economics and job promotions or awards (Hamermesh, 2018). Citation counts are also used to identify the quality of journals, which in economics is known as journal ranking (the higher the quality of the journal, the higher the number of citations; Chan et al. 2016). Several techniques have been introduced for ranking economic journals, where the main component for creating the rankings is the citations the journals received. However, each ranking potentially gives different results. Nevertheless, economists usually follow top (i.e., top 5) ranked journals, which they use during their research process, based on a specified ranking they choose to follow (Smyth, 1999).

Kapeller et al. (2017) analyzed the top 5 economic journals (see Figure 2.3) and their citation distribution between the publication years 2009 and 2013. Given their findings, more than 25% of the articles cited in the top 5 journals presented journal self-citations, indicating that economic discipline compared to other social disciplines (i.e., sociology, psychology, political science, and physics multidisciplinary) leads with more journal self-citations.

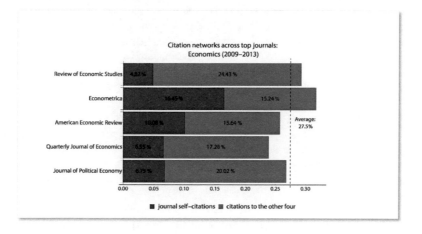

Figure 2.3: Top 5 economic journals and their citation behavior. Source: Kapeller et al. (2017, Fig. 1).

Moreover, citation counts of articles from the top 5 ranked journals in economics generally seem to be very low. The study of Hamermesh (2018) analyzed article citations from SSCI for a sample of 444 articles published in the top 5 economic journals between the publication years 1974 and 2014, showing that even articles that are published in top journals are rarely cited. But, these articles receive, on average, more citations than articles published in low-ranked journals. The author claims that the distribution of citations between the publication years of articles he studied looked the same. Hamermesh (2018) found out that empirical studies generated more citations than other studies.

Citation counts are explored for 100 journals in economics and business studies articles between the publication years 1980 and 2005, suggesting that citation peak in these disciplines is found 5 years after the article publication, which the average article received 216% more citations than the first year of publication. Nonetheless, after 5 years of publication, citations drop each year (McCabe & Snyder, 2015). The same study found that publishing in open access journals in E and BS can boost citations of articles by 10%. This benefit is seen more as skeptical rather than beneficial since the authors of articles need to pay several dollars to publish their work in such journals (McCabe & Snyder, 2015).

Another interesting study, which explores citations in economics fields, suggests that citations should first be normalized to be utilized correctly, especially when they are used as sources to evaluate economists and allocate their salaries. The study of Bornmann and Wohlrabe (2019) shows that economic journals that publish content of different economics subfields gather different citation rates. Therefore, they apply normalized indicator methods usually used in bibliometrics, that is, the mean normalized citation score (MNCS) and ($PP_{top\ 50\%}$) to normalize citation counts for economics journals. The MNCS normalization is calculated as "each paper's citation set (of a journal, researcher, institution or country) are divided by the mean citation impact in a corresponding reference set; the received normalized citations are averaged to the MNCS" (Bornmann & Wohlrabe, 2019, p. 875). However, the most vigorous normalization, in this case, is suggested by the use of percentiles where "each paper is weighted on the basis of the percentile to which it belongs in the citation distribution of its field" (the top 1%, 10%, or 20%; Bornmann & Wohlrabe, 2019, p. 884). By introducing these normalization techniques, citations can be comparable between different subfields of economics.

2.3. Journal level indicators as relevance filters

Over the years, the scientific output is growing day by day and researchers face a big challenge when it comes to filtering the relevant (quality) articles or journals for reading or publishing (Borgman, 1989). In this section, different bibliometric methods on journal level will be introduced as sources of filters (e.g., highly cited journals) and useful indicators in economics fields.

2.3.1. Journal Impact Factor as a source for filtering relevant journals

Garfield (1972) developed a journal citation pattern tool (SCI) for journal evaluation that included journals in different disciplines. Garfield (1972) declared that SCI is the most extensive database that covers the most quality journals, evaluated based on citation counts. Afterward, Journal Citation Reports (JCR) emerged, which extends the use of citations for examining journals. The system of JCR counts the references and citations to a journal and their distribution over time (Todorov & Glänzel, 1988).

Using citation counts, Garfield (1972) presented the Journal Impact Factor (JIF) for assessing a journal's quality. JIF represents the total number of citations received in a particular year by articles published in a particular journal during the two previous years, divided by the number of articles published during those 2 years (Garfield, 1972; Pisnki & Narin, 1976).

The JIF values have been investigated for the top 20 journals in economics retrieved from the two different citation databases Scopus and Web of Science, indicating different results. Scopus shows higher counts of citations and, therefore, higher JIF values for top economic journals compared to WoS, since Scopus indexes a higher number of economic articles that cite the top journals in this field (Pislyakov, 2009).

Garfield (1972) suggested that JIF is seen as a helpful indicator for libraries to identify relevant journal collections for indexing in their library systems as well as important for researchers to identify high impact journals for reading or publishing their scientific articles. Despite the fact that JIF has the ability to identify the most relevant journals, according to the citation frequency, it cannot fully identify the most important scientific articles. This issue of JIF brought debatable stories and critical voices, confirming problematic implications of citation-based indicators (e.g., Seglen, 1998; Bollen et al., 2009) and the rising resistance against the inadequate use of the JIF as a source of article evaluation (see, e.g., the Leiden Manifesto[40]). Seglen (1998) claimed that the correlation between article citation and JIF is often very poor, denoting that JIF cannot represent individual articles and should not be used as an indicator to judge the articles' quality. JIF is based on citation counts that a small number of articles have received, which, on the other hand, many articles of a particular journal receive few or no citations at all during the 2-year citation window (Elliot, 2014). The distribution of the data is highly skewed, meaning few articles receive the most substantial portion of total citations (Sugimoto & Larivière, 2018), which could be properly presented by medians (Elliot, 2014). The correlation between JIF of social sciences journals and the mean citation counts of articles is identified as low, suggesting that JIF should not be used to judge the quality of social sciences articles (Finardi, 2013). Moreover, not every scientific article published in a high impact, and therefore relevant journal is also relevant and not every article, which is of a quality and relevance, is published in high impact journals (Wets et al., 2003). Seglen (1998) reported some associated JIF problems, which are needed to take into consideration when disseminating the impact of scientific output, such as articles and journals. JIF is dependent on the discipline based on the publishing and referencing patterns since some disciplines publish less and use fewer references than other disciplines, which leads to low JIF and vice versa. Chemistry, for example, has a lower JIF than the disciplines covered in medicine (Sugimoto & Larivière, 2018). JIF can also be manipulated or increased, for instance, with the use of self-citation, where reviewers or editors suggest articles to the authors who want to publish in that particular journal.

Given the limitations of JIF mentioned above and other limitations existing in literature, JIF is seen as a flawed indicator for filtering relevant scientific articles (Neylon & Wu, 2009). And Seglen (1998) suggested that JIF should be mostly used as journal level indicator rather than an indicator that will identify the value of articles published in that journal.

The 2-year citation window is the dominant indicator for determining journal impact. Nonetheless, a 5-year JIF emerged since 2007 in JCR, which covers a bigger proportion of citations than the 2-year JIF. For social sciences, a 5-year JIF is suggested as a better indicator because in these disciplines, the citations take time to be accumulated and a longer citation window is needed (Sugimoto & Larivière, 2018).

2.3.2. *h*-index as a source for filtering relevant journals

Another indicator known as *h*-index, proposed by Hirsch (2005), is an alternative indicator to JIF, which originally was developed to measure the scientific output of researchers (researcher level), as well as the impact of journals (journal level). *h*-index is defined as: "A scientist has index *h* if *h* of his/her Np papers have at least h citations each, and the other (Np-h) papers have no more than h citations each" (Hirsch, 2005, p. 16569). This indicator combines both quantity (number of articles) and quality (number of citations these articles accumulated) in its calculation (Glänzel, 2006a). However, the *h*-index cannot be higher than the researcher's articles' count, so each additional citation for an article that reached the limit is lost in the calculation, making this indicator also flawed when evaluating researchers and journals

---

[40] Lieden Manifesto: http://www.leidenmanifesto.org

(Sugimoto & Larivière, 2018). One example of this indicator is "an author would have an h-index of 10 if ten of his papers had received at least ten citations each and his other papers have no more than 10 citations each" (Sugimoto & Larivière, 2018, p. 101). Moreover, this indicator favors the number of articles a researcher has, making it difficult to understand if it measures productivity or impact (Sugimoto & Larivière, 2018). The use of h-index benefits researchers and journals that constantly publish scientific articles, which get more than average citations (Bornmann & Daniel, 2007). The advantage of the h-index is that it does not have a fixed length of citation window as the JIF has. Any citation window could be used that favors each discipline rather than using a citation window of 2 years (Harzing & van der Wal, 2009).

The h-index is influenced by the number of articles each journal publishes; the journals that have a higher number of articles are more likely to have a higher h-index than other journals with a lower count of articles. Nonetheless, journals that publish a high number of high impact articles indicate to have a high impact in that particular field (Harzing & van der Wal, 2009), making this indicator a source for filtering and identifying journals that do publish more and are highly cited.

The study of Harzing and van der Wal (2009) showed that the h-index is positively and highly correlated (e.g., Spearman correlation, $p = 0.841$ for marketing journals) with the JIF for different subfields of E and BS disciplines (e.g., finance and accounting, and general management and strategy). Therefore, the h-index is recommended as an alternative indicator to measure the journal impact for subdisciplines in E and BS, especially when they are not fully covered in ISI (e.g., finance and accounting). Furthermore, the h-index is suggested as a more firm indicator in terms of citations covered for determining the impact of journals compared to JIF. Glänzel (2006a,b) highlighted that the h-index is another indicator that can be used additionally to other advanced bibliometric indicators for determining the impact of scientific output (i.e., journals) but not to substitute them.

2.3.3. Journal rankings as a source for filtering relevant journals

Besides indicators that are accumulated from bibliometric databases (i.e., ISI and Scopus), several other different journal rankings determining the relative value of publications (Eisend, 2011) are introduced, which are regarded as a proxy for research quality. Ranking means the position or the significance of the journal within the set of other journals (Frey & Rost, 2009). The first journal ranking in economics was published in 1971, which ranked journals based on the judgment of the members of the American Economic Association (Bornmann & Wohlrabe, 2019).

There are two different rankings, according to Frey & Rost (2009):

1. Quantitative rankings use article and citation indexes to measure the particular importance of scientific quality.
2. Qualitative rankings do not always involve the use of citations but only the editorial board memberships, so-called peer-review. The board members contribute to editorial decisions, and the evaluation of these members brings on the quality.

Journal ranking can be beneficial for different purposes, such as a guide for libraries to select journals; it raises the standard of research and academic excellence since to publish on high ranked journals, authors need to produce a higher qualitative study. For economic researchers, journal ranking plays a core role, especially when it comes to selecting the relevant journals for publishing or reading (Schläpfer, 2012; Aistleitner et al., 2018). The main idea of journal ranking is to select or filter, for example, the top 5 or top 10 journals of a greater impact that researchers would like to publish their scientific work in or read articles from (Bornmann et al., 2017). Several journal rankings have been developed (see Table 2.3) for evaluating the impact of economic journals. However, only some of them whose results can contribute to the research focus of this thesis are further covered and discussed. Each journal ranking has its own approach that is being used to rank economic journals, making it challenging to decide which rankings one should use and for what purpose. Journal rankings, nevertheless, according to Gordon (1982), are proved useful for journal selection that libraries, retrieval systems, and researchers use.

The most popular journal rankings in economics and business studies besides JIF, according to literature, are Handelsblatt ranking, RePEc, and ABS (Rafols et al., 2012; Stern, 2013; Sturm & Ursprung, 2017). Handelsblatt ranking (see Chapter 4 for more details), for example, ranks individual economists and departments and provides a journal ranking list based on weighting schemes for two different disciplines E and BS, for German-speaking countries (i.e., Germany, Austria, and Switzerland). Moreover, Handelsblatt ranking covers all journals that are ranked by JOURQUAL 2.1, a ranking developed by VHB, journals that belong to the Social Science Citation Index (SSCI) and journals that are listed in the Erasmus Research Institute of Management (EJL), making this ranking more correlated to JCR from WoS (Wohlrabe, 2013; Lorenz & Löffler, 2015), compared to other rankings (e.g., RePEc).

RePEc, as a bibliographic service for economic literature, provides rankings for researchers, institutions, journals, and countries. What makes RePEc rankings unique is that they provide co-authorship centralities between authors (e.g., identifying influential authors) registered in RePEc and evaluate other types of scientific outputs, that is, working papers which are preprints, published in informal series such as NBER[41], BREAD[42], World Bank Policy Research Working Paper Series[43] and in repositories Econstor[44], SSRN[45], or AgEcon[46], rather than in scientific journals (Ozler, 2011).

---

[41] NBER: https://www.nber.org/papers/
[42] BREAD: http://ibread.org/bread/papers
[43] World Bank Policy Research Working Paper Series: https://www.worldbank.org/en/research/brief/policy-research-working-papers
[44] Econstor: https://www.econstor.eu/about
[45] SSRN: https://www.ssrn.com/index.cfm/en/
[46] AgEcon: https://ageconsearch.umn.edu/?ln=en

Table 2.3: A list of several journal rankings existing in economics. Source: Bornmann et al. (2017, p. 3).

Study	Data Source	Ranked Journals	Approach
Coats (1971)	A.E.A. Readings	10	citation counts
Skeels and Taylor (1972)	own sampling	35	standardized citations
Billings and Viksnins (1972)	own sampling	50	citations count from three top journals
Moore (1972)	own sampling	50	authors contributions from top universities
Hawkins et al. (1973)	Survey	87	
Bush et al. (1974)	own sampling	14	citation counts
McDonough (1975)		70	meta ranking of five different rankings
Button and Pearce (1977)	Survey	20	
Kagann and Leeson (1978)	Survey	8	
Bennett et al. (1980)	own sampling	81	relative share of indexed abstracts in the JEL
Liebowitz and Palmer (1984)	WoS	108	relative impact (LP-framework)
Laband and Sophocleus (1985)	WoS	40	citation counts
Pommerehne (1986)	Survey	30	
Malouin and Francois Outreville (1987)	Survey	112	
Diamond (1989)	WoS	50	citation counts
Archibald and Finifter (1990)	WoS	104	regression approach
Enomoto and Ghosh (1993)	Survey	50	
Laband and Piette (1994)	WoS	130	relative impact (henceforth LP-framework)
Pieters and Baumgartner (2002)	WoS	42	log-multiplicative model of citations
Burton and Phimister (1995)	WoS	42	data envelopment analysis
Barrett et al. (2000)	WoS	144	relative impact (LP-framework)
Bräuninger and Haucap (2001)	Survey	150	
Liner (2002)	Textbooks	30	Citation counts
Kalaitzidakis et al. (2003)	WoS	159	relative impact (LP-framework)
Axarloglou and Theoharakis (2003)	Survey	100	
Palacios-Huerta and Volij (2004)	WoS	42	relative impact (invariant approach)
Kodrzycki and Yu (2006)	WoS	181	relative impact (invariant approach)
Ritzberger (2008)	WoS	261	relative impact (invariant approach)
Vieira (2008)	WoS	168	panel model
Wall (2009)	WoS	30	mean/median citations
Engemann and Wall (2009)	WoS	69	citation counts from seven top-journals
Combes and Linnemer (2010)	GS, WoS	1168	combines IF and citations from various sources
Bao et al. (2010)	WoS	22	relative impact (invariant approach)
Koczy and Strobel (2010)	WoS	143	tournament method
Chang and McAleer (2011)	WoS	40	various measures, meta ran-ing
Kalaitzidakis et al. (2011)	WoS	209	relative impact (invariant approach)
Halkos and Tzeremes (2011)	WoS, Scopus, RePEc	229	data envelopment analysis
Bräuninger et al. (2011)	Survey	150	
Stern (2013)	WoS	230	impact factor, uncertainty measures
Laband (2013)	GS	248	various citation measures
Hudson (2013)	WoS, other rankings	388	regression approach
Demange (2014)	WoS	37	handicap approach
Chang et al. (2016)	WoS	299	various measures, meta ranking
Vana et al. (2016)	Various	58	various measures, meta ranking
Lo and Bao (2016)	WoS	60	relative impact (invariant approach)

ABS ranking is created by the Association of Business Schools in the United Kingdom. It adopts the technique of star rating, which is based on peer-reviews, citations, and editorial judgments. However, the ABS ranking was criticized that it has negative consequences in fundings, research culture and especially for the researchers' careers since some active researchers who had received low ABS rating of the journals they published were omitted from the UK Research Excellence Framework (REF)[47] 2014 list, which is a system that assesses the quality of research in United Kingdom and that provides funding to high education institutions (Willmott, 2011; McKinnon, 2017). Removing researchers from REF list can not only negatively influence the researchers' careers but also neglect their papers to be independently evaluated between the REF and ABS ranking (McKinnon, 2017).

---

[47] REF: https://www.ref.ac.uk/

Even though journal rankings seem to assess research performance and rank journals based on their quality, these rankings are constantly boycotted and criticized (Vogel et al., 2017). First, researchers who publish articles in the top journals should adjust their writing style and research based on the criteria and the standards of these journals; these standards can limit different ways of experimenting and writing research; and according to studies, this can affect the innovation and the academic freedom. Therefore, it has been suggested that articles that are published in top ranked journals follow a specific group of research or topics, which is anticipated that can decrease the creativity in research development. Second, many economic researchers have questioned, and some of them boycotted the rankings (McKinnon, 2013). McKinnon (2013), for example, highlighted that journal rankings can discriminate relative young disciplines (e.g., logistics) and cannot identify the impact of single articles.

2.4. Discussion

Nowadays, the number of journals is increasing due to the invention of different fields of study and the need for publishing new research results, which leads to information overload (Haustein, 2012). Given the increase of journals and the number of published articles, several methods (i.e., bibliometrics) related to determining the impact of scientific journals and articles are developed. These methods, for example, help researchers to narrow the amount of literature online and filter the relevant journals for reading or publishing. Moreover, researchers and libraries could define the scientific impact of journals and articles, which helped them to select the relevant scientific output for their needs. However, these methods were generally criticized and suggested as flawed because they are not perfect, and each has its own limitations and should be used carefully depending on the purpose.

For example, JIF is not recommended as a relevant indicator when it comes to filtering articles that are highly cited and therefore show a high impact since JIF cannot represent them due to the mean value. In E and BS, journal rankings are used to help researchers selecting journals for publishing their works and as sources of reading for their work as well as libraries to select impact journals for their collections. However, journal rankings can be relevant only if they are used for the right purpose (e.g., identify highly cited journals and not the impact of the article). The other limitation is that with journal rankings, researchers are limited, for example, to top 5 journals and neglect other journals that might have published articles, which might have been of the researchers' interest.

According to Haustein (2012), the multidimensionality (i.e., journal output, journal content, journal usage and perception, journal citations, and journal management) is needed for journal evaluations because it helps to reflect on various aspects of research publications where so far still no single indicator incorporates all the aspects.

Library portals are increasingly interested in adopting retrieval technologies, which can assist in overcoming the issue of information overload using bibliometric methods such as citation counts. Citation counts in retrieval systems can retrieve and rank articles based on the user search and, therefore, can assist researchers in finding and filtering relevant articles that own a scientific impact (Lawrence et al., 1999; Yao & Yao, 2003).

Nevertheless, citation count needs time to be accumulated, especially in social sciences (i.e., E and BS), which makes it difficult to fully show the scientific impact of journal articles after a year of publication. So, the use of citation counts for newly published articles is not relevant because these articles need time to gather citations (e.g., after 2 years), and therefore, this technique is seen as not the best option to filter recently published and highly impact articles.

Citations show different citation patterns for different disciplines. For example, some disciplines can accumulate faster citations than others. The study of Abramo et al. (2011) claimed that to consider the real impact of scientific articles properly, the speed of citations from the date of articles publication should be observed. In physics, for example, the peak in citations occurs 2 years after the publication of the article, whereas in mathematics, the peak occurs after 5 years. Moreover, in E and BS, citations are very sparse, which makes it difficult for libraries to enable users the feature to filter highly cited articles for a particular journal. Since the retrieval process will only show a few articles and neglect others that didn't accumulate citations, just because some articles didn't receive many citations or no citations at all, it does not mean that these articles are not influential and, therefore, not relevant for the researchers' needs. These articles are either "essentially worthless" according to the assumption that scientific value and citations are linked or they need more time to accumulate citations, which is heavily dependent on the citation window of the discipline the articles are published in (Sugimoto & Larivière, 2018).

Chapter 3

Altmetrics as new filters

> "No one can read everything. We rely on filters to make sense of the scholarly literature, but the narrow, traditional filters are being swamped. However, the growth of new, online scholarly tools allows us to make new filters; these altmetrics reflect the broad, rapid impact of scholarship in this burgeoning ecosystem. We call for more tools and research based on altmetrics."
> Jason Priem, Dario Taraborelli, Paul Groth, and Cameron Neylon
> "Altmetrics: A Manifesto" (2010)

Different bibliometric methods (i.e., citations, JIF, and journal rankings) are used to judge the quality of scientific output (e.g., articles) and are suggested as tools for identifying and thus filtering relevant information from the rest based on their impact (Garfield, 1972; Lawrence et al., 1999; Eisend, 2011). For example, citation indices are one of the possible methods that can help to define the impact of scientific output and filter highly cited journals and articles (Lawrence et al., 1999). However, for a very long time, citations and other related indicators have been criticized for the inability to show the full impact of scientific outputs, especially journal articles (Sugimoto & Larivière, 2018) because of the limitations these indicators carry (see Chapter 2).

Given the limitations of bibliometric methods, the growth of literature and the use of social media in academia have led to the appearance of new alternative metrics known as altmetrics. Altmetrics are data derived from users action on social media platforms and other online sources (i.e., Wikipedia), which indicate the online attention of different types of scientific output (i.e., articles, books, and datasets) that are shared, mentioned, and discussed online (Priem et al., 2012).

Jason Priem suggested the term "altmetrics" in his tweet post:

> "I like the term #articlelevelmetrics, but it fails to imply *diversity* of measures. Lately, I'm liking #altmetrics." (Holmberg, 2015, p. 3)

Given the rise of users, especially researchers in social media platforms, one can see that these platforms fill the needs of researchers (i.e., by serving them throughout the research process) even though they are not inevitably focused on them (Nuredini et al., 2020). Social media platforms can instruct what kind of interaction a user can take (e.g., share e post) and which data can be freely analyzed and applied as altmetrics (Wouter & Costas, 2012; Nuredini et al., 2020). The actions of researchers (e.g., tweeting a new published scientific article) can leave traces online, which are then tracked from altmetric providers (Nuredini et al., 2020).

This chapter provides a systematic description of altmetrics, which are seen as complements to citations for evaluating scientific output in terms of online impact and therefore used as sources for filtering relevant journals or articles based on the online attention. Firstly, it discusses which researchers for what reasons use social media sources. Secondly and briefly, three classification models that aid the interpretation of altmetrics are presented. Thirdly, we discuss the state of the art of altmetric providers – two widely known altmetric providers (aggregators) are reviewed as sources for providing altmetric information for journal articles. Next, altmetrics as sources for filtering trendy topics and as impact sources for libraries will be covered. Last but not least, literature studies that explore altmetrics for E and BS disciplines, as well as journal level altmetrics, will be discussed, followed by the issues and challenges of altmetrics inherited from social media.

3.1. Scholarly use of social media

With the rise of social media, scholarly communication shifted to the web environment, and new promising ways of disseminating and evaluating research are presented (Holmberg, 2015). Social media is often used in conjunction with Web 2.0 and user-generated content, and according to Kaplan and Haenlein (2010), social media is:

> "…a group of Internet-based applications that build on the ideological and technological foundations of Web 2.0, and that allow the creation and exchange of User Generated Content." (p. 61)

Web 2.0 environment users can modify and create content online where social media is built upon the ideas and technologies of Web 2.0. Social media tools provide the ability to promote research articles digitally and encourage collaboration between researchers using blogs, wikis, bookmarking services, and bibliography systems (Kaplan and Haenlein, 2010; Procter et al., 2010). To use social media platforms, the maximum necessity is to register using an email address and join social media features (e.g., like a post) to engage with other researchers about scientific outputs. Social media features can produce meanings and can control the behavior of researchers on platforms that depicts how users (or researchers) use and interact with such platforms, especially for research purposes (Bowman, 2015).

Rowlands et al. (2011) claimed that almost 50% of researchers use social media to communicate, share, and disseminate scientific output. Researchers who use social media platforms, according to Rowlands et al. (2011), are coming mostly from Europe and Africa, and less from Asia and North America, and a large share of users of social media is male (Sugimoto et al., 2017). Experienced researchers use social media platforms (i.e., Twitter and LinkedIn) to share their research output with the public. In contrast, young researchers often use social media channels that provide questioning and answering features (e.g., StackExchange and StackOverflow) to search for helpful information or platforms that share pieces of code (e.g., GitHub; Mehrazar et al., 2018).

All these different actions that researchers perform using social media platforms present different engagements that make the nature of altmetrics multidimensional (Holmberg, 2015). For this reason, several classification systems have been suggested to interpret the nature of altmetrics better.

3.2. Classification of altmetrics[48]

Nuredini et al. (2020) highlight three possible approaches based on the existing literature that aid the interpretation of altmetrics:

1) *Source-based classification*

Social media platforms used for altmetrics have been classified into those with social media focus, those with scholarly focus, or platforms that have both dimensions (Wouters et al., 2019). According to Wouters et al. (2019), Facebook, LinkedIn, and Stackexchange have a strong social media focus. These web-based services allow researchers to create public profiles along with connections, disseminate research, and follow research outputs and are used for professional branding (Sugimoto et al., 2017). Facebook is a widely applied platform, usually used by younger researchers (Rowlands et al., 2011). LinkedIn is identified as a platform that is used highly by academics and by older generations of researchers (Rowlands et al., 2011).In contrast, Scopus or Web of Science, Mendeley, F1000, and Wikipedia citations are considered as platforms strongly related to scholarly focus, while ResearchGate and Academia.eu, which are two popular academic networks that allow researchers to upload and discover new scholarly publications, are considered as a combination of social media and scholarly focus.

2) *Engagement-based classification*

Within this approach, different levels of engagement between users and scientific outputs have been identified. Haustein et al. (2016) proposed three primary activities that are part of the engagement: "access," "appraise," and "apply." All these activities describe a different kind of interest in scientific outputs. Access can, for example, show "views," appraise can show "mentioning," and apply can capture activities such as "adoption," by re-using datasets, codes, etc.

3) *Altmetric aggregators-based classification*

Each altmetric aggregators follow different approaches when presenting altmetrics. ImpactStory[49] is an author-based service that allows researchers to promote their scientific outputs (i.e., articles, codes, slides, and videos) and track the online impact via blogs, Wikipedia, Mendeley, and more (Piwowar & Priem, 2013). The altmetrics within ImpactStory is classified into five categories: *viewed*, *saved*, *discussed*, *recommended*, and *cited*. PLOS[50], another altmetric aggregator, represents article level altmetrics and uses a similar classification system as ImpactStory. In contrast, Plum X also uses five categories: *citations*, *usage*, *captures*, *mentions*, and *social media*, but they reflect a different kind of attention compared to the categories of ImpactStory.

Since several altmetric providers are developed to track the online attention of scientific output from social media sources, a great number of studies have compared these providers with each other and identified the different characteristics these providers have in respect of representing

---

[48] Some parts of this section are substantially equivalent with the manuscript published in Nuredini, K., Lemke, S., & Peters, I. (2020). Social Media and Altmetrics. In R. Ball (Ed.), Handbook Bibliometrics. Berlin: De Gruyter.

[49] Impact Story: https://impactstory.org/
[50] PLOS: https://alm.plos.org/

altmetrics data. Peters et al. (2014) identified four altmetric tools (i.e., Altmetric.com[51], ImpactStory, Plum Analytics[52], and Webometric Analyst[53]) and compared them with each other. The findings show that different altmetric providers gather altmetric data from various social media sources with variable coverage; for example, Altmetric.com has better coverage of articles mentioned on Twitter, whereas Plum Analytics tracks better Facebook posts. Ortega (2018b) additionally found that Altmetric.com covers a higher number of blog posts and news outlets than Plum Analytics. Social media data (e.g., Twitter, Facebook, and Reddit) are supplied from Altmetric.com to ImpactStory based on individual researchers' profiles and their scientific output.

Within the group of several altmetric providers that offer altmetrics for scientific output (e.g., journal and articles), this thesis will explore Mendeley and Altmetric.com, which are the two most studied providers from the altmetric community (Haustein & Larivière, 2014; Mohammadi & Thelwall, 2014; Zahedi et al., 2014a,b; Nuredini & Peters, 2015). The following chapter discusses in detail Mendeley and Altmetric.com based on their features and altmetrics they provide, and it also highlights the findings from other existing literature that already explored Mendeley and Altmetric.com.

3.3. Mendeley and Altmetric.com

Altmetric.com and Mendeley allow crawling their database via API for different identifiers. For this thesis, two identifiers play an important role, International Standard Serial Number[54] (ISSN), which is a journal identification number, and Digital Object Identifier[55] (DOI), an identification number for journal articles. With the use of these two identifiers, altmetric information for journals in E and BS will be retrieved. Altmetric information for these journals are retrieved and explored in Chapter 5.

In contrast, PlumX does not allow to crawl their database for a particular dataset of DOIs or other articles identifiers, but rather it provides a bulk of data records consisting of any articles with altmetric information attached to them (Ortega, 2018b). The PlumX methodology does not fit this thesis purpose since the searches to retrieve altmetric data will rely on exact DOIs. Moreover, the crawl process focuses on a fixed selection of article DOIs of specified journals in economics and business studies. The selection method of journals and how Mendeley and Altmetric.com are queried for performing this thesis analysis will be described in Chapter 4.

In the next sections, we will briefly present Mendeley and Altmetric.com, followed by their features and what kind of altmetric data they provide, especially for journal articles, and some insights found from other existing literature will be mentioned.

3.3.1. Mendeley, a social reference management system

Mendeley is a social reference management system (sometimes also referred to as the academic social network) that allows users to search for articles, add them to their libraries along with

---

[51] Altmetric.com: https://www.altmetric.com
[52] Plum Analytics: https://plumanalytics.com/
[53] Webometric Analyst: http://lexiurl.wlv.ac.uk/
[54] ISSN: https://www.issn.org/
[55] DOI: https://www.doi.org/

their metadata, and organize them in folders for better retrieval. Its catalog[56] contained over 300 million documents coming from around 2 million users (Mohammadi & Thelwall, 2014). Mendeley was released in 2008 and then purchased by Elsevier in 2013 (Elston, 2019), becoming the main platform of Elsevier for research promotion and collaboration. According to William Gunn (2013), the catalog had around 90% coverage of recently published articles, especially in life sciences, math, computer science, chemistry, and social sciences. Mendeley offers a web application and Windows and Apple-based applications for users to search, share, and access literature (Elston, 2019). For registering in Mendeley, the user needs to have an email address to create an account. After registration, the users can begin searching for literature, save their desired literature in their own Mendeley library, and organize in folders for better retrieval (see Figure 3.1).

Moreover, the users can search for articles saved in their own library or, in general, Mendeley's database and keep track of recently added articles in their own library and recently read articles. Furthermore, when reading an article using the Mendeley reader feature, the user can select and highlight different parts of the text in a particular article and create comments. When the users close the current article and re-opens it again, Mendeley provides its own bookmark feature, which redirects the users to the last visited page where they left of. Users in Mendeley can follow other users and authors of articles (e.g., Stefanie Haustein) that have a Mendeley account. Users can follow different research groups (e.g., Altmetrics) that allow them to discover new articles and follow discussions based on group topics and focus.

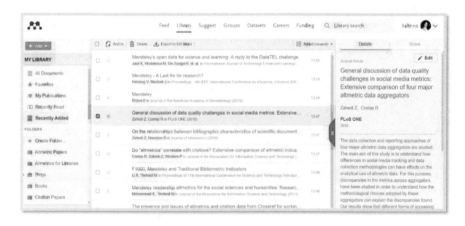

Figure 3.1: Mendeley library page of the user "Kaltrina."[57]

When using Mendeley as sources of altmetrics, meaning by retrieving readership information for scientific articles, Mendeley API is crawled. Detailed information about how Mendeley API can be accessed and crawled, especially for E and BS journals, is provided in Chapter 4. Besides

[56] Mendeley catalog: https://www.mendeley.com/guides/web/02-paper-search
[57] Mendeley library page: https://www.mendeley.com/reference-manager/library/all-references [accessed 20.09.2020]

the advantage that Mendeley offers freely available data for analysis in terms of altmetrics while crawling this provider, technical issues are involved that should be noted and mentioned. Mendeley's results can suffer from missing values, for example, missing articles' titles, journal issues, or volumes. These technical issues can have an effect on the data analysis and results; therefore, to avoid such problems, several strategies have been recommended to properly use the Mendeley API (Zahedi et al., 2014b; Nuredini & Peters, 2015).

3.3.2. Mendeley readership information

Based on Mendeley's user libraries and user demographic data, Mendeley provides readership data, which are seen as altmetric information that show the early online attention of scientific articles in particular (Maflahi & Thelwall, 2018). The Mendeley readership information is divided into four main groups, which will be described in the following sections.

3.3.2.1. Mendeley counts

Each article saved in Mendeley has a *reader count,* which is a number of unique Mendeley users (or readers) who have saved a given article in their own Mendeley library (Gunn, 2013). Viewing from the altmetrics perspective, reader counts, also known as "Mendeley Saves," is seen as a promising indicator for different studies (Li et al., 2012; Mohammadi & Thelwall, 2014; Thelwall, 2018a; Zahedi & van Eck, 2018). Mendeley counts have a positive correlation with citation counts, and this correlation determines that Mendeley counts show an early impact of later citations for journal articles (Maflahi & Thelwall, 2018). For example, a recent study of Maflahi and Thelwall (2018) investigated six journals in library and information science to find out how fast research articles can receive reader counts in Mendeley. The authors confirm that journal articles in these disciplines receive a substantial number of readers right after they are published officially, suggesting that there is no need to wait for more than a year to check the impact of an article provided by citations. Even though Mendeley counts are seen as useful early indicators for the impact, they specifically do show another academic impact compared to citations. Moreover, articles that are cited are firstly read and then referred to in future studies, depicting these articles as useful in research. In contrast, Mendeley Saves does not clearly show that "reads" represent the usefulness of the study because it is unclear whether the user has already read the article and therefore used that article in his/her study (Maflahi & Thelwall, 2018). Citations cannot decrease but rather continue to grow with time since any author can cite an article anytime he or she needs it, also even multiple times. Mendeley counts are based only on unique Mendeley readers, and if the readers remove a saved article from their Mendeley library, Mendeley counts for that particular article are automatically decreased (Zahedi et al., 2015).

Moreover, the biggest disadvantage of Mendeley, in theory, is that not all researchers use this system for their research purposes, but practically, according to studies, Mendeley reader counts are higher than citation counts, especially for the recently published articles, and still, these counts are also positively correlated with each other (Thelwall, 2017a).

3.3.2.2. Academic status

In Mendeley, users have profile pages with personal information like discipline, academic status, or currently the so-called readers' seniority and country, specifying the geographical location of the user. So, the articles that the users save into their libraries are categorized into groups via the personal information mentioned above (Gunn, 2013). For example, an article can be categorized by readers with country "Germany" or readers who are "PhDs."

In Figure 3.2, a screenshot of Mendeley readership information (i.e., academic status and discipline) is presented for the article: "Why do papers have many Mendeley readers but few Scopus indexed citations and vice versa?". According to the readership information presented below, PhDs, masters, and postgraduates are the most interested users for this article, while 52% of the readers are registered in the discipline of social sciences and 28% of the readers are registered in the discipline of computer science.

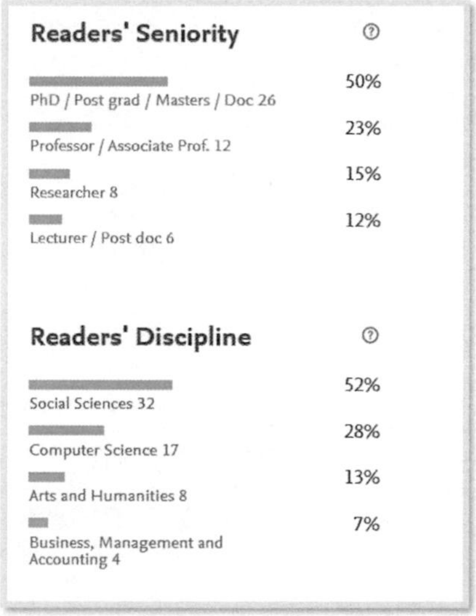

Readers' Seniority ⑦

PhD / Post grad / Masters / Doc 26	50%
Professor / Associate Prof. 12	23%
Researcher 8	15%
Lecturer / Post doc 6	12%

Readers' Discipline ⑦

Social Sciences 32	52%
Computer Science 17	28%
Arts and Humanities 8	13%
Business, Management and Accounting 4	7%

Figure 3.2: Screenshot of Mendeley readership information (Retrieved April 2, 2020).

With the information retrieved from the users' profiles in Mendeley, several studies have performed readership information analysis from Mendeley for different research articles published in various disciplines (Haustein & Larivière, 2014; Maflahi & Thelwall, 2018). It is important to note that, from the earlier research, when crawling Mendeley API, the retrieved data from the crawl are based only on the top 3 most frequent user categories for each searched article (Haustein & Larivière, 2014). For example, when crawling a specific article in Mendeley, only the three academic statuses with the highest shares per article are retrieved out of the 15 possible academic statuses an article might receive from the Mendeley users. Retrieving only the top 3 academic statuses per article as seen is a negative aspect of Mendeley API since user types which fall under the top 3 reader groups are not considered and are underestimated (Haustein & Larivière, 2014). Nonetheless, Zahedi and van Eck (2018) performed the first study that covered the full user statistics for each article found in Mendeley without any data restriction (e.g., top 3 reader groups). The authors highlighted that with the advantage of having the full received user statistics from Mendeley, one can determine more insights about the impact of research output saved in Mendeley.

However, when visiting Mendeley.com as a reader or user and not as a crawler, the top 4 academic statuses are shown instead for each article found with Mendeley page (see Figure 3.2).

Some of the academic statuses retrieved from the users of Mendeley are aggregated with each other since some of them seem to have similar function (see Table 3.1; see "Mendeley Status" and "User type"). For example, "PhD Students" are classified similar to "Doctoral Student," "Master Students" to "Postgraduates," and more (Haustein & Larivière, 2014). Mohammadi et al. (2015) and Haustein and Larivière (2014) also categorized academic statuses into educational, scientific, and professional. "PhD Students" and "Doctoral Students" are merged into "PhD Student," where these types of users are classified as "scientific" because they tend to read and publish scientific articles.

Table 3.1: Mendeley academic statuses. Source: Haustein and Larivière (2014).

Mendeley status	Sector type	User type
Assistant Professor	Scientific	Assistant Professor
Associate Professor	Scientific	Associate Professor
Doctoral Student	Scientific	PhD Student
Lecturer	Educational	Assistant Professor
Librarian	Professional	Librarian
Other Professional	Professional	Other Professional
Ph.D. Student	Scientific	PhD Student
Post Doc	Scientific	Postdoc
Professor	Scientific	Professor
Researcher (at a non-Academic Institution)	Professional	Researcher (Non-Academic)
Researcher (at an Academic Institution)	Scientific	Researcher (Academic)
Senior Lecturer	Educational	Associate Professor
Student (Bachelor)	Educational	Student (Bachelor)
Student (Master)	Educational	Student (Postgraduate)
Student (Postgraduate)	Educational	Student (Postgraduate)

These categorizations of users in "Sector type" have been suggested as helpful since it can represent the users' behaviors and different classes of impact, such as different kinds of users can read different types of articles. Zahedi et al. (2014a) claimed that scientific users might read articles with higher citation counts.

In contrast, educational users are less focused on higher citation counts, but rather on other article attributes (e.g., journal name where the article is published, the title of the article, author names, and more). The leading users of Mendeley are mostly PhDs who use this system to search for articles that will assist them in writing their own thesis or other scientific outputs (Haunschild et al., 2015a).

3.3.2.3. Discipline

Discipline is another readership information and a useful feature of Mendeley that helps to understand the saving behavior of articles by different user types (Zahedi et al., 2017). When the users of Mendeley create their profile, they don't need to assign their discipline information on their profile section (Gunn, 2013).

However, several studies that explored Mendeley readership information found that a great number of users (e.g., 99.9% of users of medicine articles) have shared their discipline information on their profile (Haunschild & Bornmann, 2015). The study of Nuredini and Peters (2015) identified 25 different Mendeley users' disciplines (see Table 3.2) based on the journal articles in economic and business studies.

Table 3.2: Mendeley user's discipline for E and BS journal articles. Source: Nuredini and Peters (2015, Figure 3).

discipline of users	Nr. of readers of Business Studies (BS) articles	Nr. of readers of Economics (E) articles
Arts and Literature	315	408
Astronomy/Astrophysics/Space Science	78	77
Biological Sciences	644	2,02
Business Administration	**35,819**	**10,688**
Chemistry	68	651
Computer and Information Science	4,136	3,017
Design	359	260
Earth Sciences	104	221
Economics	27,623	14,181
Education	1,232	1,552
Electrical and Electronic Engineering	201	555
Engineering	1,653	1,294
Environmental Sciences	558	986
Humanities	343	627
Law	416	489
Linguistics	89	119
Management Science / Operations Resear	9,143	3,036
Materials Science	30	26
Mathematics	1,164	2,66
Medicine	441	1,193
Philosophy	462	459
Physics	256	390
Phsychology	3,985	2,122
Social Sciences	8,076	25,776
Sports and Recreation	133	86

According to Table 3.2, about 37% of Mendeley users, who provided their discipline in their profiles that read E and BS journal articles, come from business administration with 35,819 readers (Nuredini & Peters, 2016). However, here it's essential to note that by crawling Mendeley API, similarly as for academic status, only the top 3 disciplines per article are retrieved, suggesting that not all users' disciplines per article are considered for the analysis.

3.3.2.4. Country

The last readership information of Mendeley is the user country. Mendeley users can save their geographical location in their profiles. Moreover, not all users provide country information on their profile pages (e.g., 17.6% of users have country information for biomedical discipline; Haunschild et al., 2015b). Similarly, when exploring Mendeley by country, studies have retrieved only the top 3 countries of users for each article (Thelwall & Mafhali, 2015).

Nuredini and Peters (2015) have explored readership information by countries for E and BS journal articles and identified 119 different countries of users that save articles, of which the top 3 countries are the United States, Germany, and the United Kingdom. Generally, the United States seems to cover the highest number of readers from almost any discipline (Haunschild et al., 2015b). According to Thelwall and Mafhlai (2015), Mendeley users tend to read more articles published by authors from their own country, and articles with international collaboration attract a higher number of Mendeley users.

3.3.3. Altmetric.com

Altmetric.com is a tool that collects information for research output found online from specific sources, such as social media platforms, traditional media, and online reference managers. Altmetric.com was founded in 2011 by Euan Adie (Liu & Adie, 2013), and in 2012, Altmetric Explorer [58] was released, which enables users (e.g., authors of articles, libraries, and researchers) to search their database and find online attention for different scientific outputs. Additionally, Altmetric.com provides an API that allows researchers (who study altmetrics) and other interested stakeholders (who integrate altmetrics to their collection) to query their database for the specific dataset of articles based using programming scripts. The API[59] calls are only made by the use of DOIs and are not queryable by ISSN. Altmetric.com tracks different scientific outputs[60] for online social information, usually tracking books, book chapters, journal articles, presentations, thesis, reports, conference proceedings, datasets, etc.

Altmetric.com monitors only scientific outputs that have unique identifiers. It tracks nine standard identifiers[61], for example, DOIs that are usually assigned to individual articles as well as to datasets and images; RePEc IDs that are used in economic research; ISBNs that are used for identifying books; and ISSNs that are used for identifying journals.

3.3.4. Altmetric Attention Score

Altmetric.com offers the Altmetric Attention Score (AAS)[62], which is a counting number that shows the total amount of the attention research outputs (i.e., articles) have already received online from social media sources. The score is based on an algorithm provided by Altmetric.com, weighting[63] different social media sources based on their reach to reflect the relative values of these sources. Moreover, Altmetric.com considers three important factors to the calculation: 1) the volume of how many times an article has been mentioned, 2) from which online sources, and 3) who created these mentions (Elmore, 2018). According to Altmetric.com, for example, a blog post has a higher weight (i.e., 6) as Twitter posts (i.e., 1) because the average blog post is more likely to bring attention to research articles than the average tweet.

The AAS is a metric that provides 1) quantity by counting the Altmetric Score, the higher the Altmetric Score, the higher is the attention as well, and 2) quality by considering the weights

---

[58] Altmetric Explorer: https://help.altmetric.com/support/solutions/articles/6000146655-introduction-to-the-altmetric-explorer

[59] Altmetric API: http://api.altmetric.com/

[60] What outputs does altmetric track: https://help.altmetric.com/support/solutions/articles/6000060968-what-outputs-and-sources-does-altmetric-track-

[61] Types of identifiers Altmetric.com tracks: https://www.altmetric.com/about-our-data/how-it-works/

[62] How is the Altmetric Attention Score calculated: https://help.altmetric.com/support/solutions/articles/6000060969-how-is-the-altmetric-attention-score-calculated-

[63] Numbers behind Numbers: https://www.altmetric.com/blog/scoreanddonut/

each source receives based on their impact (Costas et al., 2015). The AAS is represented visually as a colorful donut[64] (see Figure 3.3) of which each color represents a social media source (e.g., blue for Twitter or orange for blog posts), which contributes to the calculation of the AAS (Trueger et al., 2015). With the use of Altmetric.com, readers can find context to the attention an article has received online using the altmetric information (e.g., blog posts that discuss a particular article) aggregated for each article (Trueger et al., 2015).

Figure 3.3: Altmetric.com details page for the article "How well developed are altmetrics? A cross-disciplinary analysis of the presence of 'alternative metrics' in scientific publications." (Article's details page was retrieved from Altmetric.com on March, 2020).

The Altmetric.com details page (see Figure 3.3) provides information about the attention an article has from different attention sources. This article is mentioned in 4 blog posts; in one policy source, it is retweeted 69 times; and it is shared 2 times in Google +. Similarly, the article owns 158 citations from Dimensions, which is a citation database that Altmetric.com tracks, as well as 375 unique users who have saved this article in Mendeley and 6 users who have saved it in CiteULike. The AAS for this article is 69 and is represented by the colors of the altmetric donut. The AAS of "69" does not show where this article fits within other articles published in the same journal or within the entire dataset. Altmetric.com, on its support page, claims that if an article has an AAS of "0," then this article has no attention at all. However, finding what is a "good score" for an article AAS is challenging to be determined since not all articles with high AAS are highly mentioned and therefore have positive attention. For example, the article "The case (study) of arsenic life: How the internet can make science better" received great online attention but not necessarily a good one. The AAS of "20" on average is depicted as a "good score" compared with other articles in the dataset (Altmetric Support, 2019a).

---

[64] Colors of the donut: https://www.altmetric.com/about-our-data/the-donut-and-score/

3.3.5. Altmetric attention sources

Altmetric.com monitors 12 types of sources[65] for tracking the online activity of scientific output (e.g., books, articles, presentations, and thesis). Some source types are divided into subtypes; for example, "social media" includes services like Facebook, Twitter, LinkedIn, Google+, Weibo, and Pinterest, and "multimedia" includes Youtube, Reddit, and Q&A from Stackoverflow. The sources are tracked based on two methods: 1) by searching them with the URLs of scientific articles and 2) by examining a text (e.g., blogs) for mentions based on the article title, journal, or author names.

Table 3.3: General descriptions of altmetric sources retrieved from Altmetric.com.

Source name	Collection method	Update frequency	Notes
Twitter	Third party data provider API	Real-time feed	Demographics, support for retweets, with monitoring of suspicious activity.
Facebook	Facebook API	Weekly	Posts on public Facebook Pages only, with prioritised popular Pages.
Policy documents	PDFs collected and scanned from policy sources and repositories	Varies by policy doc (min monthly updates)	Scanning and text-mining policy document PDFs for references, which are looked up in CrossRef/PubMed and resolved to DOIs.
News	RSS feeds and API	Real-time feed	Manually curated news sources, with data provided via a third-party provider and RSS feeds direct.
Blogs	RSS feeds	Daily	Manually curated list, harvesting links to scholarly content.
Mendeley	Mendeley API	Daily	Reader counts is number of readers with the output in their Library. Not included in score.
Post-publication peer reviews	Publons API	Daily	Peer review comments collected from item records and associated by unique identifier.
Reddit	Reddit API	Daily	Includes all sub-reddits. Original posts only, no comments.
Wikipedia	Wikipedia API	Real-time feed	Mentions of scholarly outputs collected from References section. English Wikipedia only.
Q&A (Stack Overflow)	Stack Overflow API	Daily	Scan for links to scholarly outputs.
F1000Prime recommendations	F1000 API	Daily	Scan for links to scholarly outputs.
YouTube	YouTube API	Daily	Scan for links to scholarly outputs in video descriptions.
Open Syllabus	Static import from Open Syllabus	Last update September 2016	Link syllabi's contents to HLOM IDs.
Web of Science Citations	Clarivate Analytics API	Real-time feed	Citation counts from peer-reviewed literature. Not included in score. Appear in the Explorer for customers with existing Web of Science subscriptions.
Dimensions Citations	Dimensions API	Daily	Match outputs based on scholarly IDs.
Patent Citations	Static import from Dimensions	Last update October 2018	Scanning JSON patent records for links to publications and DOIs.

---

[65] Altmetric.com Sources: https://www.altmetric.com/about-our-data/our-sources/

Table 3.3 is constructed based on Altmetric.com general information page about its sources[66]. The "Source name" depicts the social media platform Altmetric.com tracks, "Collection method" presents how the data are collected, "Update frequency" depicts how often Altmetric.com updates these data, and "Notes" describes the source functionality. Twitter is tracked by its API, and the data retrieved are updated in real time. For Facebook, only the posts from public pages (e.g., institutions) are tracked and, therefore, not personal accounts posts and likes. Policy Documents in Altmetric.com are defined as reports, white papers, or documents that provide policy and guidance from government or non-government organizations (Nuredini & Peters, 2019).

Thus, policy posts include references to articles in Policy Documents. Altmetric.com searches for mentions in Policy Documents are based on links, identifiers, and text mining[67]. Text mining works by using a scraper that can match the mention in the Policy Documents with an appropriate research output based on the author's names, journal title, and time frame. This step is needed when in the Policy Documents neither URL nor DOI is found. According to the results, we confirm that in the Policy Documents, articles are mostly referenced by the URL[68] (Nuredini & Peters, 2019).

The same procedure is used in the News. Altmetric.com tracks around 2,900 news outlets via link recognition and news tracker mechanisms to pick up the mentions. The news tracker mechanism is based on the search of the text of that news based on the author's name and journals (Nuredini & Peters, 2019). Patents are intellectual properties held by the owner. Altmetric.com tracks nine different jurisdictions patents around the world. For tracking peer-reviews, two services are crawled via their APIs. PubBeer[69] is a foundation to improve research by introducing innovative methods and Publons[70], which is a company that enables researchers to keep track of the scientific impact of their works (i.e., citations and peer-reviews), all in one place. Sina Weibo[71] is tracked by Altmetric.com, which is a microblogging service similar to Twitter and the most prominent social media in China. Wikipedia is monitored, especially for the references which mention scientific outputs only in English. Google +, LinkedIn, and Pinterest are tracked only for historical data. F1000 Recommendations are monitored for the articles published in F1000Prime[72], which is an article recommendation platform for clinical, social, and behavioral sciences. Youtube API is used to find links to scientific articles mentioned in video comments. Open Syllabus Project is analyzing millions of syllabi to help and support education and research. This platform is tracked to find online mentions about books. Mendeley's data (counts for each article) are not included in the AAS. Mendeley is

---

[66] What outputs and sources does Altmetric.com track?
https://help.altmetric.com/support/solutions/articles/6000060968-what-outputs-and-sources-does-altmetric-track-
[67] How Altmetric.com tracks policy documents:
https://help.altmetric.com/support/solutions/articles/6000129069-how-does-altmetric-track-policy-documents-
[68] How news are tracked by Altmetric.com: https://www.altmetric.com/about-our-data/our-sources/news/
[69] PubBeer: https://pubpeer.com/
[70] Publon: https://publons.com/
[71] Sina Weibo: https://www.weibo.com/
[72] F100Prime: https://facultyopinions.com/prime/home

queried daily via the API. Citation data for scientific articles are represented by querying the Dimension database.

Based on the social media sources that Altmetric.com tracks and by using their affordances (e.g., likes, tweets, and posts), different altmetric indicators are created that show the online attention of scientific output in different ways (Roemer & Borchardt, 2015). In the following sections, altmetric indicators and their functionalities are categorized according to the social media source they come from.

3.3.5.1. Social media indicators

Likes and tweets belong to the toolbox of social media metrics (Roemer & Borchardt, 2015). Likes are metrics that indicate that someone positively enjoyed the research work (Roemer & Borchardt, 2015), and they can be used on different social media sites such as Facebook, YouTube, and academically on Research Gate. Since likes are part of altmetrics and altmetrics relate to "gamification," likes can be increased artificially from researchers to gain higher metric counts for their research products.

The second important metrics are **tweets and shares**. These two metrics are generated from Twitter and Facebook. According to Eysenbach (2011), tweets and citation counts are fairly strong correlated (0.40–0.70) for articles published in the *Journal of Medical Internet Research*, which means that tweets can be seen as social media activity that might increase citations or may predict citation counts. Tweets are suggested as the "earliest metrics" that appear for scientific articles, but with the shortest life, since they increase for 3 months and then continue to stay constant (Ortega, 2018c).

3.3.5.2. Usage indicators

In this category, users have options (i.e., clicks, views, and downloads) to interact with scientific outputs (e.g., journal articles or conference papers) directly. Usage metrics are early indicators, even older than citations, and are used since the time when libraries started to track the usage of their products (Glänzel & Gorraiz, 2015). But with the emergence of technology and the web, online applications started to adopt usage metrics beyond libraries (Glänzel & Gorraiz, 2015). *Views* **and clicks** are part of usage metrics that record the unique user click for that particular research product and identify the number of visitors (Roemer & Borchardt, 2015). In contrast, *Downloads* depict how many times users have downloaded a research product. According to Tattersall (2016), download counts should not be counted as a metric since they are considered as computer activity, and this might not indicate that the article or research product is used or read. In contrast, Ortega (2018c) claimed that "views and downloads" continue to grow for scientific articles, and these indicators have the longest life cycle compared to others (e.g., blogs and tweets).

3.3.5.3. Capture indicators

Capture metrics generally help users to identify the hot topics within a particular research field (Roemer & Borchardt, 2015). *Bookmarks* are one type of capture metrics that allow users to save and organize sites and URLs from different sites so that they can find them quickly anytime they want. For example, social sites like Delicious and CiteULike provide such bookmarking options. *Forks* is another capture metric that is often used by programmers to fork a source code created by someone else, and they use it as a standalone code to create a new project.

GitHub is a well-known tool that represents such fork counts. *Favorites*, as the name alone intends, present the favorite counts of specified work in a community and show a positive reaction from the users who favorited that particular work. The last type of capture metric is the *saves/readers*. This metric usually specifies the readership of the work and is usually counted within that particular tool where the work is saved (Roemer & Borchardt, 2015).

3.3.5.4. Mentions

Mentions are metrics that usually bring to light discussions generated for scholarly works across the social web (Roemer & Borchardt, 2015). One of the common places to find mentions is blog posts. Research blog has become very popular nowadays as sources of discussing scholarly communication around the web (Shema et al., 2012). Blogging about research gives the ability to share knowledge and helps researchers stay connected (Kjellberg, 2010). Shema et al. (2012) analyzed the sample blog posts from the aggregator ResearchBlogging.org, and the authors found that Life Sciences blogs were most popular in their sample, followed by Psychology, Psychiatry, Neurosciences, and Behavioral Science. The study also confirms that bloggers usually prefer to discuss papers from high-impact journals such as *Science*, *Nature*, *PNAS*, and *PLoS One*.

Bornmann (2015a,b) emphasized some advantages using blogs as sources for altmetric information: 1) a social function, which allows bloggers share opinions with a larger community, 2) a knowledge transfer from research results to non-researchers, and 3) blog posts, which can test the quality of the post-publication by allowing bloggers to peer-review and discuss them. Scientific blogs that discuss scholarly literature are complicated to track since they are spread all over the internet (Fenner, 2014; Bornmann, 2015a,b). Therefore, in this case, aggregators can play a significant role, but still, they cannot track everything available (Bornmann, 2015a,b). Nonetheless, it happens that blogs can disappear from the web after some time or move to another blog network, which leads to obsolesce links.

Other types of mentions are *comments and reviews*. Comments have a qualitative nature and mainly provide an extensive understanding of the works being shared (Roemer & Borchardt, 2015). They directly show how users understand and interact with the work being shared. Lastly are reviews, which represent a less formal procedure in altmetrics since they are coming from different kinds of users and not only from professionals. A good example of altmetric reviews is Amazon reviews or F1000 reviews (Roemer & Borchardt, 2015). F1000 is a commercial post-publication service for medical and biological research where selected researchers are able to provide reviews for articles, which are listed in different databases, to help improve their quality (Haustein et al., 2015).

3.4. Altmetric as sources for filtering highly cited articles

This section describes some valuable insights that several studies have found and suggested altmetrics as sources, especially for filtering highly cited and, therefore, high-impact articles. The focus of most of the studies that explored altmetrics is to find out to what extent altmetric information correlate with citation counts from different altmetric providers and to highlight different correlation levels between various altmetric indicators.

The study of Costas et al. (2015) confirmed a positive but weak correlation between Altmetric Scores from Altmetric.com and citation counts, indicating that altmetrics do not show the same impact as citations do. The authors also reveal that blogs tracked by Altmetric.com, for example, cannot always filter highly cited articles, but are suggested as more capable indicators compared to journal level indicators (i.e., JIF) when it comes to that point.

Zahedi et al. (2015) found a positive correlation between citation counts and Mendeley counts across five fields (e.g., biomedical and health sciences, social sciences, and humanities), suggesting that readership counts can be used as a relevant tool for filtering highly cited articles, but by only considering the limitation of this system. Mendeley Readership Information is built upon the users of Mendeley and does not consider other researchers who don't have profiles. Therefore, their behaviors are not saved within these indicators. Moreover, readership information counts are limited to users that practice Mendeley, and one should consider this limitation when using these indicators for evaluation or filter purposes.

Maflahi and Thelwall (2016) confirmed that Mendeley count can be used as early indicators to determine the article's impact. The authors explored the Library and Information Science Journal articles, which take 7 years after their publication to accumulate many Scopus citations. A positive and strong correlation between citation counts and Mendeley readership counts is found within this discipline, suggesting Mendeley readership counts as a useful indicator for determining early impact for both recently published and older articles. Moreover, Mendeley readership counts can be used as an early indicator of impact for almost all disciplines, since Mendeley counts and citations are positively and strongly correlated, but Mendeley counts appear around a year before citation counts (Thelwall, 2017a).

3.5. Altmetrics as sources for filtering "trendy topics"

Citation counts, as mentioned in Chapter 2 (Section 2.2.2), can be used as filters for identifying trendy topics published within scientific articles that had received a higher count of citations, compared to a finite set of articles for a particular discipline (Bolelli et al., 2009). The identified trends, for example, can be useful for researchers to get informed about different newly emerged topics, which are of impact, and therefore cited and referenced from the scientific community (Aleixandre-Benavent et al., 2017).

Citations, however, need their time to get present for scientific articles, about 3 years to be used as a reasonable indicator for evaluating the impact of a scientific article (Glänzel & Schubert, 2003) and thus to be useful for filtering new trends. In contrast, altmetrics, which are seen as early impact indicators compared to citations (Bronmann, 2015a,b), might be suggested as new tools for filtering trendy topics. Thelwall (2018b) claimed that the delay provided by citation counts might be undesirable for evaluating the impact of recently published articles. Similarly, this claim can be used when filtering trendy topics of those recently published articles because the first citation counts do appear 1 year after the article has been published. According to the studies performed so far, altmetric information can generally appear sooner than citation counts. Specifically, some altmetric sources (e.g., Twitter, Facebook, and Reddit) accumulate altmetric data within a few days after the articles' online publication (Fang & Costas, 2020). Twitter, for example, is suggested as a platform where users can find "trendy topics" since it allows them to post short messages (tweets) that contain a particular topic. The topics are indicated by the hash sign "#". The number of messages (tweets) that contain the same topic reflects the interest and the attention of users on a real-time basis (Naaman et al., 2011). Holmberg and Thelwall

(2014) explored how researchers use Twitter for 10 different disciplines, including economics. The author suggests that economics tweet mostly links (e.g., URL to a blog post) compared to other disciplines and was difficult and unclear to identify whether their tweets are dedicated to economics in general or to research in economics that has a scientific value.

Additionally, Mendeley counts are seen as early indicators for scientific articles and they continue to increase steadily (Maflahi & Thelwall, 2018). Besides the ability as early indicators, Mendeley counts can identify topics based on their user types (e.g., academic status). Zahedi and van Eck (2018) investigated the topic interests of users in Mendeley and identified different topics that focused on different user groups. For example, the authors mentioned that professors are usually interested in scientific topics that are related to education. In contrast, students are most interested in topics such as leadership, management, and business, and librarians are more interested in bibliometrics and information science.

The study of Wang et al. (2017) explored the top highly mentioned articles in Altmetric.com from 16 neurosurgery journals and presented the trendy topics (e.g., trauma) in regard to altmetrics scores for those articles. The authors were able to identify the most popular topics based on newly published articles with high Altmetric Scores, according to public engagement from diverse audiences (Wang et al., 2017).

Within this thesis, trendy topics using Mendeley and Altmetric.com altmetrics will be explored and discussed in Chapter 5. However, the focus for identifying trendy topics will be on economic and business studies journal articles. Moreover, articles that are published recently are supposed to have high Mendeley counts and AAS. The results will be considered for discussion in Chapter 5.

3.6. Altmetric studies for economic literature

Several studies investigated altmetric information for social science publications in general (Zahedi et al., 2014a), but a couple of studies focused specifically on economic and business studies journal articles only and investigated altmetric information for these disciplines (Nuredini & Peters, 2015, 2016; De Filippo & Sanz-Casado, 2018; Drongstrup et al., 2019). Zahedi et al. (2014a) claimed that since citation counts are not well represented generally in social sciences, the correlation between Mendeley counts and citations is found positive and moderate ($p = 0.49$). The authors suggest Mendeley as a relevant platform for this discipline since, according to the correlation, citing an article and reading it (i.e., saving it in Mendeley) are seen as related activities. Similarly, the study of Fraser et al. (2019), which analyzed Open Access articles for different disciplines, confirmed that Mendeley counts and also tweets are higher for social science articles compared to other altmetric indicators and other disciplines.

Nuredini and Peters (2015, 2016) explored Mendeley and Altmetric.com for the top 30 economic (E) and business studies (BS) journals and found a high coverage of the articles within these disciplines with 77.5% in Mendeley and 38% in Altmetric.com. The authors noted that Mendeley and Twitter are the most used sources for journal articles in E and BS. The results of the study from Nuredini and Peters (2015) revealed that Mendeley's information might be helpful for economic researchers to determine the suitable journal or article for reading or publishing based on the target groups of Mendeley. Furthermore, the authors also highlighted that based on the low but positive correlations between Journal Impact Factors and Altmetric Score on journal level, altmetrics could be used as complement indicators of traditional bibliometrics for indicating the impact of journals.

Nuredini et al. (2017) investigated the altmetric information for the top 4 Open Access (OA) journals in economic and business studies. The authors highlighted that OA journals in these disciplines are not well covered in Altmteric.com, but they have higher coverage of articles (65%) compared to closed journals (44%). Week correlation is found between altmetrics and citation counts, suggesting that the more the journal is cited, the less altmetrics the journal gets or vice versa. According to the case study the authors performed, the openness of journals doesn't lead to a more online attention.

Nuredini and Peters (2019) explored altmetric information for working papers (or preprints) published within the economic and business studies disciplines. The authors identified different issues and challenges (i.e., based on the handle or URL of the article) when retrieving altmetric information for this types of scientific output, and they found a negative correlation between citations from Crossref and Altmetric Scores.

The study of De Filippo and Sanz-Casado (2018) analyzed 76,400 articles published between 2013 and 2015 in economic journals, and they found that less than one-third are found in social media platforms, most commonly being mentioned in Twitter and blog posts and fewer in Facebook. A significant number of economic articles (87%) that received online attention are also cited. However, citation counts and altmetrics (e.g., tweets) are found positive but low correlated, meaning that most cited articles did not necessarily gain high altimetric counts and vice versa.

Drongstrup et al. (2019) investigated scientific articles from 22 economic subdisciplines (e.g., accounting and finance) for altmetric information with an emphasis on online mentions for Policy Documents. The authors suggest that Policy Mentions can be used as indicators to show a broader impact of economic research since a large number of articles have been found with at least one policy mention, and the articles from top journals in economics receive higher policy counts.

3.7. Journal level altmetrics

Besides article level altmetrics (ALM) that seek to measure the online impact on article level (e.g., PLOS ALM), several research studies introduced aggregation of altmetrics on journal level to evaluate the impact of scientific journals. Moreover, altmetrics on journal level are created by summing up of all social media mentions for each article published by a specific journal (Loach & Evans, 2015).

Since altmetrics appear faster than citation counts and offer a nuanced view for scientific output, journal level altmetrics are suggested as new measures to complement the use of Journal Impact Factors for evaluating journals (Loach & Evans, 2015). Altmetric.com provides journal level[73] information for 11,000 journals in 18 different disciplines and created individual journal metric

---

[73] Journal Analytics in Altmetric.com: https://www.altmetric.com/press/press-releases/cabells-to-feature-altmetric-data-in-journal-whitelist-analytics/

pages (see Figure 3.4) with aggregated social media mentions per journal as well as the average the online attention of individual articles published on a specified journal.

Cabells[74], which is a scholarly services company that provides information about whitelist and blacklist journals, is helping researchers to find the right journals for publishing their research work. According to Altmetric.com news page[75], Cabells adopted the Altmetric.com journal level metric page. Cabells suggested that the use of journal level information from Altmetric.com in real-life applications is very beneficial for its users since it provides helpful insights and an accurate overall picture of the journal importance.

Altmetric.com supports the aggregation of altmetrics on journal level only if some important points are met by encouraging researchers to develop correct journal level altmetrics. Four main important steps that should be met when developing journal level altmetrics are as follows:

- **Account for known skew** using coverage percentiles (e.g. "% articles with an attention score in a journal"), geometric means, or medians (technically allowed, but discouraged).
- **Address biases** related to subject area, location, and other confounding variables, for example, by using subject-area normalization.
- **Look beyond the boundaries of specific journals** toward network analysis, communications theory, and topic-based analysis.
- **Are transparent and otherwise in line "responsible metrics" practices** described by the Leiden Manifesto. (Altmetric.com, Using Altmetric data to develop journal level metrics, 2019b, para 2).

Altmetric.com suggests that when using journal level altmetrics, the median of the AAS per article should be considered and the articles online attention. Similarly, like citation counts, which are differently covered for different disciplines and therefore need to be normalized, altmetrics also needs to be first normalized to disciplines (subject areas). The study of Bornmann (2014a,b) shows that altmetrics should better be normalized on the level of topics since some articles receive online interest from many people outside of that scientific discipline. Altmtetric.com also encourages researchers to base their developed metrics on Leiden Manifesto[76] principles and practices for better research evaluation guidance.

---

[74] Cabells: https://www2.cabells.com/
[75] Altmetrics in the news: https://www.altmetric.com/press/press-releases/cabells-to-feature-altmetric-data-in-journal-whitelist-analytics/
[76] Leiden Manifesto: https://www.nature.com/news/bibliometrics-the-leiden-manifesto-for-research-metrics-1.17351

Figure 3.4: *Behavioral Ecology* journal metric page with journal level altmetrics in Altmetric.com. (Source: Altmetric.com, retrieved 06.04.2020.)

Apart from Altmetrc.com journal level altmetrics, several research studies aggregated altmetrics on journal level and explored the correlation between this metric with JIF (Loach & Evans, 2015; Nuredini & Peters, 2016). Nuredini and Peters (2016) claimed that the correlation between AAS and citation counts is low on article level and increases on journal level for the top 30 E and BS journals (Spearman correlation $r = 0.614$). The authors reveal that old published articles in E and BS journals still have low altmetrics, although the availability of altmetrics increased for more recent articles. However, when considering altmetrics data for real-world applications (e.g., in libraries), higher aggregation levels, such as journal level, can overcome the sparsity of altmetrics data well. By doing so, it will be ensured that for every record, altmetric information could be displayed, which lowers, or even avoids, user frustration.

However, not all studies support the use of journal level information. Holmberg and Park (2018) suggested journal level altmetrics as not reliable because only a few articles have gained a great number of online attention and their popularity can influence these indicators. Therefore, journal level indicators are not useful indicators for journal evaluation, especially for Korea-based scientific journals.

3.8. Altmetric challenges[77]

Despite the fact that altmetrics are identified as indicators complementary to citations and useful sources to evaluate scientific output (Priem et al., 2010; Wouters et al., 2019), they do have challenges. This section will highlight the challenges that are introduced to altmetrics by the characteristics that social media platforms offer and the limitations of altmetric providers.

The first main challenge, which is evident when using altmetrics, is the data quality (Haustein, 2016). Each altmetric provider or aggregator has its own data retrieval strategies for social media counts, and one should be careful when using the provided methods (Zahedi et al., 2014b). For example, Altmetric.com tracks tweets from Twitter in real time regularly, whereas Lagotto tracks only a portion of the tweets (Zahedi et al., 2014b), resulting in altmetric data inconsistencies. The quality of altmetric data is also dependent on metadata. If the metadata (usually DOIs) of research products are not available and correct, altmetric data might result in missing values. For instance, if an article does not have a DOI and the altmetric information is requested based on the article's title, it can happen that this article might not be found with altmetric information because the altmetric provider is not able to identify the article based on its title only. This phenomenon is most evident for articles with missing metadata often originated from Mendeley (Zahedi et al., 2014b; Nuredini and Peters, 2015). Hassan et al. (2017) used the Altmetric.com data dump shared in June 2016, of which many articles tracked from Altmetric.com had DOIs rather than other article identifiers, which leads to an issue of not being able to cover all data since not all articles covered on their study had DOIs and therefore altmetric information attached to it. Nuredini and Peters (2015) explored Mendeley for the top 30 journals in economic and business studies and confirm that searching Mendeley by a journal name might not be the best solution if we want to retrieve all articles related to that journal. They report that if a journal name is searched to retrieve all the articles that are published in that journal, this search will retrieve all entries that have a minimum of two words in common with that specified journal title. Therefore, to avoid data duplication, missing values, and search issues, the authors used DOIs for gathering readership data from Mendeley and the CrossRef API to retrieve the DOIs for all publications selected in their dataset.

The second challenge that characterize altmetrics is their heterogeneity nature of these indicators (Holmberg, 2015). Altmetrics capture different types of scholarly output mentioned in different online platforms used by diverse user communities (Haustein et al., 2016), and they create different impacts, which makes it difficult to capture what they present (Holmberg, 2015). For example, sharing an article on Facebook does not have the same impact as bookmarking the paper in a reference management system (Haustein, 2016; Lemke et al., 2017). In that sense, a tweet can self-promote researchers' work and is usually used by experienced researchers (Lemke et al., 2017), whereas download counts can imply the readership of an article used from young researchers. Wouters et al. (2019) identified the internal heterogeneity of altmetric indicators, which is an important feature that one should be careful for. They consider indicators that come from the same platforms, but they imply different actions. For

---

[77] Some parts of this section are substantially equivalent with the manuscript published in Nuredini, K., Lemke, S., & Peters, I. (2020). Social Media and Altmetrics. In R. Ball (Ed.), Handbook Bibliometrics. DeGruyter.

example, a tweet and a re-tweet arguably have different roles and should be valued differently. Altmetrics that are accumulated from Mendeley or F1000 recommendations are conceptually near citations or peer review and those that come from Twitter or Facebook show another impact (believed as social impact). Mendeley readership information are being identified with a positive correlation to citations meaning that these two metrics are related. On the other hand, F1000 recommendations known as metrics of quality face a low number of articles that are recommended on these services, and the correlation between these counts with citations is weak, meaning that they are not related.

Third, altmetrics data can be decreased over time because users might delete their social media accounts or remove the article from their library on their reference management systems leading to eliminate altmetrics that have been accumulated for those research products (Haustein, 2016). Robinson-García et al. (2014) highlighted that Altmetric.com and other altmetric providers have source limitations. The authors state that altmetric providers usually do not provide an empirical or conceptual explanation of the sources they use. In this case, they track Twitter but don't track, for example, Tumblr, so articles mentioned in other media are neglected and that, of course, leads to information loss. However, the authors proclaimed that the sources, which altmetric providers select, usually are more popular and provide APIs, which are practical for collecting their data.

Mohammadi and Thelwall (2014) performed an altmetric analysis for social science literature in Mendeley, especially looking at the correlation between citation counts and readership information. The authors mentioned that their research results are of limitations because the readership counts are limited only to the researchers that are registered in Mendeley as their reference manager system. In contrast, there are researchers that use other reference manager systems (i.e., EndNote), or there are others that don't use any of them.

3.9. Discussion

With the use of the web and social media tools in academia, new metrics, that is, altmetrics, have been proposed for measuring the online impact of scientific outputs. Altmetrics, in this case, are used as early impact indicators, which show the online attention or sometimes referred to as the societal impact of different scientific outputs. According to some research studies published by the altmetric community, altmetric information (e.g., blog posts) correlates positively with citation counts, reflecting a similar interest toward scientific outputs as citations. Nevertheless, altmetrics still differ from citations in different levels (e.g., altmetrics show the attention of scientific output from a wider audience and appear sooner than citations). Even though altmetrics show the online attention of scientific outputs, there are serious concerns that altmetrics carry for research assessments (Haustein, 2016). For example, altmetrics are heterogeneous, meaning that different social media sources represent different things; for example, sharing an article on Facebook is not the same as saving the article in a reference management system. Therefore, one should be careful about how to use these sources for research assessments (Haustein, 2016), since it is important to understand which altmetric information is useful for what kind of discipline of study and for what purpose.

Altmetric information, particularly for scientific outputs, is created from researchers and other audiences based on social media platform features. These actions that researchers leave online are tracked by several altmetric providers, each of them tracking different social media platforms. Mendeley and Altmetric.com are the most investigated altmetric providers from the altmetric community and therefore cover a significant number of journal articles with online attention, also for economic and business studies journal articles.

Mendeley readership information are being identified with a positive correlation to citations meaning that these two metrics are related. This correlation determines that Mendeley counts show an early impact of later citations for journal articles. According to studies performed so far, academic status and discipline are the most covered readership information from Mendeley for almost all disciplines, indicating that these two indicators might be helpful since they can represent the user behaviors and different classes of impact. Altmetric.com, however, tracks different social media platforms, for example, Twitter in which tweets and citation counts are fairly strong correlated (0.40–0.70) for articles. This means that tweets can be seen as social media activity that might increase citations or may predict citation counts. Moreover, blogs tracked by Altmetric.com are suggested as better indicators to filter highly cited articles.

Since citation counts can identify trendy topics, but sometimes it is needed for them to get accumulated, altmetric information might be used as alternative indicators for identifying trendy topics instead, within a shorter time period than citations. Generally perceived, using the advantage of altmetrics, which can identify articles that have gained higher online attention (i.e., Altmetric Scores or Mendeley counts) than the rest, researchers might be able to filter trends in a specific scientific discipline, even with recently published articles.

Journal level altmetrics are also suggested as a useful tool from the altmetric community since they give researchers or libraries the sense of the non-citation attention of journals beyond the Journal Impact Factor. Given the fact that journal level information (e.g., Journal Impact Factor) cannot identify the impact of individual articles, Altmetric.com has suggested possible ways that journal level altmetrics can be useful in the right way to "judge" the (online) impact of articles within that journal.

Introducing altmetrics to libraries plays an important role because it will help researchers to be aware of possible choices that can help them to evaluate the impact of scholarly literature and make current selections (Lapinski et al., 2013). Similarly, Thelwall et al. (2013) confirmed that there is a need for digital libraries to use altmetrics since researchers need alternative strategies to identify the most relevant articles from all the data the library suggests. Moreover, since citations need time to appear, the use of altmetrics can help to promote, for example, the high-impact articles (those articles that right after publication receive higher online attention) found in the large dataset faster than citations.

Chapter 4

Methodology: data and technical approaches

In this chapter, we present the data methodology, techniques, and technical issues for creating the datasets that will be used to explore altmetric information. We will briefly show the data selection and data preparation phases for crawling three different providers, as well as the data challenges and technical approaches for creating the datasets. The datasets described in this chapter will be used for analysis and results in Chapter 5.

4.1. Journal selection strategy

The dataset for this study is formed with the use of journals from Handelsblatt journal-ranking[78]. Handelsblatt journal ranking evaluates the performance of research outputs in economics and business studies for German-speaking countries (i.e., Germany, Austria, and Switzerland) (Krapf, 2010). Handelsblatt ranking ranks journals for two different disciplines: economics (in German known as "Volkswirtschaftslehre"—VWL) and business studies ("Betriebswirtschaftslehre"—BWL) (Krapf, 2010). These rankings are the so-called prominent rankings in academia used for research evaluation, which lasted for a long time because of their public visibility and data quality (Sturm & Ursprung, 2017).

Handelsblatt published several rankings starting from 2009 onwards, which were re-published over and over the years since they were enhanced in data methodology and accuracy (Krapf, 2010; Lorenz & Löffler 2015). The dataset for our research is based on the new versions of Handelsblatt ranking for economics and business studies journals.

1) Handelsblatt ranking for economic journals[79]

The newest Handelsblatt ranking for economic journals (E)[80] was published in 2017. This ranking includes the SCImago[81] journal indicator (SJR) that measures the influence of scientific journals based on the number of citations received by the journal (Forschungsmonitoring, 2017). Citations used in the SJR come from the Scopus database. Journals with higher SJR values have greater influence compared to other journals. According to Handelsblatt ranking calculations, the top 5 journals with the highest SJR (i.e., *American Economic Review*, *Econometrica*, *Journal of Political Economy*, *Quarterly Journal of Economics*, and *Review of Economic Studies*) in economics receive a weight of 1.

Other journals that have an SJR score that is equal or greater than the average SJR score of the top 5 journals will also gain a weight of 1, specifically, in this ranking, 11 journals have a weight of 1 according to Forschungsmonitoring (2017). Journals that are selected in Handelsblatt

---

[78] Handelsblatt: https://www.handelsblatt.com/politik/deutschland/journal-ranking/9665428.html?ticket=ST-6344762-wsWoaDjTg5DUtdhWzyMD-ap3
[79] Forschungsmonitoring Economic journal ranking methodology:
https://www.forschungsmonitoring.org/Description_VWL_Main_Journal_weights.pdf
[80] In this thesis, the acronyms BS or BWL for Business Studies journals and E or VWL for Economics journals are used interchangeably.
[81] SCImago: https://www.scimagojr.com/

ranking start with a weight of 0.025 and are all journals that are listed in EconLit[82]. EconLit is an economic literature database that covers articles published in the field of economics beginning in 1969. Since SJR values can change every year, because of the new citation counts that publications receive, they are corrected by considering the relative difference within publication years. The SJR value for a journal is the average number of citations received in the current year divided by the number of publications over the last 3 years. Moreover, the mean of the corrected SJR values over the following 3 years is considered (Forschungsmonitoring, 2017). In accordance with SJR values, journals are classified into classes from A+ to F. Journals with weight one belong to class A+, followed by journals that have the highest SJR values which belong to class A, the remaining journals of the top 10% belong to B, and the journals of 25%, 50%, and 100% are classified as C, D, and E, respectively. Lastly, journals that are in EconLit but do not have SJR values belong to the class F (Forschungsmonitoring, 2017).

2) Handelsblatt ranking for business studies journals[83]

Handelsblatt published the newest ranking for business studies journals in 2018. The last ranking before was published in 2014 where the journals selected in the ranking belonged to several rankings that classified journals based on their quality, such as JOURQUAL rank from VHB, Social Science Citation Index (SSCI), and Erasmus Research Institute of Management (ERIM) journal list (EJL) (Lorenz & Löffler 2015). The JOURQUAL [84]is collected by the German Academic Association for Business Research (VHB), where the weighting scheme is based on surveying the members of VHB to judge the quality of journals (Krapf, 2010). The ERIM[85] journal list (EJL) is based on judgments from ERIM members[86] and ISI scores. The EJL divides journals into three categories: STAR journals, A-primary, and B-secondary journals (Krapf, 2010). The methodology of how journals are ranked by the newest ranking is described in the Forschungsmonitoring (2018) description document, where two of their weighting schemes are highlighted. The first scheme for ranking business studies journals is based on the SJR citations and the second scheme is based on VHB-Jourqual 3[87], which is published by the members of VHB (German Academic Association for Business Research) who arrange the journals in different categories.

The SJR scheme is used here similarly as in the ranking for economic journals mentioned above. The SCImago ranks scientific journals based on the number of citations received by the journal and on the importance of the journal where the citations come from. Journals that belong to the category A+ in the VHB-Jourqual 3 (i.e., *Academy of Management Journal*, *Administrative Science Quarterly*, *Academy of Management Review*, and *Management Science*) obtain a weight of 1. The other journals are calculated based on the average values of the SJR, which follows the same principle as the methodology for ranking economic journals. In the end, 23 journals from the Handelsblatt journal ranking list for business studies have a weight of 1. The other journals start with a weight of 0.025, which covers 14% of the journal list. The SJR is the average of citations the SJR has in the current year divided by the number of articles for the last

---

[82] Econlit: https://www.aeaweb.org/econlit/
[83] Forschungsmonitoring Business Studies journal ranking methodology:
https://www.forschungsmonitoring.org/Description_BWL_Main_Journal_weights.pdf
[84] Jourqual: https://vhbonline.org/en/service/jourqual/vhb-jourqual-3/
[85] Jourqual list: https://www.erim.eur.nl/about-erim/erim-journals-list-ejl/
[86] ERIM members: https://www.erim.eur.nl/about-erim/erim-journals-list-ejl/provisions/
[87] VHB-Jourqual -3: https://vhbonline.org/vhb4you/jourqual/vhb-jourqual-3/

3 years. The VHB-Jourqual 3 scheme ranks journals based on the judgment of more than 1,000 VHB members. These members created a threshold of which the journals should be classified. From the journal list, 651 journals out of 934 have passed the threshold of 25 reviews and received a rating. It should be noted that journals listed in VHB-Jourqual include journals that publish interdisciplinary research articles. For example, the list[88] contains the journal *Value in Health*, which is depicted under the category "Gesundheitswesen" or "Healthcare system".

4.2. Top 1,000 journals from economics and business studies

The total number of journals in Handelsblatt ranking from both disciplines (economics and business studies) is 3,664 (including the identical journals for both disciplines). Our study is focused on the top 500 journals from the economics (E) Handelsblatt ranking list (2017) and the top 500 from the business studies (BS) Handelsblatt ranking list (2018). The reasons we selected the top 500 from each discipline are the following:

1) *Crossref coverage*: At the beginning of our study, we selected all journals (3,664) that are listed in Handelsblatt ranking for both E and BS disciplines. All journal ISSNs were used to crawl Crossref to retrieve the journal's metadata, especially articles' DOIs. Crossref is a data service that provides the connection between journals and articles and their metadata and their citations (see Section 4.3.1 for more details). The DOIs of articles found in E and BS journals were important for this thesis because for querying altmetric providers (i.e., Mendeley and Altmetric.com) and retrieving altmetric data, article identification numbers were needed. When crawling Crossref for metadata, around 50% of the ISSNs metadata (i.e., DOIs) could not be retrieved from it. This issue was addressed to Crossref and they assume that those journals are not indexed in their database. One reason for not finding journals in Crossref can be that publishers perhaps have used other Registration Agencies (e.g., DataCite[89] and mEDRA[90]) to deposit their journals and articles beside Crossref. For example, Table 4.1 lists some of the journal names not retrieved with metadata from Crossref for Handelsblatt ranking journals in E and BS (crawled 12.02.2019).

Table 4.1: Example of journals not indexed in Crossref.

Journal names	ISSNs
International Journal of Economic Issues	0974-603X
International Policy Review	1088-7326
Social and Economic Studies	0037-7651
Journal of Small Business Strategy	1081-8510

---

[88] List of journals in VHB-Jourqual-3 https://vhbonline.org/vhb4you/vhb-jourqual/vhb-jourqual-3/gesamtliste
[89] DataCite: https://datacite.org/
[90] meEDRA: https://www.medra.org/

2) *Journals that don't provide DOIs*: Another possible reason for not indexing these journals in Crossref might be that some journals listed in Handelsblatt ranking do not usually offer DOIs for their publications. For example, the journals *MIT Sloan Management Review*, *Land Economics Monographs*, *Economia Internazionale*, and *Arthaniti* are not found in Crossref because they do not provide DOIs. The article "Can you measure the ROI of your social media marketing" published in the *MIT Sloan Management Review* is found with no available DOI in EconBiz[91] as well as at the journal web page. This issue makes it difficult to crawl altmetric providers and to retrieve altmetric information without an identification number of articles such as DOIs.

The journals that are listed in the top 500 are found with good coverage in Crossref (e.g., for BWL, 474 journals are found with metadata, see Chapter 5). The journals listed below 500 for both disciplines were found less because of the issues presented above at 1) and 2). These issues will lead to low article coverages for these journals, which would affect the results of this study. The bias would happen when representing different ranges of journal coverages; specifically, some journals (above 500) would present higher numbers of articles where other journals (below 500) would present a lower number of articles. Therefore, to avoid biased coverages between journals caused by missing data, we decided to select the top 500 journals for each discipline. Two different datasets are saved for journals: top 500 journals in business studies and top 500 journals in economics. The datasets from Handelsblatt ranking came in Excel sheets with columns such as journal ISSNs, journal names, and their classes (e.g., A+). Two datasets with the top 500 journal names and their ISSNs are used for data pre-processing. The data pre-processing technique, usually used in data mining, is a process where the incomplete real-world dataset is transformed into a consistent and complete dataset for further analysis (Kotsiantis et al., 2006). This step helps us to retrieve more accurate results when querying Crossref for the journal's metadata. Our study will adopt some of the data pre-processing steps that are needed to prepare our dataset for further processing. ISSNs are the main attributes that will be used to query Crossref for retrieving its metadata, and therefore, data pre-processing will be applied only to the ISSN column. The names of the journals and other metadata will be retrieved from querying Crossref.

Data pre-processing steps involved in creating the accurate dataset are as follows:

- *Data cleaning*: With this step, we detect and remove journals that might not be useful for creating our dataset. According to the study of Nuredini and Peters (2015), multidisciplinary journals like *Nature* and *Science* are excluded from the dataset because of the large number of articles they include, which can lead to bias of the results. The authors mentioned that *Nature* is ranked among the top 15 journals in the Handelsblatt ranking, but because of its comparably large number of articles published (66,813) that would bias the results *Nature* was excluded and replaced with *Quarterly Journal of Economics* (Nuredini & Peters, 2015; p. 382). Similarly, for this study,

---

[91] Article in EconBiz: Can you measure the ROI of your social media marketing
https://www.econbiz.de/Record/can-you-measure-the-roi-of-your-social-media-marketing-hoffman-donna/10008859294

Nature and *Science* are excluded from the list and are replaced with the following journals right after the top 500.

- *Missing values*: With this step, two journals lists (E and BS) retrieved from Forschungsmonitoring are checked for missing values. For this part, we found some journals without ISSNs and some journals that had incomplete ISSN numbers (e.g., missing the first numeral "0" or Excel rounded the ISSN numbers leading to different numbers). Therefore, we manually proofed all the journal ISSNs and updated the missing values. In both disciplines, 20 journals have either missing ISSNs or incomplete ISSNs.

- *Removing duplicates*: Next, a script in python is written to check whether the top 500 journals contain duplicates. We removed the duplicates and therefore added other journals that are placed below the 500 for both E and BS journals. For example, in the top 5 journals, the journal *Energy Policy* is the common journal for both disciplines. To avoid duplicates of data for the journal list in economics, we removed the *Energy Policy* and replaced that journal with the journal *Economics Letters* following the top 5.

- *Replaced journals online ISSNs with print ISSNs*: Our study is generally based on journal print ISSNs, first, because most of the journals in Handelsblatt ranking came with print ISSNs, and second, based on Nuredini and Peters (2015, 2016), Crossref provided good article coverage for print ISSNs.

4.3. Data collection phase

Social Media Analytics includes the process of gathering a large volume of data (e.g., structured or unstructured) from social media platforms and analyzing these data using different analytical techniques (Batrinca & Treleaven, 2015). There are different text formats that can be analyzed within the Social Media Analytics, for example, HTML[92], XML[93], JSON[94], and CSV[95] files.

This thesis is focused on retrieving structured data from three important providers: Crossref, for metadata, Mendeley for readership information, and Altmetric.com for social and online media data. All three services offer APIs, whose responses are based on JSON format. The advantage of structured data is that they can be parsed in MySQL database management system, stored into tables, and also joined together (Bali et al., 2017). The data stored into tables can be queried using Structured Query Language (SQL). The workflow in Figure 4.1 presents the main steps taken to accomplish the data selection and collection phase. This study is based on three phases. The dataset retrieved from three services are based on "historical data," because they are once crawled in 2019 and are not updated since then. Once we retrieved the data from the APIs, and we looked up if we should pre-process (e.g., data cleaning) them before analysis. For example, to retrieve better results with a high accuracy, we added "-" between the digits of ISSNs of the journals since they were missing (see Section 4.2 for more information about data inconsistencies).

---

[92] HTML: HyperTextMarkup Language, consists of HTML elements: tags (e.g., <div>)
[93] Extensible Markup Language, structuring textual data using <tag>…<\tag> to define elements
[94] JavaScript Object Notation (JSON), human-readable data interchange, derived from JavaScript
[95] CSV-a comma-separated values (CSV) file contains the values in a table (ASCII text lines)

Phase 1: The top 500 ISSN journal list for BS and the top 500 list for E are created. The journal ISSNs are checked, updated, edited, and removed based on the pre-processing steps shown in the section above.

Phase 2: Afterwards, these two journal lists are used to query Crossref by ISSNs to retrieve the number of articles each journal has as well as their metadata like title, publisher, etc. (for more details about Crossref see Section 4.3.1). The data received from Crossref are sent to the MySQL database for further analysis.

Phase 3: After Crossref is crawled and DOIs for articles are retrieved, altmetric providers such as Mendeley and Altmetric.com are queried. The querying process for Mendeley is described in Section 4.3.3. Mendeley is queried using the API, whereas altmetric information from Altmetric.com is downloaded via the Altmetric Explorer. More information about how data are downloaded from Altmetric.com are shown in Section 4.3.4. The data received from Mendeley and Altmetric.com are sent to the MySQL database for further analysis.

These phases are applicable for other disciplines as well, as long as their input data are based on ISSNs and DOIs.

For this research, a server machine with specifications shown in Table 4.2 is used to handle the datasets retrieved from three platforms. The OS of the server is Linux.

Table 4.2: Server specifications used for this research study.

Processor	Memory	System architecture
Processor: Intel(R) Xeon(R) Gold 6154 CPU @3.00GHz 4 cores	16 GB RAM	System Architecture x86_64

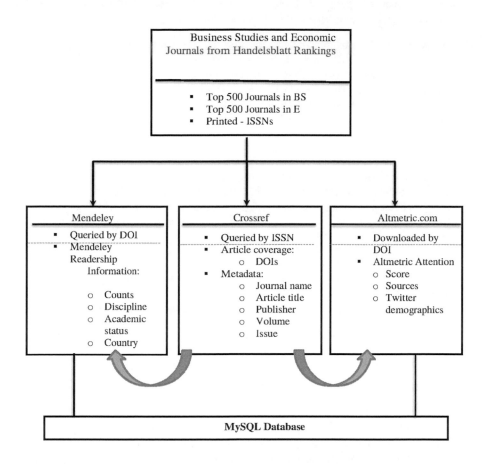

Figure 4.1: General workflow of data selection and collection for economic and business studies journals.

4.3.1. Crawling Crossref as data service for E and BS journals

Crossref is a DOI Registration Agency and is known as a milestone for scholarly information, providing links between the sets of references listed at the end of an article to their online full texts (Pentz, 2001). Additionally, Crossref registers DOIs and bibliographic metadata for articles that publishers have deposited (Lammey, 2015). Crossref collaborates with more than 4,000 publishers providing 70 million DOIs to scientific outputs such as articles, books, conference, and proceedings. It holds only bibliographic metadata to articles but not the full text; nevertheless, it provides the link where the content can be found online. Crossref offers a free Application Programming Interface (API) where users can search, filter, and retrieve the data for free. There are different libraries built for using Crossref API developed in various programming languages such as R, Python, Ruby, and Javascript (Lammey, 2016). Besides these programming languages, the Crossref database can be queried via PHP as well. PHP is a programming language used especially for web development.

This study uses Crossref for three reasons, first, because Crossref makes the data easily available by using its REST API[96]; second, the API can be queryable by ISSNs; and third, Crossref covers more articles than other data services. There are other data services[97] such as DataCite[98] that offer an API but cannot be crawled via ISSN; the crawling can be done only via DOIs. DataCite, for example, currently includes 1,950 repositories and 17,894,865 research works. Crossref[99], as of April 28, 2020, includes 77,843 journals and 82,712,895 journal articles (i.e., DOIs).

For our study, the script used to crawl Crossref is written in PHP. In the following section, we will explain the PHP script and describe some main parts used for querying the Crossref API. The script itself uses the cURL function that enables the interaction with the API. The Crossref API was requested two times, first when we retrieved data for the list of journal ISSNs in E and second for the journals in BS. The retrieved data are saved automatically in a MySQL data table.

Since Crossref API provides freely available data, there is no need to generate an authorization key first to use the API. The URL for Crossref API is http://api.crossref.org/. Crossref takes ISSNs as input, which in our case, ISSNs are listed in a text file. To return all articles for a particular ISSN, the API call should take this resource component into consideration:

/journals/{issn}/works - > which returns a list of works (i.e., articles) in that given journal[100]

as well as the parameter:

filter={filter_name}:{value} -> which filters results based on a specific field, in our case publication year.

To apply this component and the parameter in our code, the function "getResponse" (shown as snipped code in Figure 4.2) is used to retrieve all journal data found in Crossref with particular ISSNs and then select all articles of the listed journals that are published between 01.01.2011 and 31.12.2018.

The crawling of Crossref started 12.02.2019 at 13:00. The selection of articles is based on the suggestions from the study of Nuredini and Peters (2015) which claimed that recent articles accumulate more altmetric information than older ones by suggesting publication years (from 2011 onwards) as better sources when exploring altmetric information in general. Therefore, articles published between the years 2011 and 2018 for this thesis are considered.

---

[96] REST API: Representational State Transfer
[97] Other DOI Registration Agencies: https://www.doi.org/registration_agencies.html (accessed 19.02.2020)
[98] DataCite: https://datacite.org/
[99] Crossref Status Report: https://data.crossref.org/reports/statusReport.html
[100] API doc: https://github.com/CrossRef/rest-api-doc

```
    $pageWithResults = getResponse('journals/'.
urlencode($issn)
.'/works?rows=1000&offset='.$offset.'&cursor=*&filter=fro
m-pub-date:2011-01-01,until-pub-date:2018-12-31');
```

Figure 4.2: Snipped code for the getResponse function in Crossref.

Crossref API provides pagination that can be used when the data are larger than 1,000 records per page since by default, the script will terminate when the records hit 1,000. Therefore to fetch all results needed for this study, the API Crossref is queried for pagination. With pagination, the API provides two additional parameters known as "rows" and "offsets" that can control the pagination process.

The pagination in Crossref is based on these rules:

Page 1: http://api.crossref.org/v1/works?rows=1000&offset=0
Page 2: http://api.crossref.org/v1/works?rows=1000&offset=1000
Page 3: http://api.crossref.org/v1/works?rows=1000&offset=2000

We navigated through pages with the rows and offset values. The first page has rows 1,000 and offsets 0, and if the data are larger than 1,000, the iteration will move to offset 1,000, which will retrieve the records from Page 2.

The same script iterates for all ISSNs for both disciplines E and BS, and the data that are fetched are automatically added in MySQL database. A snipped JSON response of Crossref API for a particular article is shown in Figure 4.3.

Based on the data we retrieved from Crossref API, we selected the main fields that played an important role for our dataset, for example, the title of the article, the journal name, which, in this case, in Crossref is named as "publisher," the publication date of the article, and DOI.

```
     . . . . .
          "reference-count": 114,
          "publisher": "Academy of Management",
          "issue": "6",
          "content-domain": {
            "domain": [],
            "crossmark-restriction": false
          },
          "short-container-title": [
            "AMJ"
          ],
          "published-print": {
            "date-parts": [
              [
                2017,
                12
              ]
            ]
          },
          "DOI": "10.5465/amj.2015.0852",
          "type": "journal-article",
          "created": {
            "date-parts": [
              [
                2016,
     . . . . . .
```

Figure 4.3: Snipped JSON response from Crossref.

4.3.2. Datatable design for Crossref in MySQL

The data received from Crossref are sent to the MySQL database for further analysis. In MySQL, a database called "Journals" is created. In this database, two separate tables, "crossref_bwl" for journals in business studies and "crossref_vwl" for journals in economics, are created. The table structure for both disciplines is constructed as follows:

Table 4.3: Crossref datatable for economic journals and articles.

```
MariaDB [journals]> desc crossref_vwl;
+-------------------+--------------+------+-----+---------+----------------+
| Field             | Type         | Null | Key | Default | Extra          |
+-------------------+--------------+------+-----+---------+----------------+
| id                | int(11)      | NO   | PRI | NULL    | auto_increment |
| issn              | varchar(500) | YES  |     | NULL    |                |
| journalname       | varchar(500) | YES  |     | NULL    |                |
| doi               | varchar(100) | YES  |     | NULL    |                |
| title             | varchar(800) | YES  |     | NULL    |                |
| publisher         | varchar(100) | YES  |     | NULL    |                |
| volume            | varchar(100) | YES  |     | NULL    |                |
| issue             | varchar(100) | YES  |     | NULL    |                |
| referencecount    | int(11)      | YES  |     | NULL    |                |
| isreferencedbycount | int(11)    | YES  |     | NULL    |                |
| journalissue      | varchar(100) | YES  |     | NULL    |                |
| discipline        | varchar(50)  | YES  |     | NULL    |                |
+-------------------+--------------+------+-----+---------+----------------+
12 rows in set (0.00 sec)
```

Table 4.4: Crossref datatable for business studies journals and articles.

```
MariaDB [journals]> desc crossref_bwl;
+-------------------+--------------+------+-----+---------+----------------+
| Field             | Type         | Null | Key | Default | Extra          |
+-------------------+--------------+------+-----+---------+----------------+
| id                | int(11)      | NO   | PRI | NULL    | auto_increment |
| issn              | varchar(500) | YES  |     | NULL    |                |
| journalname       | varchar(500) | YES  |     | NULL    |                |
| doi               | varchar(100) | YES  |     | NULL    |                |
| title             | varchar(800) | YES  |     | NULL    |                |
| publisher         | varchar(100) | YES  |     | NULL    |                |
| volume            | varchar(100) | YES  |     | NULL    |                |
| issue             | varchar(100) | YES  |     | NULL    |                |
| referencecount    | int(11)      | YES  |     | NULL    |                |
| isreferencedbycount | int(11)    | YES  |     | NULL    |                |
| journalissue      | varchar(100) | YES  |     | NULL    |                |
| discipline        | varchar(50)  | YES  |     | NULL    |                |
+-------------------+--------------+------+-----+---------+----------------+
12 rows in set (0.00 sec)
```

The following metadata are extracted from JSON and gathered for the journals in E and BS: ISSN, journal name, DOI, title, publisher, volume, issue, reference count, is referenced by count, and journal issue. Most of the attributes mentioned above are self-explanatory. For example, the ISSN is the identification number that a journal possesses. "Reference count" represents the number of references used in that particular article. "Is referenced by count" represents the number of citations that a particular DOI has, based on the Crossref data. The metadata retrieved are sent to the MySQL tables shown in Tables 4.3 and 4.4.

4.3.3. Crawling Mendeley for E and BS journals

Mendeley API allows users to programmatically access and manage resources of different types (e.g., catalogs and datasets) by giving the users the available API methods. The API is free of use; however, Mendeley claims that in the future, it plans to offer fee-based services to academic institutions[101].

---

[101] Mendeley data: https://data.mendeley.com/faq?q=versions

The Mendeley API is crawled by python to retrieve the Mendeley readership information for all journals/articles in business studies and economics. Python is a high-level programming language invented by Guido van Rossum with the first release in 1991 (Van Rossum & Drake, 2011). Mendeley provides the documentation which is needed to access the API, and it offers the possibility to explore the API via an interaction window (see Figure 4.4) that can be accessed via this link: https://api.mendeley.com/apidocs/docs. The "catalog" feature of Mendeley shown in Figure 4.4 allows exploring the retrieval of Mendeley readership information for a specific article type (e.g., DOI).

Figure 4.4: Mendeley API interactive window for the "catalog" feature.

Authorization data are needed to make use of the API. For our script, a Mendeley python library[102] is installed that provides access to the Mendeley API. The credential data for the client, such as the ID and secret key, are retrieved by creating an application in https://dev.mendeley.com/myapps.html and are used for authorization purposes (see Figure 4.5).

Figure 4.5: Mendeley form for registering new app and retrieving the secret key.

As can be seen in the study of Nuredini and Peters (2015), searching Mendeley by title or keywords is problematic because, for example, if a journal name is searched to retrieve all the

---

[102] Python library for Mendeley: https://pypi.org/project/mendeley/

articles published in that journal, this search will retrieve all entries that have a minimum of two words in common with that specified journal title. This procedure will lead to data duplications, data that are not needed for our research, and missing articles that should have been retrieved but were not because their journal names are not correctly saved in the Mendeley's metadata. Therefore, in this case, we will use DOIs of journal articles for E and BS, which are already collected from Crossref, and for each DOI, make a Mendeley call.

Other studies confirm that searches by DOI provide more complete results as searches by title (Thelwall, 2017a). It is important to note that even searching by DOI sometimes can lead to errors. There are cases where a DOI has been misspelled by the users and results in no hits, or some DOIs point to the same article but are written differently or even return more articles than desired. Similar issues are reported in the study of Bar-Ilan et al. (2012).

Mendeley was crawled on 24.03.2019 to retrieve readership information for E and BS journals. The readership counts for articles retrieved from Mendeley are based on the counts that had been accumulated on the day that Mendeley was crawled.

The Mendeley "catalog" is being used for collecting the readership information requested for each DOI found in E and BS journals. Each call made in the "catalog" is characterized by the DOI as input and "views". Views are categorized in Mendeley into five categories:

- *bib*: It will return the bibliographic data of the articles searched within the catalog. Bibliographic data of articles included here are pages, volume, location, publication date, and more.
- *client*: It will return the core fields of the article (e.g., DOI, title, and author names).
- *stats*: It will return the core fields and readership information (i.e., statistics) for an article, respectively, countries, academic status, and discipline.
- *all*: It will return all fields from all the groups above (i.e., bib, client, and stats).

Since the metadata for all articles in E and BS were retrieved from Crossref, Mendeley is queried for the "view=stats," which retrieves the articles' core fields and the Mendeley readership information. Figure 4.6 shows a small snipped code of python script for crawling Mendeley API.

```
from mendeley.exception import MendeleyException
import json
from os.path import join

dump_dir = "DOIS"
DOIs = []
for doi in DOIss:
    try:
        foo =
session.catalog.by_identifier(doi=doi,
view="stats")
        DOIs.append(foo)
        try:
            issn=foo.identifiers['issn']
            title=foo.title
            doii=foo.identifiers['doi']
            count=foo.reader_count
            year=foo.year
            journalname=foo.source

academicstatus=foo.reader_count_by_academic_stat
```

Figure 4.6: Snipped code in Python for crawling Mendeley.

Mendeley data are structured; mainly, they are retrieved in JSON format. A screenshot of the Mendeley JSON file is shown in Figure 4.7. In the screenshot, the academic status and discipline are revealed for a selected article. For example, based on the data below, we can see that 11 associate professors and 49 master students read this article. Most of the readers are coming from business, management, and accounting disciplines.

The "reader_count_by_user_role" or similarly known as "the academic status" of users in Figure 4.7 lists 10 different academic statuses: "Unspecified," "Professor-Associate Professor," "Librarian," "Researcher," "Bachelor Student," "Master Student or Postgraduate," "PhD or Doctorate," "Other," "Lecturer," and "Senior Lecturer." More details about the readership information or user statistics of Mendeley can be found in Chapter 3.

```
"reader_count_by_user_role": {
    "Unspecified": 5,
    "Professor > Associate Professor":
11,
    "Librarian": 1,
    "Researcher": 18,
    "Student   > Doctoral Student": 11,
    "Student   > Ph. D. Student": 28,
    "Student   > Postgraduate": 9,
    "Student   > Master": 49,
    "Other": 4,
    "Student   > Bachelor": 21,
    "Lecturer": 2,
    "Lecturer > Senior Lecturer": 6
    },
  "reader_count_by_subject_area": {
    "Unspecified": 9,
    "Agricultural and Biological
Sciences": 6,
    "Arts and Humanities": 2,
    "Business, Management and
Accounting": 26,
. . . .
```

Figure 4.7: Snipped JSON file retrieved from Mendeley.

The Mendeley readership data requested by DOIs are saved in a MySQL database. By crawling Mendeley, the retrieved data did not only match our ISSNs but also retrieve more ISSNs than requested. Therefore, we have to perform data cleaning by merging the journal ISSNs from Mendeley with the journal ISSNs from Crossref. The retrieved ISSNs from Mendeley were without dashes in the middle between the four numbers in ISSN (e.g., 03044076). To match the ISSNs with the journals from Crossref, we need to add dashes between the ISSN numbers (e.g., 0304-4076), which was done with an SQL query. The journals found without matches from Mendeley and Crossref are excluded from the query.

The readership information from Mendeley is saved in the table called "tbl_doi" with the metadata. The table structure is shown in Table 4.5. Most of the field names are self-explanatory besides the count, electronic and discipline. The count is depicted as a number, which determines how many times a DOI has been saved or read in a Mendeley library. The electronic field saves some more additional data for journals with additional electronic ISSNs but is not used in our data analysis since not all journals have data that belong to this field. Therefore, when SQL queries are performed, we exclude this field by writing "electronic is null." The discipline field represents which articles are found in business studies journals and which articles belong to economic journals.

The main table "tbl_doi" is linked with the other three tables (all three presented in Table 4.6) through a 1:N relationship, which means that one article from the main table can be repeated often within the other tables. For example, one article can be read by different users with different disciplines, and it should, therefore, be included in the table that saves the disciplines of that article more than once. Based on the "views=stats," we get full readership information from Mendeley (see Figure 4.6)—first, the academic status of the readers; second, the country of the readers; and third, the discipline of the readers. Each category of the readership information for this research study includes all user statistics values without any limitations, as in earlier Mendeley research studies (see Chapter 3 for more details about Mendeley readership information).

The articles saved in the main table are also saved in these three tables for readership information. The communication between the tables is made based on the joins. A sample SQL code for selecting and aggregating the articles that received readers with academic status is shown below. This query shows the list of all academic statuses that Mendeley provides and their reader numbers each status received for articles that belong to BS journals only.

Table 4.5: Main Mendeley table for saving reader counts in MySQL.

```
MariaDB [journals]> desc tbl_doi;
+------------+------------------+------+-----+---------+----------------+
| Field      | Type             | Null | Key | Default | Extra          |
+------------+------------------+------+-----+---------+----------------+
| id         | int(11) unsigned | NO   | PRI | NULL    | auto_increment |
| doi        | varchar(50)      | NO   | UNI |         |                |
| count      | int(11)          | NO   |     | 0       |                |
| year       | varchar(50)      | NO   |     |         |                |
| issn       | varchar(500)     | YES  |     | NULL    |                |
| title      | varchar(1000)    | YES  |     | NULL    |                |
| publisher  | varchar(200)     | YES  |     | NULL    |                |
| discipline | varchar(20)      | YES  |     | NULL    |                |
| electronic | varchar(150)     | YES  |     | NULL    |                |
+------------+------------------+------+-----+---------+----------------+
9 rows in set (0.00 sec)
```

Since the table's academic status does not provide information about the discipline of the articles, there is a need to link this table with the main table and to filter the desired data. The link between the two tables is done by connecting the same "ids" that belong to both tables.

```
SELECT a.status, SUM(a.count)
FROM tbl_reader_count_academic_status AS a, tbl_doi AS d
WHERE a.id_doi=d.id AND d.electronic IS NULL AND d.discipline="bwl"
GROUP BY a.status;
```

Table 4.6: Mendeley categories for readership information.

```
MariaDB [journals]> desc tbl_reader_count_academic_status;
+--------+-------------------+------+-----+---------+----------------+
| Field  | Type              | Null | Key | Default | Extra          |
+--------+-------------------+------+-----+---------+----------------+
| id     | int(11) unsigned  | NO   | PRI | NULL    | auto_increment |
| id_doi | int(11)           | NO   | MUL | NULL    |                |
| status | varchar(100)      | NO   |     |         |                |
| count  | int(11)           | NO   |     | 0       |                |
+--------+-------------------+------+-----+---------+----------------+
4 rows in set (0.00 sec)

MariaDB [journals]> desc tbl_reader_count_country;
+---------+-------------------+------+-----+---------+----------------+
| Field   | Type              | Null | Key | Default | Extra          |
+---------+-------------------+------+-----+---------+----------------+
| id      | int(11) unsigned  | NO   | PRI | NULL    | auto_increment |
| id_doi  | int(11)           | NO   | MUL | NULL    |                |
| country | varchar(100)      | NO   |     |         |                |
| count   | int(11)           | NO   |     | 0       |                |
+---------+-------------------+------+-----+---------+----------------+
4 rows in set (0.00 sec)

MariaDB [journals]> desc tbl_reader_count_subdiscipline;
+------------+-------------------+------+-----+---------+----------------+
| Field      | Type              | Null | Key | Default | Extra          |
+------------+-------------------+------+-----+---------+----------------+
| id         | int(11) unsigned  | NO   | PRI | NULL    | auto_increment |
| id_doi     | int(11)           | YES  | MUL | NULL    |                |
| category   | varchar(100)      | NO   |     |         |                |
| discipline | varchar(150)      | NO   |     |         |                |
| count      | int(11)           | NO   |     | 0       |                |
+------------+-------------------+------+-----+---------+----------------+
5 rows in set (0.00 sec)
```

4.3.4. Downloading information from Altmetric.com

Altmetric information from Altmetric.com is downloaded from the Altmetric Explorer[103]. The account for using the Altmetric Explorer is free since it is only used for research purposes in this case. The Altmetric Explorer[104] enables the user to download altmetric information for a set of identifiers (i.e., DOIs, ISSNs, and PubMed IDs).

The "Advanced search" form is shown in Figure 4.8. In our study, we searched Altmetric Explorer for DOIs, where the limited number for each search is 25,000 DOIs. Because of this limitation, we performed the search multiple times, each chunk containing 25,000 DOIs, and the results were downloaded as a .csv file. Altmetric.com was queried between 10.05.2019 until 15.05.2019.

---

[103] Altmetric Explorer: https://www.altmetric.com/explorer/
[104] Altmetric Explorer Advanced Search: https://help.altmetric.com/support/solutions/articles/6000146545-basic-and-advanced-search-

Figure 4.8: Altmetric Explorer search form.

All .csv files retrieved from Altmetric.com are checked for errors before loading in the MySQL database. Some of the data rows, for example, as shown in Figure 4.9, were disconnected from their row. For example, row 588 is disconnected where its data lie underneath the row. We copied the "Homo sapiens" and "Evolved via Selection" data and pasted to the "Survival of the friendliest." A similar methodology is used for the other identical data rows. These types of data were merged manually by copying the row below and pasting to their belongings rows.

Figure 4.9: Altmetric data errors in CSV files.

After all, data are checked, and the bad rows are updated. The CSV data are stored in the MySQL database using a PHP script. For altmetric information, two tables in the database are created: an altmetric table for business studies journals and an altmetric table for economic journals. The structure and altmetric data downloaded from Altmetric Explorer are shown in Table 4.7. Nineteen different AAS (i.e., blogs, news, Wikipedia, etc.) are retrieved and saved in the database. More information about the sources can be found in Chapter 3. The other attributes (i.e., ISSNs) are self-explanatory. Online ISSNs were also delivered from Altmetric.com but only for few numbers of journals. The detailed page and the badge URLs of articles are only retrieved but not they are necessarily important for this thesis since they offer only the URL where the article can be found in Altmetric.com with altmetrics information.

Table 4.7: Altmetrics information saved in the MySQL for both E and BS journals.

```
MariaDB [journals]> desc altmetrics_bw1;
+----------------------+--------------+------+-----+---------+----------------+
| Field                | Type         | Null | Key | Default | Extra          |
+----------------------+--------------+------+-----+---------+----------------+
| id                   | int(11)      | NO   | PRI | NULL    | auto_increment |
| altmetric_score      | int(11)      | YES  |     | NULL    |                |
| title                | varchar(500) | YES  |     | NULL    |                |
| journal_name         | varchar(500) | YES  |     | NULL    |                |
| print_issn           | varchar(500) | YES  |     | NULL    |                |
| online_issn          | varchar(500) | YES  |     | NULL    |                |
| subjects             | varchar(500) | YES  |     | NULL    |                |
| affiliation          | varchar(500) | YES  |     | NULL    |                |
| publication_date     | varchar(100) | YES  |     | NULL    |                |
| doi                  | varchar(500) | YES  |     | NULL    |                |
| news                 | int(11)      | YES  |     | NULL    |                |
| blog                 | int(11)      | YES  |     | NULL    |                |
| policy               | int(11)      | YES  |     | NULL    |                |
| patent               | int(11)      | YES  |     | NULL    |                |
| twitter              | int(11)      | YES  |     | NULL    |                |
| peer_review          | int(11)      | YES  |     | NULL    |                |
| weibo                | int(11)      | YES  |     | NULL    |                |
| facebook             | int(11)      | YES  |     | NULL    |                |
| wikipedia            | int(11)      | YES  |     | NULL    |                |
| google               | int(11)      | YES  |     | NULL    |                |
| linkedIn             | int(11)      | YES  |     | NULL    |                |
| reddit               | int(11)      | YES  |     | NULL    |                |
| pinterest            | int(11)      | YES  |     | NULL    |                |
| f1000                | int(11)      | YES  |     | NULL    |                |
| qa                   | int(11)      | YES  |     | NULL    |                |
| videos               | int(11)      | YES  |     | NULL    |                |
| syllabi              | int(11)      | YES  |     | NULL    |                |
| mendeley             | int(11)      | YES  |     | NULL    |                |
| dimensions_citations | int(11)      | YES  |     | NULL    |                |
| details_page         | varchar(500) | YES  |     | NULL    |                |
| badge_url            | varchar(500) | YES  |     | NULL    |                |
+----------------------+--------------+------+-----+---------+----------------+
31 rows in set (0.00 sec)
```

Altmetric Explorer is also used to download Twitter demographics for the selected articles. This type of file is handled in Excel for further analysis, where it presents the countries of the Twitter users that tweeted about the E and BS articles.

4.4. Conclusion

Within this chapter, the methodology and technical approaches of retrieving altmetric data are described. This research includes the main methods, which are part of Social Media Analytics, for retrieving social media data. Here we gather altmetrics for journals and articles. First step to gather the data was to use Handelsblatt ranking journals ISSNs to create the dataset of journals for analysis. To retrieve altmetric data from two Altmetric providers, this study needed the identification numbers of articles (i.e., DOIs) published in those journals. Therefore, we performed searchers for metadata within the Crossref data service for three reasons: first, because Crossref makes the data (i.e., metadata) easily available by using its API; second, its API can be queryable by ISSNs; and third, Crossref covers more articles than other data services. In detail, we described how Crossref is crawled by introducing the main components and parameters needed to retrieve the data from its API. Afterward, we presented the Mendeley API, its methods, and parameters to appropriately crawl and retrieve Mendeley data. At the end of this chapter, we present the altmetric data retrieved from Altemtric.com and the steps needed to take into consideration for making the dataset more consistent. Additionally, we presented the MySQL tables and their structures that were useful to store the data retrieved from all three providers. Mendeley information retrieved from the API generally is free for use from both researchers and developers. Afterward, Mendeley information has no limitations as long as there is an authentication process involved in the code. In contrast, Altmetric.com is free for use only when the retrieved altmetric data are used for research purposes. Otherwise, when adopting such data, Altmetric.com should be further contacted to discuss the availability and prices for commercial use. This approach, presented in this thesis, of course, can be generalizable for other disciplines as well, as long as there is a list of journal ISSNs and DOIs, which should be explored for altmetric information.

Chapter 5

Top 1,000 economic and business studies journals and their altmetric information[105]

In this chapter, we explore altmetric information from two altmetric providers for journals in economics (E) and business studies (BS). First, the coverage of E and BS journal articles in Crossref will be presented, which creates the Dataset I. Dataset I includes all E and BS journal articles found with metadata (e.g., DOIs), published between 2011 and 2018. Second, with the use of Dataset I, specifically the DOIs of journal articles, Mendeley and Altmetric.com are investigated for their altmetric information. Moreover, Mendeley is explored for the coverage and readership information, which creates the Dataset II. Altmetric.com is examined for coverage, the Altmetric Attention Score, and different attention sources, which creates the Dataset III. Last but not least, the correlation between citations from Dimensions and altmetric data is explored, followed by identifying trendy topics for E and BS disciplines.

5.1. Dataset I: Crossref coverage for journals in E and BS

In this section, Crossref for journals in E and BS is explored. Crossref is used to locate the articles for all top 1,000 journals (from Handelsblatt ranking) and to retrieve their metadata (i.e., DOI, title, journal name, publisher, volume, and issue).

This study identified 621,585 articles from Crossref for the publication years 2011–2018, of which 58% of articles belong to BS journals and 42% of articles belong to E journals. From the top 1,000 journals for both E and BS disciplines, 918 journals are found with metadata in Crossref, which are around 92%.

For BS journals, we found a total of 474 journals, which is a coverage of 95% (see Table 5.1). The total number of article DOIs between the publication years 2011–2018 is 359,433 within the BS disciplines and 262,152 within the E disciplines. Based on the metadata found in Crossref, three journals (i.e., *Environmental Science and Technology*, *Value in Health*, and *Journal of Cleaner Production*) have published more than 8,000 DOIs within 8 years.

In contrast, E journals in Crossref have 89% coverage with 444 ISSNs out of 500 ISSNs, showing a lower coverage compared to BS journals. Only one journal in E (i.e., *Energy* with ISSN 0360-5442) has more than 8,000 articles' DOIs found in Crossref. The general coverage of E and BS journals in Crossref is shown in Table 5.1. The percentage of total articles found in Crossref for E and BS journals cannot be calculated since we retrieve only the number of articles that Crossref indexed for each journal, but we are not aware of how many articles the journals publish in total.

---

[105] This chapter is partly published in Nuredini, K. (2021). Investigating altmetric information for the top 1,000 journals from Handelsblatt ranking in economic and business studies. *Journal of Economic Surveys*.

Table 5.1: Journal coverage in Crossref for the top 1,000 journals in E and BS.

Top 500 E journals found in Crossref			
Total no. of journals	%	Total no. of articles (2011-2018)	%
444	89%	262,152	
Top 500 BS journals found in Crossref			
Total no. of journals	%	Total no. of articles (2011–2018)	%
474	95%	359,433	
Total E and BS journals		Total E and BS journal articles	
918	92%	621,585	

Table 5.2 lists the journal output (i.e., ISSN, number of DOIs, and number of issues per year) for the top 10 journals found in Crossref with the highest number of DOIs. The first top five journals belong to BS discipline and the other five journals belong to E discipline. The complete list of journals from both E and BS and their number of articles with DOIs found in Crossref are presented in Appendix I and II.

The top 10 journals from Handelsblatt ranking that publish a high number of articles do not necessarily publish only economic articles but also publish articles in other disciplines or articles that have interdisciplinary research. For example, the journal *Value in Health*[106] publishes literature within the topics in pharmacoeconomics, Health economics, outcomes research, and healthcare research.

Table 5.2: Description of journal output for the top 10 journals in economics and business studies.

	ISSN	Journal name	Total no. of articles found in Crossref	No. of issues per year
1	0013-936X	*Environmental Science and Technology*	8,963	24
2	1098-3015	*Value in Health*	8,807	6
3	0959-6526	*Journal of Cleaner Production*	8,659	30
4	0957-4174	*Expert Systems with Applications*	7,421	24
5	0301-4215	*Energy Policy*	5,469	12
6	0360-5442	*Energy*	8,847	11
7	0002-8762	*The American Historical Review*	5,688	5
8	0377-2217	*European Journal of Operational Research*	5,251	24
9	0043-1397	*Water Resources Research*	4,663	12
10	0165-1765	*Economics Letters*	3,708	12

---

[106] The journal "Value in Health": https://www.journals.elsevier.com/value-in-health

Figure 5.1 shows the article distribution of the E and BS journals found in Crossref based on publications from 2011 to 2018. Journals that belong to BS appear to publish more articles than journals in E. In 2011, more articles were published and registered in Crossref compared to other publication years for both disciplines E and BS.

However, a considerable drop for articles published between 2014 and 2018 and registered in Crossref is shown. This drop was addressed to Crossref to identify any issue. Crossref confirmed that the data retrieved for this study are properly crawled and the reason why this drop is presented remains unknown. One assumption for this drop might be that publishers perhaps have used other DOI Registration Agencies (e.g., DataCite and mEDRA) to deposit articles beside Crossref.

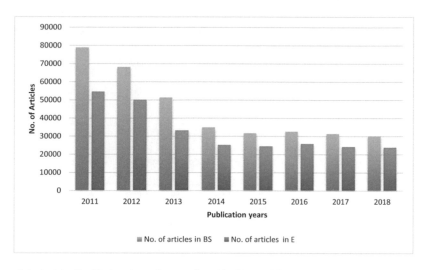

Figure 5.1: Article distribution through years found in Crossref for E and BS journals.

5.2. Dataset II: Mendeley coverage for journals in E and BS

This section explores Mendeley as a source of altmetrics. Specifically, it looks up at Mendeley readership information for economic and business studies journals that create the Dataset II. Details about the methodology and the techniques of how the data are collected from Mendeley can be found in Chapter 4. Mendeley, as a platform, is described in detail in Chapter 3.

We identified a total of 719 (72%) journals from both E and BS that have articles saved in Mendeley, where 92% of the business studies journals and 51% of the economic journals are covered in Mendeley. The general coverage of journals and articles in economics and business studies in Mendeley is shown in Table 5.3.

Mendeley, for readership information, is queried based on the article DOIs found from Crossref (Dataset I). From the total number of articles (621,585) in both disciplines, 295,582 (48%) articles are found by the Mendeley crawl. Half of the articles from Crossref are not found either because of missing DOIs in Mendeley's metadata or because the articles are not of interest to the Mendeley community. These results confirm other studies when investigating the coverage of Mendeley from different disciplines (Mohammadi & Thelwall, 2014; Zahedi et al., 2015). For example, the study of Mohammadi and Thelwall (2014) explored the coverage of journals in social sciences and humanities for the publication year 2008, and they found 44% of the articles with DOIs in Mendeley.

Several studies have explored the coverage and usage of research articles in Mendeley (Haustein, & Larivière, 2014; Nuredini & Peters, 2015; Zahedi et al., 2015). Haustein and Larivière (2014) explored 1.2 million articles from four different disciplines (biomedical research, clinical medicine, health, and psychology), showing that the percentage of articles found in Mendeley with at least one reader is higher than the coverage on other social media platforms. Nuredini and Peters (2015) investigated Mendeley coverage for the top 30 journals in economic and business studies over 20 years of publication history, and they found a relatively good coverage of the articles in these disciplines with 77.5%. However, according to Mohammadi and Thelwall (2014), the coverage of articles in Mendeley seems to be more significant for science and medicine research rather than for social sciences and humanities (Mohammadi & Thelwall, 2014). Table 5.3 presents the journal coverage for both disciplines E and BS. The BS journals appear to be better present in Mendeley compared to E journals. The number of articles found with DOIs in Mendeley for BS is a way broader than for E.

Table 5.3: Journals and article coverage in Mendeley for the top 1,000 journals in E and BS.

Top 500 E journals found in Mendeley			
Total No. of journals	%	Total No. of articles	%
257	51%	77,161	29%
Top 500 BS journals found in Mendeley			
Total No. of journals	%	Total No. of articles	%
462	92%	218,341	61%
Total E and BS journals		Total E and BS journal articles	
719	72%	295,582	47%

The description of journal coverage from all top 719 journals found in Mendeley and their readership counts on journal level are presented at the end of this thesis in Appendix I for BS and Appendix II for E journals.

5.2.1. Mendeley readership information: reader counts

Each article saved in Mendeley has a reader count, which is a number of unique Mendeley users (or readers) who have saved a given article in their own Mendeley library, assuming that the articles are read by the users of Mendeley. However, Mendeley readership information (also known as statistics) does not certainly reflect the "read" activity of articles, meaning readers of

Mendeley do not inevitably read all articles that they have saved in their Mendeley library (Zahedi et al., 2017).In this section, we explore readership counts from Mendeley for E and BS journals. Figure 5.2 presents the top 10 journals with the highest readership counts in Mendeley on journal level from both E and BS and the number of articles (DOI count) found in Mendeley and Crossref for these journals. The readership count on journal level is calculated by the sum of all counts each article of that journal has received. The top 10 journals in BS are presented on the left side of the chart and the top 10 journals in E are presented on the right side of the chart. This list of journals is used for further investigation examples in this thesis.

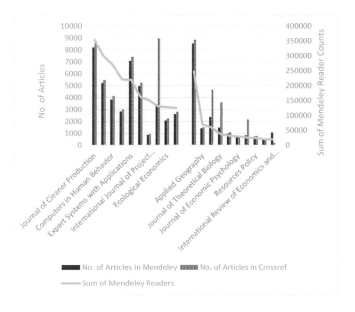

Figure 5.2: Top 20 journals with highest Mendeley reader counts in BS and E (shaded).

Figure 5.2 presents that BS journals have higher reader counts in Mendeley than E journals, suggesting that many articles from BS journals are not just more saved on Mendeley but also more read by the Mendeley community compared to E journals. In BS journals, the *Journal of Cleaner Production* has the highest Mendeley reader count (354,352) and the highest number of articles found in Mendeley (8,194). In E journals, *Energy* has the highest Mendeley reader count (246,443) and the highest number of articles found in Mendeley (8,526).

The journal *International Journal of Project Management* from BS falls in the top 10 journals with the highest Mendeley reader counts, but it has the lowest number of published articles in comparison with other journals, even though the article coverage for this journal in Mendeley is around 90%. The *Energy* journal from E is the best covered in Mendeley and *Environmental Science and Technology* is least findable, although it has the largest number of articles published. It is important to note that, since Handelsblatt ranking covers all journals that are ranked by JOURQUAL 2.1, a ranking developed by VHB (German Academic Association for

Business Research), journals that belong to the Social Science Citation Index (SSCI), and journals that are listed in the Erasmus Research Institute of Management (EJL), the list covers multidisciplinary journals, for example, the journal *Energy* is listed in the ranking since this journal publishes economic[107] and policy issues articles as well. The top 20 journals with high Mendeley reader counts for both E and BS belong to the classes B and C in Handelsblatt ranking. Given this insight, journals that are not highly ranked in Handelsblatt ranking are, however, mostly read in Mendeley.

When investigating the readership counts for each publication year and the number of articles found in Mendeley, it can be seen that readers in Mendeley, after a drop from 2013 to 2015, add current articles to their libraries more often each year, resulting in good coverage of newer research. However, when it comes to reader counts, older articles found in Mendeley from publication years 2011–2013 gain comparably higher counts than recently published articles (see Figure 5.3). Although the coverage of newly published articles is high in Mendeley (72%), the reader counts for these articles are low compared to other articles published earlier than 2018. In 2018[108], articles received 33% less Mendeley counts than that in 2017.

One of the possible reasons that lead to the decrease of Mendeley readership counts for recent publications, according to Zahedi et al. (2017), is that the readers of Mendeley are not much aware of very newly published articles, and there is a delay until they notice them and save them to their libraries. Despite the fact that Mendeley readership counts seem to have a strong correlation with citations for journal articles, Mendeley counts can appear 1 year before citations (Thelwall, 2018b). They are seen as more beneficial because of the ability to show an earlier impact of scientific outputs compared to citations (Thelwall, 2017a).

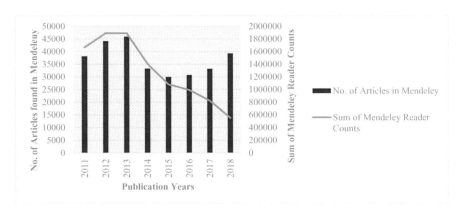

Figure 5.3: The year-wise distribution of articles and readers in Mendeley.

For the publication year 2018, around 72% of articles found in Crossref from both E and BS had at least one Mendeley reader count in Mendeley. The steady increase of Mendeley reader counts for early publications and decreasing patterns of Mendeley reader counts for recently

---

[107] About the "Energy journal": https://www.journals.elsevier.com/energy

[108] The publication year of articles "2018" for our study depicts the recently published articles in E and BS since the altmetric data for articles are retrieved in the beginning of 2019.

published articles were also spotted at the study of Zahedi et al. (2017) for WoS publications between 2004 and 2013 and of Mafhlahi and Thelwall (2016) for Library and Information Science journals between 1996 and 2013.

One-third (33.83%) of the articles found in Mendeley, which have the highest reader counts, already cover more than 80% of the total readers. Even 5% of articles cover more than 30% of readers (see Table 5.4). The total count of readers (rcB) from all BS journal articles is 8,904,827 and is calculated as a sum of all readers for all articles the BS journals have achieved. Similarly, the reader count of economic journal is calculated (rcE) and is 1,423,597.

Table 5.4: Percentage of readers for all articles in Mendeley.

No. of articles	1–15,000	15,001–100,000	100,001–200,000	200,001–295,582
% of articles	5.07%	28.76%	33.83%	32.34%
Total no. of readers	3,336,576	5,088,238	1,689,513	214,097
% of readers	32.30%	49.26 %	16.36 %	2.07%

5.2.2. Mendeley readership information: discipline

In the study of Nuredini and Peters (2015), 25 disciplines were identified for the top 30 journal articles in BS and E. But by exploring the top 1,000 journals in the similar disciplines (E and BS), 29 different disciplines (see Table 5.5) are identified in Mendeley. In terms of discipline, when retrieving the data from the Mendeley API, for each article, within this research, we received all possible disciplines that the user might have. Moreover, the results of this study cover all disciplines an article can receive from its readers.

The discipline names retrieved in 2015 from Mendeley are distinct from the discipline names retrieved in 2019. For example, the discipline "arts and humanities" retrieved from this study cannot be found in the study of 2015 since Mendeley provided two categories: one category for "arts" and the second category for "humanities." Besides the new representation of discipline names, Mendeley also added new disciplines that appeared at the 2019 crawl and were not listed in the 2015 study. Four new disciplines are "veterinary science," "immunology and microbiology," "energy," and "decision sciences." Most of the readers from the journals in BS found in Mendeley have a background in "business management and accounting" where for the journals in E the readers have a background in "economics, econometrics, and finance."

In Table 5.5, all the disciplines of E and BS journals are shown. The first column represents the names of the disciplines that the articles from both E and BS journals received based on Mendeley users. Each discipline in Mendeley has a reader count, which is a number that represents the readers of that particular discipline (in this case, this reader count is named as rcDB for business studies and rcDE for economics). The rcDB is presented in the second column that lists all the readers each discipline achieved from BS journal articles. rcDB is calculated by the sum of all readers' disciplines each article accumulated and aggregated on discipline level. For example, "agricultural and biological sciences" discipline has 43,460 readers meaning that 0.49% of all Mendeley readers have this discipline saved in their profile information for BS journals. The third column presents the % of readers for each discipline. The percentage of readers for each discipline is calculated with the fraction of:

The percentage (%) of readers for each discipline = $\frac{rcDB}{rc}$ for business studies journals, where rc are all reader counts for articles that received readers in Mendeley.

The percentage (%) of readers for each discipline = $\frac{rcDE}{rc}$ for economic journals, where rc are all reader counts for articles that received readers in Mendeley.

"The unspecified" discipline means that none of the users saving these articles into their Mendeley library do not show their discipline on their profile and Mendeley categorizes these articles as an unspecified category. Even though only 25.82% of users for both E and BS have their discipline public, more than 90% of articles (268,350) have readers that provide discipline information on their profiles. For BS journals, 6% of the readers are coming from the discipline "business, management, and accounting," and for E journals, 8.48% of the readers have the same discipline.

Since not all Mendeley users save discipline information on their profiles, we calculated another percentage of readers only for those that have published discipline information on their profiles (rcBD for BS journals and rcED for E journals).

The percentage (%) of readers with shared discipline information = $\frac{rcDB}{rcBD}$ for BS journals, where rcBD are all reader counts for BS articles that received readers in Mendeley.

The percentage (%) of readers with shared discipline information = $\frac{rcDE}{rcED}$ for E journals , where rcED are all reader counts for E articles that received readers in Mendeley.

We found out that 30% of readers for BS journals and 24.57% of readers for E journals with published discipline information on their profile are coming from business management and accounting discipline.

Table 5.5: Users discipline for journal articles in E and BS.

Disciplines from Mendeley	No. of readers per discipline in BS	% of all readers for each discipline in BS	% of readers with published discipline information	No. of readers per discipline in E	% of all readers for each discipline in E	% of readers with published discipline information
Agricultural and biological sciences	43,460	0.49%	2.40%	8,878	0.62%	1.81%
Arts and humanities	19,534	0.22%	1.08%	10,063	0.71%	2.05%
Biochemistry, genetics and molecular biology	6,138	0.07%	0.34%	1,079	0.08%	0.22%
Business, management and accounting	546,926	6.14%	30.20%	120,783	8.48%	24.57%
Chemical engineering	3,903	0.04%	0.22%	345	0.02%	0.07%
Chemistry	19,378	0.22%	1.07%	1,170	0.08%	0.24%
Computer science	54,693	0.61%	3.02%	33,667	2.36%	6.85%
Decision sciences	7,574	0.09%	0.42%	2,781	0.20%	0.57%
Design	5,385	0.06%	0.30%	3,272	0.23%	0.67%
Earth and planetary sciences	17,247	0.19%	0.95%	3,144	0.22%	0.64%
Economics, econometrics, and finance	322,643	3.62%	17.82%	29,060	2.04%	5.91%
Energy	4,043	0.05%	0.22%	1,452	0.10%	0.30%
Engineering	83,345	0.94%	4.60%	67,472	4.74%	13.72%
Environmental science	81,576	0.92%	4.50%	12,091	0.85%	2.46%
Immunology and microbiology	855	0.01%	0.05%	158	0.01%	0.03%
Linguistics	3,039	0.03%	0.17%	1,723	0.12%	0.35%

Disciplines from Mendeley	No. of readers per discipline in BS	% of all readers for each discipline in BS	% of readers with published discipline information	No. of readers per discipline in E	% of all readers for each discipline in E	% of readers with published discipline information
Materials science	3,570	0.04%	0.20%	733	0.05%	0.15%
Mathematics	26,616	0.30%	1.47%	4,052	0.28%	0.82%
Medicine and dentistry	15,524	0.17%	0.86%	9,291	0.65%	1.89%
Neuroscience	5,459	0.06%	0.30%	1,250	0.09%	0.25%
Nursing and health professions	4,424	0.05%	0.24%	3,878	0.27%	0.79%
Pharmacology, toxicology, and pharmaceutical science	1,367	0.02%	0.08%	388	0.03%	0.08%
Philosophy	3,146	0.04%	0.17%	1,028	0.07%	0.21%
Physics and astronomy	4,807	0.05%	0.27%	1,334	0.09%	0.27%
Psychology	109,088	1.23%	6.02%	34,984	2.46%	7.12%
Social sciences	215,840	2.42%	11.92%	75,745	5.32%	15.41%
Sports and recreations	2,551	0.03%	0.14%	3,819	0.27%	0.78%
Unspecified	198,206	2.23%	10.95%	57,891	4.07%	11.77%
Veterinary science and veterinary medicine	461	0.01%	0.03%	134	0.01%	0.03%

5.2.3. Mendeley readership information: academic status

Mendeley's academic status is another important readership information that helps to determine what kind of impact the research articles have based on the academic status of readers. Mohammadi et al. (2015) emphasized that the status of academics can affect the usage of research articles. The authors, for example, highlighted that younger researchers read and cite more articles in contrast to senior researchers. Additionally, PhD students seem to browse and often use articles more than professors. For the academic status, we received the full scale of Mendeley data characterizing this information. Moreover, the results of this section are based on full data (i.e., academic status) of Mendeley users for the articles published in E and BS journals.

Early studies on Mendeley readership information confirm that PhD students are the core Mendeley readers for different disciplines performed by various research studies (Haustein & Larivière, 2014; Mohammadi et al., 2015; Nuredini & Peters, 2015). For example, Mohammadi et al. (2015) explored Mendeley user categories for different research fields, (i.e., clinical medicine, engineering and technology, social science, physics, and chemistry) and found that the majority of Mendeley readers are PhD Students (90.7%). Within this study, similar to earlier studies performed for Mendeley, we found that PhDs are the core readers of E and BS journal articles. In Table 5.6, all occupational categories from Mendeley, however, restricted to our 1,000 journals, are shown additionally with readers counts received in E and BS journals.

Table 5.6: Presents the academic status of journals in E and BS.

Academic Status	No. of readers for E journals	No. of readers for BS journals
Student > PhD student	366,551	2,322,798
Student > Master	257,874	1,744,267
Researcher	176,777	865,264
Student > Doctoral student	109,431	772,209
Student > Bachelor	115,408	738,669
Unspecified	99,687	603,281
Professor > Associate professor	70,817	431,060
Professor	58,579	363,942
Student > Postgraduate	50,512	331,829
Lecturer	47,980	299,066
Other	44,128	268,839
Lecturer > Senior lecturer	18,271	115,916
Librarian	9,642	57,127

PhD students are the central Mendeley readers for both E and BS journals and are represented with 35% for BS journals and 33% for E journals (see Table 5.7). Next, master students are found with 23% for BS and 22% for E journals. The number of readers for BS and E journals is calculated based on the sum of counts each academic status received for all journals. The "% of readers" is the number of readers for each academic status over the total number of readers that have academic statuses.

Several academic statuses listed by Mendeley (see Table 5.7) are similar, for example, PhD student and doctoral student or master students and postgraduates. Following the study of Mohammadi et al. (2015) and Haustein and Larivière (2014), Mendeley's academic statuses are merged into single fields (see Table 5.7) and into categories such as scientific, educational, or professional (see Table 5.8). For example, assistant professor and lecturer are merged into assistant professors who are intended for the educational category. Associate professor and senior lecturer are merged with associate professor, PhD student is merged with doctoral student and categorized as scientific, and master student is merged with postgraduate student and categorized as educational. Besides the publication year 2013, where master students are identified as main readers in our dataset, from 2011 to 2018, PhD students are the leading readers in Mendeley identified with the highest counts.

Table 5.7: Percentage of readers for each academic status in both BS and E journals.

Business studies journals			Economics journals			
Academic status	No. of readers	% of readers in BS	Academic status	No. of readers	% of readers in E	Category type
Student > PhD student	3,095,007	34.75%	Student > PhD Student	475,982	33.43%	Scientific
Student > Master	2,076,096	23.31%	Student > Master	308,386	21.66%	Educational
Researcher	865,264	9.71%	Researcher	176,777	12.41%	Scientific
Student > Bachelor	738,669	8.29%	Student > Bachelor	115,408	8.10%	Educational
Professor > Associate professor	546,976	6.14%	Professor > Associate professor	89,088	6.25%	Scientific
Professor	363,942	4.08%	Professor	58,579	4.11%	Scientific
Lecturer	299,066	3.35%	Lecturer	47,980	3.37%	Educational
Librarian	57,127	0.64%	Librarian	9,642	0.67%	Professional
Other	268,839	3.01%	Other	44,128	3.09%	Professional
Unspecified	603,281	6.77%	Unspecified	99,687	7.00%	Unspecified

For both E and BS journals, most of the readers are scientific, and very few readers of these journals are professional (e.g., librarians). The grouping of the academic statuses shows how research articles are used by different user types, reflecting their role and purpose when using Mendeley (Zahedi & van Eck, 2018). For example, the scientific group includes professors and PhD students, and we assume they use Mendeley for publishing where master students and bachelor students reflect more the educational way of using the literature.

Table 5.8: Percentage of readers in three different categories.

	BS journals	E journals
Categories	% of readers	% of readers
Scientific	54.68%	56.2%
Educational	34.95%	33.13%
Professional	3.65%	3.76%

The top 10 journals for both E and BS, which received higher Mendeley reader counts, are shown in Table 5.9 with their top three academic statuses. The first top 5 journals belong to BS having PhD students as core readers, followed by master students and researchers. The top 5 journals with the highest Mendeley reader count that belong to E also have PhD students as their primary readers followed by master students and bachelor students, except for the *Journal of Theoretical Biology* and *Forest Policy and Economics* that have the same academic statuses as the other E journals; the only difference is that instead of bachelor students, they have researchers in their top 3.

Table 5.9: Top 10 journals for both E and BS and their top 3 academic statuses.

Top 5 BS journals with high Mendeley counts	Top 3 Mendeley academic statuses	Top 5 E journals with high Mendeley counts	Top 3 Mendeley academic statuses
Journal of Cleaner Production	Student > PhD	*Energy*	Student > PhD
Energy Policy		*Applied Geography*	Student > Master
Computers in Human Behavior	Student > Master	*Water Resources Research*	Student > Bachelor
Journal of Business Research		*Journal of Theoretical Biology*	Student > PhD
Expert Systems with Applications	Researcher	*Forest Policy and Economics*	Student > Master
			Researcher

5.2.4. Mendeley readership information: country

Among 195 countries around the world[109], Mendeley users for articles in E and BS are coming from 119 different countries. The top 15 countries for E and BS journals are shown in Table 5.10. The top 3 countries with the most readers in E and BS are the United States, the United Kingdom, and Brazil.

Country readership information from Mendeley is found for 146,484 or 49.5% of articles. The Mendeley readership information country is calculated based on the users' demographic

---

[109] Countries around the World: https://www.worldometers.info/geography/countries-of-the-world/

information on their profiles for users that have saved articles from the top 1,000 journals in their Mendeley library.

Table 5.10: Percentage of readers in the top 15 countries for BS and E journals.

Country	No. of readers in BS	% of readers in BS	Country	No. of readers in E	% of readers in E
United States	87,249	15.83%	United States	15,580	17.93%
United Kingdom	59,074	10.72%	United Kingdom	9,369	10.78%
Brazil	39,905	7.24%	Brazil	4,915	5.66%
Germany	37,639	6.83%	Germany	4,898	5.64%
Spain	23,459	4.26%	Spain	3,404	3.92%
Netherlands	16,244	2.95%	Colombia	3,124	3.59%
Portugal	15,729	2.85%	Japan	2,741	3.15%
Malaysia	14,879	2.7%	India	2,656	3.06%
Canada	14,298	2.59%	Canada	2,407	2.77%
India	14,226	2.58%	Italy	2,391	2.75%
Indonesia	14,185	2.57%	France	2,226	2.56%
France	13,916	2.52%	Netherlands	2,143	2.47%
Italy	13,509	2.45%	Malaysia	2,079	2.39%
Japan	12,923	2.34%	Portugal	1,997	2.3%
Colombia	12,658	2.3%	Australia	1,858	2.14%

Around 16% of the readers for journals in BS are coming from the United States, about 11% from the United Kingdom, and 7% from Brazil. The readers for E journals have similar countries but with less number of readers. In general, 4.35% of all users (that have saved at least one of the top 1,000 journal articles from E or BS) have provided country information in their Mendeley profile, whereas 22.6% of users are found with academic status and 25.82% of users have discipline information in their profile. Even though the country information is not favorably represented for all users of E and BS articles—this readership information can still play an important role for readers. It has been investigated that readers of Mendeley tend to read articles that are authored from their own country. This insight can further help readers of E and BS articles to check for country information an article has, based on Mendeley users, which might indicate which specialism their country is interested in (Thelwall & Maflahi, 2015).

5.3. Dataset III: Altmetric.com coverage for journals in E and BS

Within this section, we explore Altmetric.com that collects information for research output found online from specified sources such as social media platforms, traditional media, and online reference managers. Altmetric.com is examined for E and BS journals which creates the Dataset III. The methodology and techniques of how the data are collected from Altmetric.com can be found in detail in Chapter 4.

We identified a total of 913 (91.3%) journals from both E and BS that have articles saved in Altmetric.com. BS journals are found with 95% and E journals are found with 87.6%. The general coverage of journals from E and BS in Altmetric.com is shown in Table 5.11. In Dataset I, we found a total of 621,585 research articles in Crossref from both disciplines, of which 272,507 (43.8%) articles are found in Altmetric.com with DOIs. Although less than 50% of articles are found with altmetrics, most of the journals are saved at least once in Altmetric.com.

Table 5.11 presents the journal coverage for both disciplines E and BS found in Altmetric.com. BS journals appear to be a better present than E journals and also the number of articles found with DOIs in Altmetric.com for BS is larger than for E.

Table 5.11: Journals and article coverage in Altmetric.com for top 1,000 journals in economics and business studies.

Top 500 E journals found in Altmetric.com			
Total no. of journals	%	Total no. of articles	%
438	87.6%	106,649	40.6%
Top 500 BS journals found in Altmetric.com			
Total no. of journals	%	Total no. of articles	%
475	95%	165,856	46%
Total E and BS journals		Total E and BS journal articles	
913	91.3%	272,507	43.8%

5.3.1. Altmetric.com—Altmetric Attention Score

The Altmetric Attention Score (AAS) is a number that presents the total amount of the attention research outputs (e.g., journal articles) have received online from social media sources. The AAS is based on an algorithm provided by Altmetric.com (not yet empirically tested by the altmetric community), weighting different social media sources based on their reach to reflect the relative values of these sources. For example, blog posts might have a higher weight than Twitter posts because the average blog post is more likely to bring attention to research articles than the average tweet. The Altmetric Attention Score is a metric that provides 1) quantity by counting the Altmetric Score; the higher the Altmetric Score, the higher is the attention; and 2) quality by considering the weights each source receives based on their impact (Costas et al., 2015). Several studies have explored Altmetric.com for the coverage of journal articles and explored altmetric sources for different disciplines (Costas et al., 2015; Nuredini & Peters, 2016; Hassan et al., 2017).

Costas et al. (2015) explored one and a half million articles with publication years 2011–2013, of which 52% were covered by Altmetric.com, but only a low number had received attention scores (15%–25%). The authors highlighted that social media shares are mostly related to newly published articles. For the publication year 2013, the authors found more than 25% of articles that received online attention. The study of Hassan et al. (2017) explored 15 different disciplines in Altmetric.com, and they confirm that there is a rapid increase of altmetric data from 2011 until 2015 by 20.46%.

In this section, we examine the AAS for the journals in E and BS. Figure 5.4 presents the top 10 journals from E and BS that have the highest AAS, which is the sum of all articles' AAS. The first five journals shown in green have the highest AAS in BS and the other five belong to the E journals with the highest AAS, shown in blue shaded. The journal *Psychological Science* has the highest AAS from the entire dataset III with a total of 149,303, which is 10% of the total AAS accumulated by all BS journals in this study.

The journal *Environmental Science and Technology* has the highest number of articles compared to other journals shown in Figure 5.4, meaning its articles are at least mentioned online in average. For economics journals, *American Economic Review* is identified with the highest Altmetric Score of 25,023, which is 4% of the total AAS accumulated by all E journals in this study. The entire list of journals from both disciplines and their AAS on journal level is shown in Appendix I and II.

The E journals *American Economic Review*, *Journal of Economic Perspectives*, *Journal of Consumer Research*, and *Quarterly Journal of Economics* all belong to the classes A+ or A in the Handelsblatt ranking.

These journals are highly ranked based on Handelsblatt ranking and also have received a higher AAS than other journals. According to the top 5 highly ranked journals in E, we can suggest that these journals are also popular on social media platforms. In contrast, the top 5 journals from BS that received high AAS fall into the classes B, C, or D in Handelsblatt ranking, showing that also journals that do not belong to the highly ranked classes A or A+ can be popular on social media platforms.

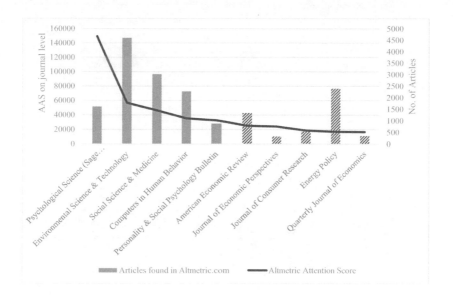

Figure 5.4: Top 10 journals with highest AAS in BS and E (shaded).

Figure 5.5 shows a year-wise representation of the total number of articles found in Crossref (Dataset I) and Altmetric.com for journals in BS and the sum of their AAS received online for each publication year. Although the number of articles published found from Crossref is higher in 2011, the coverage of articles in Altmetric.com is greater for the years 2017 (15%) and 2013 (14.9 %) as for 2011. The year 2018 has a very low coverage of journal articles in Altmetric.com (3.4% found with altmetrics) and, therefore, the lowest coverage of AAS (7,322). The reason for finding more articles published in 2017 with altmetrics is that Altmetric.com tracks recent publication years of articles. Articles published in 2016 have 24% more shares than articles published in 2015, and articles published in 2017 have 39% more attention than those in 2015. According to the study of Yu et al. (2017), altmetric sources from Altmetric.com may not be as immediate as anticipated because each social media source has different levels of immediateness. Moreover, the authors explored the different levels of the immediacy of altmetrics, specifically between Weibo altmetrics Twitter and general altmetrics from Altmetric.com. Yu et al. (2017) claimed that Weibo altmetrics are more immediate and are captured within 180 days (for 69% of articles), where general altmetrics happen more after 364 days (for 46% of articles) after the publication date. Based on this insight, we might claim that articles in E and BS published in 2018 and retrieved with altmetric information in early 2019 have low altmetric coverage and shares because more time is needed for them to accumulate altmetric information. Fang and Costas (2020) explored the immediacy of altmetrics from Altmetric.com for WoS articles published between 2012 and 2016 and have a DOI. They found out that the immediacy of altmetrics depends on the AAS tracked by Altmetric.com, the type of document that is shared online and the discipline of that research work.

Some altmetric attention sources (e.g., Twitter) collect altmetrics as soon as the article is published online, whereas sources such as Policy Documents, for example, accumulate online attention slowly. Documents such as "Editorial material" and "Letters" collect faster altmetrics than the type "Review" and journal articles. The authors also highlighted that the discipline "physical sciences and engineering" and "life and earth sciences" collect faster altmetrics from different altmetric attention sources compared to other disciplines such as "social science," "biomedical and health sciences," "mathematics," and "computer science."

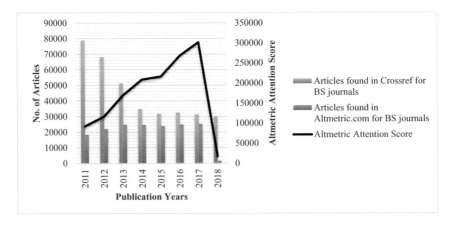

Figure 5.5: Year-wise representation of articles found in Crossref and Altmetric.com for business studies journals.

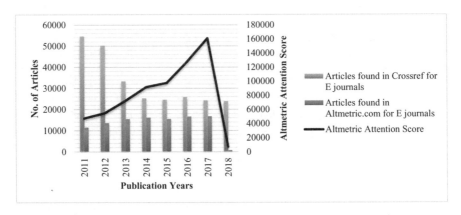

Figure 5.6: Year-wise representation of articles found in Crossref and Altmetric.com for economic journals.

Similarly, like BS journal articles, E journal articles (see Figure 5.6) also have a higher AAS in the publication year 2017. The coverage of articles published in 2018 is higher for economic journals than for BS journals. Current published research is being more often shared than the older articles from 2011. The AAS for both E and BS journals is significantly increasing by around 23% on average each year from 2011 to 2017.

5.3.2. Altmetric.com attention sources

When exploring Altmetric.com, it should be noted that although Altmetric.com shows Mendeley reader counts for each research article, the AAS is calculated only for those articles for which at least one other social media metric (such as Twitter and news) has been found. Mendeley is not included in the AAS[110] of Altmetric.com. Hence, some studies working with data from this provider exclude Mendeley (data tracked by Altmetric.com) from their analyses (e.g., Costas et al., 2015).

Nineteen different altmetric attention sources are identified while exploring Altmetric.com data for our top journals in E and BS (see Table 5.12). Robinson-García et al. (2014) identified 16 altmetric attention sources for research articles explored in 2014. Nuredini and Peters (2015) identified 13 attention sources.

Table 5.12 also lists the type of source the Altmetric Attention Sources fall into. For example, Twitter falls in social media groups, whereas Videos and Q&A fall in Multimedia and other online platforms. This categorization of altmetric attention sources is based on the Altmetric.com general information page about its sources[111]. These sources tracked by Altmetric.com are described in detail in Chapter 3.

Table 5.13 provides information for altmetric attention sources for journals in economics. The total number of articles found in the sources shows the number of DOIs found in Altmetric.com that accumulated attention in each of the sources. It is important to note that there are articles that are found in both Twitter and blogs or other attention sources. Therefore, if we sum up all articles found with altmetrics in all sources from Table 5.12, the number is greater than the article coverage found in Altmetric.com (e.g., 106,649 articles for E journals).

---

[110] How is the Altmetric Attention Score is calculated:
https://help.altmetric.com/support/solutions/articles/6000060969-how-is-the-altmetric-attention-score-calculated-
[111] What outputs and sources does Altmetric.com track?
https://help.altmetric.com/support/solutions/articles/6000060968-what-outputs-and-sources-does-altmetric-track-

Table 5.12: Altmetric attention sources identified in Altmetric.com for E and BS journals.

No.	Altmetric attention sources	Type of the source
1	News	Mainstream Media[112]
2	Blogs	Blogs
3	Policy	Policy Documents
4	Patent	Patent Citations
5	Twitter	Social Media
6	Peer review	Peer review Platforms
7	Weibo	Social Media
8	Facebook	Social Media
9	Wikipedia	Wikipedia
10	Google +	Social Media
11	LinkedIn	Social Media
12	Reddit	Multimedia and other online platforms
13	Pinterest	Social Media
14	F1000	Research highlights
15	Q&A	Multimedia and other online platforms
16	Videos	Multimedia and other platforms
17	Syllabi	Open Syllabus Project
18	Mendeley	Online Reference Managers
19	Dimension Citations	Citing Database

The total number of counts per source is calculated by the sum of each count the source has reached. The "% of total no. of articles per source" is the total number of articles found per source divided by the total number of articles found generally in Altmetric.com. The "% of total no. of counts per source" is the sum of all counts per source divided by the sum of all counts for all sources.

For E journals, Twitter has the highest coverage of articles with 57.98% followed by Facebook with 11% and Policy Posts with 9.64%. Twitter is the most active medium for mentioning economic journal articles. Besides the highest coverage of articles, Twitter also has the highest number of shares with 83.69%.

---

[112] The list of Mainstream Media outlets that Altmetric.com tracks: https://www.altmetric.com/about-our-data/our-sources/news/

Table 5.13: Distribution of articles from E journals within different altmetric attention sources.

Altmetric attention sources	Total no. of articles per source	% of total no. of articles per source	Total no. of counts per source	% of total no. of counts per source
News	7,142	6.60%	28,229	5.15%
Blogs	9,994	9.23%	16,119	2.94%
Policy	10,439	9.64%	17,664	3.22%
Patent	241	0.22%	373	0.07%
Twitter	62,733	57.98%	457,999	83.69%
Peer review	86	0.08%	103	0.01%
Weibo	226	0.21%	403	0.07%
Facebook	11,745	11%	18,448	3.37%
Wikipedia	2,776	2.57%	3,577	0.65%
Google +	1,514	1.39%	2,437	0.44%
LinkedIn	10	0.009%	10	0.001%
Reddit	834	0.77%	1,319	0.24%
Pinterest	16	0.01%	19	0.003%
F1000	83	0.07%	86	0.015%
Q&A	109	0.10%	124	0.022%
Videos	237	0.22%	308	0.05%
Syllabi	0	0%	0	0%

Similarly, we also show altmetric attention sources for journals in business studies in Table 5.14. Journal articles in BS are mostly found on Twitter with 103,697 (56.62%) articles that have a total of 83.47% of tweets, Facebook with 11%of shares , and blogs with 8.94% of posts . Twitter is also the medium in which BS journal articles are frequently mentioned. These results are similar to the findings of Hassan et al. (2017), highlighting that Twitter has a higher coverage of articles and altmetric attention than other social media sources.

Since Mendeley data tracked from Altmetric.com are not considered at the calculation of AAS, Mendeley is calculated separately from the aforementioned sources. In E journals, 104,171 articles are found with Mendeley Saves, which covers 97.7% of articles retrieved with altmetrics. In BS journals, 162,890 articles are found with Mendeley Saves, which covers 98% of articles retrieved with altmetrics.

Based on the retrieved data from Altmetric.com, only 2% (3,167) of articles from BS journals have accumulated Mendeley reader counts and have not received any extra attention from other sources, and only 2.6% (2,762) of articles from E journals have accumulated Mendeley counts.

These types of articles are not counted at the calculation of AAS. There are 46,520 articles with AAS = 0 for BS and 32,065 articles with AAS = 0 for E journals.

Table 5.14: Distribution of articles from BS journals within different altmetric attention sources.

Altmetric attention sources	Total no. of articles per source	% of total no. of articles per source	Total no. of counts per source	% of total no. of counts per source
News	13,228	7.03%	84,417	7.03%
Blogs	16,365	8.94%	30,170	2.51%
Policy	13,187	7.20%	21,515	1.79%
Patent	1,005	0.18%	2,249	0.18%
Twitter	103,697	56.62%	1,001,988	83.47%
Peer review	2,055	1.12%	2,490	0.20%
Weibo	371	0.20%	938	0.08%
Facebook	21,732	11%	37,988	3.16%
Wikipedia	4,459	2.43%	5,676	0.47%
Google +	3,913	2.13%	8,574	0.71%
LinkedIn	92	0.05%	99	0.0008%
Reddit	1,621	0.88%	2,566	0.21%
Pinterest	32	0.02%	34	0.003%
F1000	163	0.09%	169	0.01%
Q&A	199	0.11%	236	0.02%
Videos	834	0.50%	1,080	0.09%
Syllabi	1	0.0006%	102	0.008%

Mendeley is by far the most prominent attention source for both E and BS journals. For BS journals, 98.2% of articles found in Altmetric.com have at least one Mendeley count and so do 89% of articles for E journals. Although Mendeley counts are higher than any other source tracked by Altmetric.com, they are excluded from the table when listing the top 5 attention sources for articles in E and BS journals (see Table 5.15). Dimensions citations showcase citation data for articles in E and BS journals. In BS journals, 91.6% of articles have received Dimensions citations and so do 89% of articles in E journals. A recent published study of Fang and Costas (2020) that explored the immediacy of altmetrics for 12 Altmetric.com attention sources suggests that Twitter, Reddit, News, Facebook, Google+, and Blogs accumulate altmetrics faster compared to other sources such as Peer-review, Policy Documents, Wikipedia, Video, F1000Prime, and Q&A.

5.3.3. The impact of the top 5 Altmetric.com attention sources

In Table 5.15, the top 5 altmetric attention sources and their counts found in Altmetric.com for journals in E and BS are presented. Given these results, the online attention is higher in Twitter with 83.47% of tweets for BS journals and 83.69% of of tweets for E journals. Given these results, online activity is higher on Twitter than that on other mediums.

Mendeley counts are excluded from the top 5 social media sources because, as mentioned in Section 5.3.2, Altmetric.com excludes this indicator for the calculation of AAS. The findings of Robinson-García et al. (2015) presented the top 5 sources with 95% of shares (i.e., Twitter, Mendeley, CiteULike, Facebook, and Blogs), identifying CiteULike as another source tracked from Altmetric.com. CiteULike, however, was not identified within our dataset, either because it is not tracked anymore by Altmetric.com or because economic and business studies journal articles have not received CiteULike data (Robinson-García et al., 2014). Besides "Policy Documents" (which is a new source identified in this research), we confirm the findings of Nuredini and Peters (2016).

Table 5.15: Top 5 altmetric attention sources for both disciplines.

Altmetric.com attention sources in BS journals	% of counts	Altmetric.com attention sources in E journals	% of counts
Twitter	83.47%	Twitter	83.69%
News	7.03%	News	5.15%
Facebook	3.16%	Facebook	3.37%
Blogs	2.51%	Blogs	2.94%
Policy Documents	1.79%	Policy Documents	3.22%

Twitter is the most prominent source and covers the highest number of articles with 56.62% in BS and 57.98% in E journals. Several studies have investigated the usage of Twitter for scholarly communications (Priem & Castello, 2010; Eysenbach, 2011; Bar-Ilan et al., 2012). These studies claim that researchers use Twitter to share and discuss scientific articles (Priem & Castello, 2010). Tweets are suggested as a tool that can be used to measure the social impact of articles.

News is the second most prominent altmetric attention source for our dataset, with 7.03% of mentions for BS journal articles and 5.15% for E journal articles. News includes mainstream media outlets and magazines. There is proof that the mention of articles in news media can result in higher citation rates (Shipman, 2012). Facebook counts are also confirmed as a metric that might be used to measure the social impact of research, including a broader range of readers (Bornmann, 2015a,b). In our dataset, Facebook counts are identified with 3.16% for BS journals and 3.37% for E journals. Blogs have also been recognized as a source for scholarly impact and owning a strong correlation with citation counts (Shema et al., 2014). In our study, blogs are identified with 2.51% counts for BS journals and 2.94% for E journals. Last but not least, on the top 5 attention sources, E and BS journals are also found at Policy Documents with 1.79% for BS and 3.22% for E journals.

Furthermore, we further investigated only the set of articles that have been mentioned in a particular altmetric source and meanwhile are found with Mendeley readership information (see Table 5.16). First, we explored only the set of articles that have received Twitter counts from Altmetric.com, and this dataset (DOIs) is then queried for Mendeley academic status. For BS, we found 4,330 articles that have Twitter counts only and Mendeley academic status. These articles are read mostly from PhDs with 34% followed by master students with 20% and professors (including lecturers) with 17%. With Facebook counts, we found 240 articles, of which 33% of readers are PhD students. Articles mentioned only in News or only in Blogs seem to not have still accumulated Mendeley academic status. Articles that have been mentioned by Policy Documents only are 56, and 30% of the readers of these articles are PhDs followed by master students with 15%.

Table 5.16: BS articles found only in single sources and with academic status from Mendeley.

Altmetric attention sources for BS articles	Twitter	News	Facebook	Blogs	Policy Documents
No. of articles	4,330	50	240	169	56
Academic status	PhD students (32%) Master students (21%) Professors (17%)	Null	PhD students (33%) Master students (21%) Professors (17%)	Null	PhD students (30%) Master students (15%) Unspecified (14%)

Similarly, we performed the same analysis for E articles (Table 5.17). Articles mentioned in News or Blogs are mostly covered in Mendeley with academic status PhD (36%) followed by professors and lecturers with 18%.

Table 5.17: E articles found only in single sources and with academic status from Mendeley.

Altmetric attention sources for E articles	Twitter	News	Facebook	Blogs	Policy Documents
No. of articles	3,891	55	157	175	54
Academic status	PhD students (34%) Master students (19%) Professors (15%)	PhD students (33%) Professors (19%) Master students (17%)	PhD students (33%) Master students (20%) Professors (19%)	PhD students (36%) Professors (18%) Master students (17%)	PhD students (35%) Professors (23%) Master students (13%)

Additionally, for this study, we also investigated Twitter demographics[113] from Altmetric.com for both E and BS journal articles. Altmetric.com classifies users of Twitter (that have shared articles) based on the geolocation they have provided on their Twitter profile.

Tables 5.18 and 5.19 show the top 10 countries with a high number of posts for E and BS journals, together with the number of posts tweeted per country and the number of readers of those countries. According to the Twitter demographics, tweets are mostly posted by users from the United States with 17.26% for BS journals and 24.74% for E journals.

Table 5.18: Top 10 countries from Twitter demographics for BS journals.

BS journals				
Countries	No. of posts	% of posts	No. of readers	% of readers
United States	179,674	17.26%	88,456	18.48%
United Kingdom	144,564	13.89%	59,636	12.46%
Canada	31,836	3.06%	16,880	3.53%
France	14,413	1.38%	6,775	1.42%
Australia	27,356	2.63%	13,682	2.86%
Japan	13,622	1.31%	6,705	1.4%
Spain	19,171	1.84%	10,946	2.29%
Germany	14,009	1.35%	6,928	1.45%
Netherlands	17,365	1.67%	7,999	1.67%
Sweden	6,933	0.67%	3,706	0.77%

Table 5.19: Top 10 countries from Twitter demographics for E journals.

E journals				
Countries	No. of posts	% of posts	No. of readers	% of readers
United States	97,861	24.74%	45,020	23.29%
United Kingdom	51,795	13.09%	22,594	11.69%
Canada	12,380	3.13%	6,840	3.54%
Australia	10,166	2.57%	5,401	2.79%
Spain	8,718	2.2%	5,475	2.83%
France	7,511	1.9%	3,530	1.83%
Japan	4,288	1.08%	2,457	1.27%
Germany	6,633	1.68%	3,427	1.77%
Netherlands	6,199	1.57%	3,233	1.67%
Italy	4,910	1.24%	2,639	1.37%

---

[113] Twitter Demographics : https://help.altmetric.com/support/solutions/articles/6000060978-how-are-twitter-demographics-determined-

5.3.4. Correlation of citation counts with all altmetric attention sources

Altmetric.com integrates Dimensions badges on their platform by presenting citation data from Dimensions database[114] for journal articles they track. The Dimensions database was launched in 2018, consisting of 128 million documents, of which 89 million are articles (e.g., from journals or conference proceedings) and the rest are patents, clinical trials, Policy Documents, etc. (Orduña-Malea & López-Cózar, 2018). The Dimensions database is partly free for access and partially paid and attaches citation data for 50 million documents and altmetric data for 9 million documents. Orduña-Malea and López-Cózar (2018) explored Dimensions for citation counts, and the authors found that Dimensions have good coverage of recent articles. Compared to the Scopus database, Dimensions offer considerably lower citation data. However, the citation counts from Dimensions and Scopus are found to be strongly correlated with each other, suggesting Dimensions citations as alternative metrics to Scopus citations. A subscription for the Scopus citation database is needed to retrieve citation data for journal articles, where Dimensions citations are freely extracted from Altmetric.com. Hence, for this study, Dimensions citations are used instead as sources to explore the relationship between citation counts and altmetric information for E and BS journals.

In this section, we will explore the correlation between the citation counts retrieved from Dimensions badges in Altmetric.com and AAS as well as Tweets and Mendeley Readership counts retrieved from Altmetric.com.

We use the Spearman correlation (ρ) instead of the Pearson correlation (r) to explore the correlation between citation counts and altmetrics because of the skewness of our data (Thelwall, 2018b). Citations and altmetrics are seen as skewed since not all articles have received citations and altmetrics; some have received more and some have received less.

The Spearman correlation (ρ) statistically measures the strength and direction of the monotonic relationship between two variables (Siegel, 1957). In a monotonic relationship, two variables have a tendency to change together but not always at a constant rate (Schober et al., 2018). The Spearman correlation is usually used for ordinal data or data that are ranked and follow some order instead of raw values (Siegel, 1957). In contrast, the Pearson correlation (r) statistically measures the strength and direction of the linear relationship between two variables and is usually performed for continuous variables.

We calculated the Spearman rank correlation based on the formula:

$$\rho = 1 - \frac{6 \sum d_i^2}{n(n^2 - 1)}$$

where d_i is the difference between a pair of ranks and n is the total number of observations (Spearman, 1987).

The correlation coefficient (ρ) can be interpreted based on the following points: the closer ρ is to +1, the stronger is the correlation between the values. The closer ρ is to 0, the weaker is the

---

[114] Dimensions database: https://www.dimensions.ai/

correlation; if the coefficient is 0, then there is no correlation at all. However, if ρ gets closer to -1, the correlation becomes stronger again, although negative (Ratner, 2009).

The calculation of the Spearman correlation is performed in SPSS[115]—a software used for advanced statistical analysis. The Spearman correlation is calculated for article level and journal level. For article level, Spearman correlation is calculated between citations, AAS, Twitter (tweets), and Mendeley Readership Counts. When calculating the Spearman correlation in SPSS, the "Sig (2-tailed)" annotation is used. The Sig (2-tailed)[116] is used in statistical hypothesis testing in mathematics to evaluate the null hypothesis against the alternative and is equal to the probability of observing a greater absolute value of t under the null hypothesis.

The Spearman correlations on article level are shown in Table 5.20 for BS journals and Table 5.21 for E journals. The correlation between Dimensions citations and AAS is ρ = 0.106, showing that there is a very low correlation between these two variables. Similarly, a low correlation is spotted on article level for E journals between those two variables, ρ = 0.110 (see Table 5.21). Tweets are very low or not correlated at all with citations from Dimensions on article level for BS ρ = -0.020 and for E ρ = -0.038.

Another interesting insight from the correlation on article level is that Mendeley Readership counts have a strong and positive correlation with Dimensions citations on article level. The Spearman correlation for BS journals on article level is ρ = 0.705, and for E journals, it is ρ = 0.730, suggesting that articles with high Mendeley count most likely have high citation counts.

Table 5.20: Spearman correlation between citation counts, tweets from Twitter, Mendeley counts, and AAS on article level for BS journals.

Correlations

			Altmetric Attention Score	Twitter	Mendeley Readership Counts	Dimensions Citations
Spearman's rho	Altmetric Attention Score	Correlation Coefficient	1.000	.761**	.169**	.106**
		Sig. (2-tailed)	.	.000	.000	.000
		N	165856	165856	165856	165856
	Twitter	Correlation Coefficient	.761**	1.000	.078**	-.020**
		Sig. (2-tailed)	.000	.	.000	.000
		N	165856	165856	165856	165856
	Mendeley Readership Counts	Correlation Coefficient	.169**	.078**	1.000	.705**
		Sig. (2-tailed)	.000	.000	.	.000
		N	165856	165856	165856	165856
	Dimensions Citations	Correlation Coefficient	.106**	-.020**	.705**	1.000
		Sig. (2-tailed)	.000	.000	.000	.
		N	165856	165856	165856	165856

[115] SPSS Statistical analysis software : https://www.ibm.com/analytics/spss-statistics-software
[116] SPSS annotated output: https://stats.idre.ucla.edu/spss/output/t-test/

Table 5.21: Spearman correlation between citation counts, tweets from Twitter, Mendeley counts, and AAS on article level for E journals.

Correlations

			Altmetric Attention Score	Twitter	Mendeley Readership Counts	Dimensions Citations
Spearman's rho	Altmetric Attention Score	Correlation Coefficient	1.000	.714**	.165**	.110**
		Sig. (2-tailed)	.	.000	.000	.000
		N	106649	106649	106649	106649
	Twitter	Correlation Coefficient	.714**	1.000	.044**	-.038**
		Sig. (2-tailed)	.000	.	.000	.000
		N	106649	106649	106649	106649
	Mendeley Readership Counts	Correlation Coefficient	.165**	.044**	1.000	.730**
		Sig. (2-tailed)	.000	.000	.	.000
		N	106649	106649	106649	106649
	Dimensions Citations	Correlation Coefficient	.110**	-.038**	.730**	1.000
		Sig. (2-tailed)	.000	.000	.000	.
		N	106649	106649	106649	106649

We also calculated the Spearman correlation on journal level between citation counts from Dimensions, AAS, Twitter, and Mendeley readership counts. For BS journals, we spotted a strong correlation $\rho = 0.732$ between citations and the AAS (see Table 5.22). For E journals, this correlation is higher than that for BS journals with a value $\rho = 0.814$ (see Table 5.23). AAS and Dimension citations are strongly correlated on journal level rather than that on article level, meaning that journals with high citation counts are also receiving substantial attention online.

We also calculated the correlation between tweets and citations from Dimensions on journal level, resulting in a strong correlation for BS journals with $\rho = 0.666$ and for E journals with $\rho = 0.739$. Another strong correlation is found between the Mendeley counts and Dimensions citations. For BS journals, the correlation is $\rho = 0.958$, and for E journals, it is $\rho = 0.970$, denoting that highly saved journals in Mendeley seem to be highly cited as well.

Table 5.22: Spearman correlation between AAS, Twitter, Mendeley readership information and Dimensions citations on journal level for BS journals.

Correlations

			Altmetric Attention Score	Twitter	Mendeley Readership Counts	Dimensions Citations
Spearman's rho	Altmetric Attention Score	Correlation Coefficient	1.000	.936**	.724**	.732**
		Sig. (2-tailed)	.	.000	.000	.000
		N	475	475	475	475
	Twitter	Correlation Coefficient	.936**	1.000	.656**	.666**
		Sig. (2-tailed)	.000	.	.000	.000
		N	475	475	475	475
	Mendeley Readership Counts	Correlation Coefficient	.724**	.656**	1.000	.958**
		Sig. (2-tailed)	.000	.000	.	.000
		N	475	475	475	475
	Dimensions Citations	Correlation Coefficient	.732**	.666**	.958**	1.000
		Sig. (2-tailed)	.000	.000	.000	.
		N	475	475	475	475

Table 5.23: Spearman correlation between AAS, Twitter, Mendeley readership information and Dimensions citations on journal level for E journals.

Correlations

			Altmetric Attention Score	Twitter	Mendeley Readership Counts	Dimensions Citations
Spearman's rho	Altmetric Attention Score	Correlation Coefficient	1.000	.947**	.818**	.814**
		Sig. (2-tailed)	.	.000	.000	.000
		N	438	438	438	438
	Twitter	Correlation Coefficient	.947**	1.000	.743**	.739**
		Sig. (2-tailed)	.000	.	.000	.000
		N	438	438	438	438
	Mendeley Readership Counts	Correlation Coefficient	.818**	.743**	1.000	.970**
		Sig. (2-tailed)	.000	.000	.	.000
		N	438	438	438	438
	Dimensions Citations	Correlation Coefficient	.814**	.739**	.970**	1.000
		Sig. (2-tailed)	.000	.000	.000	.
		N	438	438	438	438

The correlation between citations from Dimensions and other altmetric attention sources are shown in Appendix III. For example, the Spearman correlation between Blogs and citations for BS journals is found to be $\rho = 0.618$, which shows a positive correlation; however, this value is lower compared to other sources (e.g., Mendeley). News is identified with a Spearman correlation of $\rho = 0.694$ for BS journals and $\rho = 0.762$ for E journals, showing a strong and significant correlation, especially for E journals. The correlations found in this thesis between different indicators are generally stronger on journal level than on article level. This happens because a great number of articles have low values or even no values at all for some of the indicators, which has a negative effect on the correlations. By summing up multiple articles for higher aggregation (i.e., journal level), this negative effect of those articles is reduced, leading to stronger correlated values. Similar findings have been highlighted in the study of Costas et al. (2015) as well.

Within this study, we also calculated the Spearman correlation between citation counts from Dimensions and AAS as well as citation counts and Mendeley counts for articles grouped based on their publication years (see Figure 5.7). These correlations are performed for both E and BS journal articles. The correlation between citation counts and AAS is positive but low. The correlations seem to be stronger for articles published in 2011, followed by a drop of the Spearman coefficient each year.

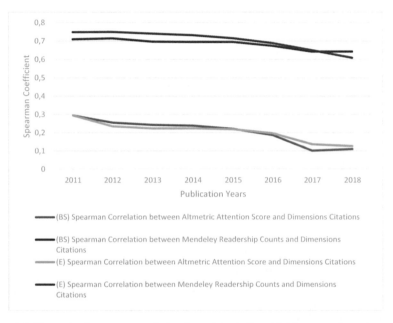

Figure 5.7: Year-wise Spearman correlation for articles in E and BS between altmetric attention scores, Mendeley and citation counts.

5.3.5. Identifying trendy topics using altmetrics (proof-of-concept with Latent Dirichlet Allocation)

Within this section, the AAS, Mendeley counts, and citations from Dimensions are investigated, to identify trendy topics in E and BS journal articles. Within this thesis, trendy topics are those that are retrieved from articles that have received high online attention and are recently published. However, we don't take into account the number of articles published within that topic, but instead we compare the average values of AAS, citations, and Mendeley counts for each topic. The average values are calculated as a fraction of the sum of the indicators (e.g., AAS) divided by the total number of articles found within that topic.

To retrieve the topics of E and BS articles, we have used topic modeling. Topic modeling analyzes a large amount of text data and clusters similar articles together (Blei et al., 2003). The approach that is used in this study is based on the Latent Dirichlet Allocation (LDA) algorithm, which considers each document as a group of topics and each topic as a group of words (Blei et al., 2003; Griffiths & Steyvers, 2004).

As discussed in Chapter 3, trendy topics besides the use of citations can also be identified using altmetrics. The main advantage here is that altmetrics do appear within a shorter time than citations, and this feature can be used mainly for identifying trendy topics for recently published articles.

The dataset of this thesis is based on the articles published between 2011 and 2018, and their altmetric information was retrieved in the beginning of 2019. Therefore, within this research, the recently published articles are those that are published in 2018, and therefore, only those articles will be considered for this part. However, it is important to keep in mind that articles published in 2018 have not necessarily been written in that year. These articles might have been submitted, for example, in 2016 and been published in 2018. Nevertheless, here, we do not take into consideration when the article is written, and we focus more on the official online publication date of that article and consider that date as recently published. Within this regard, future studies should shed light on the publication window of the articles and more precisely define which articles should be considered as "trendy."

Table 5.24 presents the total number of articles that have been retrieved for both BS and E journals in Mendeley and Altmetric.com with a publication year 2018. Moreover, we have only selected articles that have accumulated AAS (i.e., AAS > 0) as well as articles that have accumulated Mendeley (i.e., counts>0).

Table 5.24: Total number of articles from E and BS journals published in 2018 and found in altmetric providers.

Altmetric provider	Publication year	No. of articles in BS	No. of articles in E
Mendeley	2018	48,282	16,843
Altmetric.com	2018	1,272	648

To perform LDA and retrieve the topics for each of the articles, first we have to do pre-processing (e.g., data cleaning) for the article titles that have been found within this query. First, we converted the words into their base word and removed stop words. The main data cleaning stages that were performed for both titles retrieved from Mendeley and Altmetric.com were linked to remove punctuation, special characters, and digits. Nonetheless, for articles that were retrieved from Mendeley, additional data cleaning methods have been used compared to the data retrieved from Altmetric.com. For example, some amount of the article titles in Mendeley had special characters attached at the strings (e.g., "€performance relationship"), which should be removed beforehand to retrieve better results when performing LDA. However, article titles retrieved from Altmetric.com were pretty clean.

It is important to note that for 1,272 articles retrieved from Altmetric.com, we assigned 15 topics, whereas for Mendeley data (48,282), we assigned 30 topics. Since this part is just a proof of concept, we assigned the number of topics depending on how good the code performed. However, for future studies and precise analysis, one should try to build many LDA models with different number of topics and select the one that has the highest coherence (by using, e.g., *compute_coherence_values()*; Prabhakaran, 2020). The code for building the model and retrieving the topics is written in python.

After performing LDA, we retrieved the topics (see Appendix IV, for topic descriptions) in each discipline, and for each topic, we calculated the sum of the AAS and Mendeley counts. In Figure 5.8, topics of articles published in BS and found in Altmetric.com are presented. Topic 10 (which is related, e.g., to data and innovation) has higher citation counts compared to other topics. Topic 14 (which is related to health) has the higher number of AAS. Topic 8 (which is related to social analysis) has less AAS compared to other topics. Topic 4 (which is related to industry) has less citation counts. Topic 14 has both high citations and AAS.

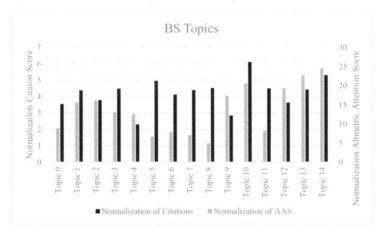

Figure 5.8: Topic distribution of BS articles found in Altmetric.com.

In Figure 5.9, topics of articles published in E and found in Altmetric.com are presented. Topic 13 (which is related to economic growth) has higher AAS compared to other topics. Topic 14 (which is related to trading or investments) has the higher number of citations. Topic 8 (which is related to finance) has less AAS compared to other topics. Topic 1 (which is related to inequality) has less citation counts. Topic 14 has both high citations and AAS.

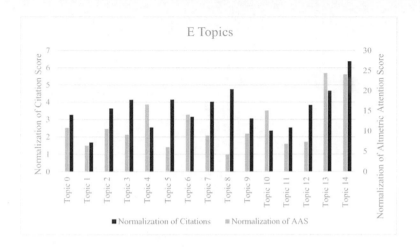

Figure 5.9: Topic distribution of E articles found in Altmetric.com.

In Figure 5.10, topics of articles published in BS and found in Mendeley are presented. Topic 29 (which is related to innovation and management) has the highest number of Mendeley counts followed by topic 9 which is related to "Big Data." Topics 5 (related to social media) and 8 (stochastic based algorithms) show low number of Mendeley scores.

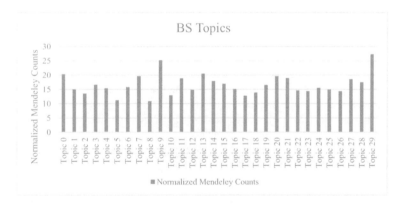

Figure 5.10: Topic distribution of BS articles found in Mendeley.

In Figure 5.11, topics of articles published in E and found in Mendeley are presented. Topic 3 (which is related to energy, electricity, and optimization) has the highest number of Mendeley counts. Topic 0 (related to distribution and models), topic 16 (inflation and trading), and topic 26 (market and credit) show low number of Mendeley counts.

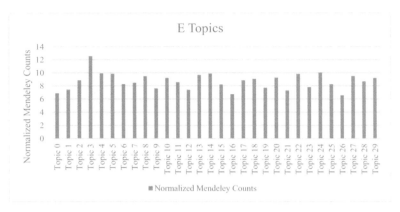

Figure 5.11: Topic distribution of E articles found in Mendeley.

Based on results retrieved in this part, topics with the highest AAS of BS and E are related to health and economic growth, whereas topics that have the highest Mendeley counts in these disciplines are related to innovation, management, and energy. We conclude the findings of this part by suggesting new studies that can further explore identifying trendy topics. There is still an open question, whether trendy topics can also be those that cover a higher number of publications or those that have a higher number of online attention.

5.4. Discussion and conclusion

From the top 1,000 E and BS journals in Handelsblatt ranking, in Crossref we found 92% of journals with article DOIs and their metadata. In Mendeley, 72% of journals with article publication years 2011–2018 are found, of which around 48% of articles have at least one Mendeley reader. BS journals are more findable in Mendeley compared to E, in which similar results are also found within the study of Nuredini and Peters (2015), with the top 30 journals. In Altmetric.com, 91.3% of E and BS journals are found, and we discovered moderate shares of articles (around 44%) for publication years 2011–2018. However, the publication year 2011 includes full-scale Almetric.com data from July 2011 onwards; therefore, when considering a full-scale altmetrics for libraries, altmetrics from the publication year 2012 are suggested for use instead (Thelwall et al., 2013). Moreover, this analysis reveals that altmetrics from both providers are still sparse, even when considering many journals and articles. Therefore, when using altmetrics for library portals, especially those with economic focus, journal level aggregations are suggested since, for each library record, altmetric information could be shown. These findings relate to the earlier results of Nuredini and Peters (2016).

The AAS for both E and BS journals significantly increased by around 23% on average each year from 2011 to 2017. The AAS trend shows that altmetrics for articles published between 2012 and 2017 could be used as helpful sources in library systems, for example, for filtering research trends (articles published within the past 2 years and having received high online attention).

Mendeley readership information such as discipline, academic status, and country tends to show users' reading behavior in Mendeley for both E and BS journal articles. These fields are not mandatory; therefore, only 4.4% of all users (that have saved at least one of the top 1,000 journal articles from E or BS) have provided country information in their Mendeley profile, whereas 22.6% of users are found with academic status and 25.8% of users have discipline information in their profile. Compared with the earlier Mendeley research for E and BS journals (Nuredini & Peters, 2015, 2016) that only considered the top 3 user statistics for each article, this study determines the behavior of Mendeley readers correctly because the results are based upon the Mendeley readership information for each article. Based on the insights, we can conclude that E and BS journals generally have similar Mendeley user patterns independent of the journals' position in the Handelsblatt ranking. For example, in Mendeley, most of the central users are PhDs, which confirmed this fact within this study and in the study of Nuredini and Peters (2015) that investigated Mendeley only for the top 30 journals. Given this case, Mendeley might be suggested as a good altmetric source to find research articles in E and BS journals for economists with the academic status PhD.

A large scale of Mendeley users in this study are coming from "business, management, and accounting" discipline for BS journal articles with 30% of readers and from "economics, econometrics, and finance" for E journal articles with 18% of readers, whereas in the study of Nuredini and Peters (2015), most of the readers of the top 30 journal articles for both disciplines are coming from business administration. However, this discipline seems to be recently updated in Mendeley and replaced with "business, management, and accounting."

Even though the country information is not favorably represented for all users of E and BS articles—this readership information can still play an important role for readers. It has been investigated that Mendeley readers tend to read articles authored from their own country. This insight can further help readers of E and BS articles to check for country information an article has, based on Mendeley users, which might indicate which specialism their country is interested in (Thelwall & Maflahi, 2015). Within this study, the top 3 user countries are United States, United Kingdom, and Brazil, of which the users of Mendeley read E and BS journal articles (for the top 1,000 journals), whereas in Nuredini and Peters (2015) study, the top 3 countries are the United States, Germany, and United Kingdom. According to this information, one possible suggestion could be that Mendeley users from Germany might read more articles that are published in the top 30 journals from Handelsblatt ranking. The most prominent sources found from Altmetric.com for articles in E and BS journals are Mendeley, Twitter, News, Facebook, Blogs, and Policy Documents; similar results are also shown within the study of Nuredini and Peters (2016).

Journal articles in BS are mostly found on Twitter (56.6% of articles) followed by Facebook that covers 11% of articles and by blogs with 8.9% of articles. For E journals, Twitter has the highest coverage of articles with 58% followed by Facebook with 11% and Policy Posts with 9.6%. Moreover, since Twitter as a source tracked by Altmetric.com was found with a large number of E and BS journal articles, we encourage economic researchers to check for tweets, which can make it easier for them to find recently published articles for reading. Twitter, moreover, is believed to show a societal impact of scholarly articles (Eysenbach, 2011) and predict highly cited articles right after their publication. Therefore, we also encourage economists who are authors to share their articles by promoting them on social media, especially on Twitter, which is supposed to increase the number of citations (Ortega, 2016).

Additionally, we also investigated articles found with attention in only one source of Altmetric.com and have received Mendeley readership information such as academic status. In this way, we determined which articles are read by different groups of Mendeley users and have a specific online attention. Our results show that most of the readers of these articles are PhD students followed by master students and professors. Articles found in News or in Blogs beside PhDs are also read more by professors.

Within this study, we found that top highly ranked journals (with classes A+ and A) in E from Handelsblatt ranking are highly mentioned in the sources tracked by Altmetric.com, making them also popular in social media platforms (i.e., attention sources). Additionally, we learned that besides the popularity of highly ranked journals in social media platforms, journals ranked below class A, which have been assigned to classes B and C in Handelsblatt ranking, are highly saved in Mendeley. These journals also do not necessarily always publish only articles with an economic focus but also publish other scientific findings from different disciplines. Some possible reasons why low ranked journals from Handelsblatt are highly saved in Mendeley might be first because of the heterogeneous nature of those journals (publishing a variance of scientific content besides economics). Second, a large scale of Mendeley readers, in this case, master students, do read/save the articles but do not often author their own, leading to low citation counts and low rankings of these journals (Thelwall, 2017b). And the other option can be that the readers of these journals (e.g., researchers) might not author articles that are indexed in Scopus—Scopus is the main contributor of citations to Handelsblatt ranking, and therefore, we believe that the Handlesblatt ranking (based on citations) for these journals is lower.

Based on the correlation coefficients retrieved for our datasets, Altmetric Score and Tweets are less correlated with Dimensions citations on article level. Therefore, we could not suggest Altmetric Score or Twitter as an indicator that will filter articles with high online impact and that are therefore highly cited soon after their publications. AAS and Tweets are, however, strongly correlated with citation counts on the journal level, which might be used as an indicator that helps to filter highly cited journals instead. Blogs and News are also positively correlated with citation counts on journal level, which are used as sources that can identify highly cited journals for E and BS journals.

During the altmetric investigation process for E and BS journal articles, we found a strong correlation between Mendeley counts and Dimensions citations for E and BS on both journal and article levels. This correlation suggests Mendeley readership information for E and BS journal articles as alternative indicators to citations, reflecting the scientific impact of articles within a shorter time frame than citation counts. With this finding, we could recommend Mendeley counts to libraries as useful indicators respectively as popularity factors (complementary to citations) that might help to provide a better ranking of search results for library services. However, to precisely confirm the level of immediacy of altmetrics, especially Mendeley counts, in future studies we will observe these indicators for E and BS journal articles on a monthly basis.

5.4.1. Limitations

The research explored in this study is confined by two essential limitations: 1) the selection of journals based on a specific discipline and 2) limitations related to altmetric providers (Altmetric.com and Mendeley). Moreover, the research analysis and results of this study consider only the top 1,000 journals in E and BS disciplines and do not consider the entire list of journals in the Handelsblatt ranking ($n = 3,664$). The limitation of journals to 1,000 is based on several data retrieval issues, which are mentioned in the methods and data sources. These issues (e.g., not every article published in one of the 3,664 journals had a DOI) made it difficult to include all journals for this research. The altmetric information suggested in this study is dependent on the lifetime of the two altmetric providers. Altmetric information is also limited because Altmetric.com only tracks certain sources and neglects other social media sources or attention sources that might be useful and relevant for the readers of E and BS journal articles. For example, Altmetric.com has permission to track data from Wikipedia but not from other encyclopedias such as Britannica. This limitation misrepresents the online attention scientific articles gain since there is a bias toward the included sources, whereas missing sources are neglected (Gumpenberger et al., 2016). Last but not least, one should mention that Mendeley's information generally suffers from missing and incorrect values in the metadata, which makes the whole crawling process challenging. Also, the data that are retrieved from Mendeley are only based on the users who practice Mendeley.

Chapter 6

Questionnaire in evaluating altmetrics usage for journals in economic and business studies

In this chapter, we answer the last research question No.4 (from Chapter 1) by exploring whether altmetric information plays a vital role for economists during the article selection process. In the following section, we first present the setup of the questionnaire and the mockup with four fictive articles in economics and business studies, enriched with different related journal information (i.e., bibliometrics, journal ranking, and altmetrics). The questionnaire, including the mockup, is sent to a group of economists in academia. After that, we analyze the responses of the economists we received from the survey and present the results.

6.1. Does the filtering of journal articles work using altmetrics?

This thesis utilized three parts to examine the research questions of this study. The first part discusses the literature review based on the use cases derived from the ZBW personas (shown in Chapter 3). The second part included the gathering of altmetric data for the top 1,000 journals in economics (E) and business studies (BS) and analyzing them, as described in Chapters 4 and 5, which according to the results we retrieved can answer the primary research questions of the thesis. Subsequently, the third part will answer the last research question by using a survey that aims to explore whether altmetric information can help economists to filter out an article (from other articles) for reading first.

According to the results retrieved in Chapter 5, altmetrics for E and BS journal articles (published between 2011 and 2018) are moderately covered in Mendeley (47%) and Altmetric.com (43.8%), showing that not all articles of these journals accumulated altmetrics. Moreover, the study of Nuredini and Peters (2015), which explored altmetrics for the top 30 journal articles in E and BS between the publication years 1994 and 2013, found that altmetrics are better present for articles published in recent years. From the publication year 2011 onwards, every year, more than 10% of the articles searched are found with altmetric attention, suggesting that from 2011 there is a steadily increasing amount of E and BS journal articles available on social media platforms. These results are in line with other studies (Haustein et al., 2014; Costas et al., 2015), suggesting that altmetrics are better present for recently published articles since Altmetric.com started to collect data from 2011 onwards.

Given the fact that altmetrics are generally moderately present for E and BS journal articles, as well as that altmetrics are more present toward articles published during the recent years (e.g., from 2011 onwards), when suggesting altmetrics for library online portals, many library records (i.e., articles) will have no altmetrics at all. Therefore, higher aggregation levels, that is, journal level altmetrics, are suggested as alternative metrics that can be attached to most articles indexed in library portals. Journal level altmetrics can overcome the sparsity of altmetrics by ensuring that for each journal article, altmetrics are presented, which can avoid user frustration when using altmetrics as a source for selecting an article or a journal for reading. In this case, however, the user of the library should be aware or informed that journal level altmetrics cannot identify the online attention of an article but can be used as a metric that can further assist with their decision-making. Moreover, journal level altmetrics can be used to identify the online attention of journals based on different altmetric categories (e.g., a journal read by mostly PhD students), which in this case can help users to make decisions on what to read.

Since one should be careful about what kind of altmetric information should be used and how to present them to libraries, this survey will explore whether journal level altmetrics for four articles, presented to the respondents, can play any role for their article selection and therefore contribute to drawing conclusions about the usefulness of altmetrics for users in real-world applications.

Specifically, the survey will help to evaluate the behavior of economists in academia during the article selection process using different scholarly evaluation metrics. Moreover, we will present both bibliometric and altmetric indicators attached to four journal articles of which the participants are encouraged to make a decision which article they want to read first. This study, however, is focused more on finding out the usefulness of altmetric information when selecting an article for reading rather than the bibliometric indicators in general. The study of Rousseau and Rousseau (2017) already surveyed economists and their knowledge about different bibliometric indicators, highlighting that the Journal Impact Factor is the best-known indicator from economists, followed by the h-index.

A small unit of the collected altmetric information for E and BS journal articles from Chapter 5 will be used in the questionnaire to learn about the economist's behavior for article selection purposes and to find out the role of altmetrics in this manner.

6.2. The setup of the questionnaire

To answer the research questions mentioned above, we used a questionnaire. According to Fink (2003), the surveyor can collect useful information about the related target of people and their behavior about the field that is studied by using a questionnaire.
The questionnaire is created on the LimeSurvey[117] Version 2.73.1+171220 software package, which is an open-source platform for producing professional online questionnaires. A LimeSurvey instance is hosted and maintained by the Christian-Albrechts-Universität zu Kiel, Kiel[118], Germany.

The questionnaire of this study has five parts. In the first part, the participants are informed about the purpose of the questionnaire and the time it takes approximately to complete it. The second part includes the privacy policy that the participants should agree with before filling out and submitting the survey. The privacy policy informs the participants explicitly that filling out the survey is voluntary and that they are free to leave the survey at any time. The third, fourth, and fifth parts of the questionnaire are described in detail in the following sections.

---

[117] LimeSurvey: https://www.limesurvey.org/
[118] University of Kiel: https://www.uni-kiel.de/en/

The entire questionnaire design is attached at the end of the thesis under Appendix V.

The questionnaire is sent via a mailing list managed by ZBW – Leibniz Information Centre for Economics, instructing participants to follow the link sent via email. The questionnaire, the mockup, and the experimental data received from this survey[119] are subsequently published on Zenodo [120] (an open access repository operated by CERN) to support the open science movement.

The main content of the questionnaire is designed mainly into three parts:

6.2.1. First part: The demographic information

The first part of the questionnaire included demographic information such as age, discipline, country, gender, and academic status. The "Age" field only receives an integer as an input with a two-character limit. The "Discipline" is a dropdown box that provides three different discipline options: "Economics (VWL)," "Business Studies (BWL)," and "Other." The "Country" field is a dropdown box that displays 196 built-in generated country names from the LimeSurvey platform. Next, the field "Gender" is presented with three radio buttons for "Female," "Male," and "No Answer." The last question from the demographic information section is the "Academic Status" which is a dropdown box containing nine different academic statuses: "Bachelor Student," "Master Student," "PhD Student," "Researcher," "PostDoc," "Assistant Professor," "Professor," "Associate Professor," and "Other."

6.2.2. Second part: The task assigned to the participants and related questions

This section focuses on the task assigned to the participants upon which the following questions of the questionnaire are based. The task encouraged participants to analyze the mockup-based graphic (see Figure 6.1) presented to them before answering the questions of the survey. At the mockup (graphic), four different article items and their related information, such as their metadata and metrics-based data, are simultaneously represented. Generally, a mockup is a user interface prototype that usually presents software concepts that are valuable for developers (Ricca et al., 2010). The mockups can help to develop web applications where user requirements are gathered and are understandable for end-users. Based on the information shown on the graphic, the participants were advised to select one article they would like to read first.

6.2.2.1. Mockup design

The graphic (see Figure 6.1), which is presented at the questionnaire, illustrates four E and BS journal articles, their metadata, and metric associated data (e.g., citations on journal level). For creating the graphic, four real articles with altmetrics from E and BS journals (Chapter 5) are manually selected and integrated into the EconBiz portal. The selection process of the four articles is based on three criteria: First, recently published articles are taken into account since they are supposed to generate more altmetric information (Nuredini & Peters, 2016); second, articles that meet the first criteria and are found with altmetric information in both Mendeley

---

[119] Questionnaire, results, and mockup: https://doi.org/10.5281/zenodo.3783722
[120] Zenodo: https://zenodo.org/

and Altmetric.com; and third, the results from the first and second criteria are limited to articles that have high altmetrics from both providers. Four articles are selected for performing a survey because the more articles we represent the more time-consuming the questionnaire would have been for the participants.Using the EconBiz portal layout, the graphic with four articles is created. All four articles' data are represented at once with the intention to make the questionnaire task as easy as possible and save the participants' time. The altmetrics on journal level attached to the four articles in EconBiz are available only for creating this study and therefore accessed only internally from the EconBiz team.

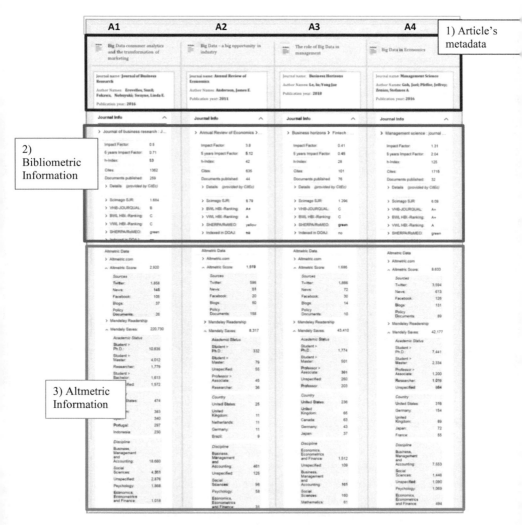

Figure 6.1: The visualization of the mockup-based graphic for the four articles and their data.

Each article at the graphic is based on three important data parts:

1) Article level information such as its metadata

The article level information that is shown at the graphic are the titles, journal names, author names, and publication years. The abstracts are intentionally not used at the graphic because most of the economists use the abstract as the main criteria to judge whether an article is worth reading entirely (Dahl, 2009). Since we wanted to explore altmetrics as a tool for filtering and to select an article for reading, we refrained from showing the abstracts to get more meaningful data on how economists would form their decisions if their primary criterion (abstracts) is not available to them.

Meanwhile, all four articles used in the mockup had a heterogeneous nature meaning each article represented a different topic and the representation of various topics would have made it difficult for participants to make any comparison. In this case, for the graphic representation at the survey, the real article names are renamed to fictive names to overcome the topic heterogeneity of the articles, with the intention to make it easier for the participants to evaluate similar related topics. Nevertheless, other associated data such as journal names, author names, and journal info sections (e.g., Altmetric Scores) for those four articles are based on real data that are retrieved from the EconBiz database and the dataset of this thesis (Chapters 4 and 5).

The four fictive article names of which participants are encouraged to select one based on the journal information are as follows (see Figure 6.1):

1) Big Data consumer analytics and the transformation of marketing
2) Big Data—a big opportunity in industry
3) The role of Big Data in management
4) Big Data in economics

2) Bibliometric information

The bibliometric information presented at the graphic is retrieved from the dataset that EconBiz collected, but it is not yet officially published at the EconBiz portal because this part is still under a research process. The team behind the EconBiz portal is investigating different bibliometric indicators that are Open Access and, therefore, meaningful to use for the economic literature. CitEc[121] is a RePEc service that is adopted by EconBiz because it offered a complete journal list (CSV file) and respective bibliometrics matched with ISSNs found in EconBiz. In addition, CitEc data are freely available, supporting the Open Access movement in comparison with other bibliometric providers such as Scopus[122], WorldCat[123], and WoS. Their data are behind a paywall, or the collected data are inconsistent since their APIs are still work in progress, which makes them difficult to use in EconBiz. The CitEc database includes 1,437,499 articles and 15 million citations. The citations in CitEc are generated by the articles that are

---

[121] CitEc: http://citec.repec.org/s/2018/gamjpubli.html
[122] Scopus: https://www.scopus.com/home.uri
[123] WorldCat: https://www.worldcat.org/

available in RePEc and are limited only to articles that focus on E and BS disciplines. A warning[124] message highlighted by the CitEc service suggests that their data might contain errors (e.g., omissions in the identification of references), which they are still working on to improve the platform's quality and increase the accuracy level. These limitations should be considered when using these data for evaluation purposes.

For each journal article, the Impact Factor from the CitEc database is shown, followed by the 5 years Impact Factor, h-index, and citation counts. All these data are represented on the journal level. In addition to CitEc, there is a list of other journal ranking sources such as SCImago SJR, VHB-JOURQUAL, BWL and VWL HBI. Ranking, SHERPA/RoMEO, and whether this journal is indexed in DOAJ directory. SCImago SJR[125] is a platform that ranks journals based on the citations derived from Scopus. The SCImago journal ranking coefficients are freely available (as an excel file) from the service itself. VHB[126] is the German Academic Association that provides the journal ranking known as VHB-JOURQUAL for business research. The journal ranking is built upon the judgments of the VHB members (1,000) and is described in Chapter 4 in detail.

Similarly to SCImago, VHB-JOURQUAL makes their journal ranking list freely available. Next, HBI or Handelsblatt ranking for both VWL and BWL (see Chapter 4) is also used within the bibliometrics, considering that their data are also freely accessible. Since for EconBiz Open Access is an important movement, it also considers SHERPA/RoMEO[127], which is an online service that determines and analyses the publisher's open access policies as well as DOAJ[128] , which indexes Open Access journals.

Even though bibliometric information on journal level is shown at the questionnaire graphic, for this research, bibliometric information is mostly used as a comparison toolbox toward altmetric data, and therefore, not much detailed information is needed for this part. The focus of this study primarily relies on exploring the behavior of economists only for altmetric information. However, general insights can still be drawn from the results for bibliometric information as well.

3) Altmetric information

Generally, Altmetric.com provides more than 16 altmetric sources (see Chapter 3) where the research output is mentioned. However, based on the results in Chapter 5, we found the top 5 sources from Altmetric.com that E and BS journal articles are mostly mentioned online. The top 5 altmetric sources for E and BS journals are Twitter, News, Facebook, Blogs, and Policy Documents. Each source has its counting number, which is derived from the sum of all articles published in a particular journal mentioned on that source. A screenshot of one article and its Altmetric.com sources aggregated on journal level is shown in Figure 6.2.

Similarly, like the altmetric information from Altmetric.com, Mendeley readership information is aggregated on journal level. Mendeley readership information has three categories (i.e., academic status, country, and discipline), of which each category reader counts is aggregated on journal level. For example, the number of users with a particular academic status (i.e., PhD)

---

[124] CitEc warning: http://citec.repec.org/warning.html
[125] SCImago: https://www.scimagojr.com/
[126] VHB: https://www.vhbonline.org/en/
[127] SHERPA/RoMEO: http://sherpa.ac.uk/romeo/index.php?la=en&fIDnum=|&mode=simple
[128] DOAJ: https://doaj.org/

134

who read articles published in one journal is summed up. Mendeley readership information to economists is presented to see whether this information attached to the article will help them make article judgments and whether economists with the same academic status will be interested in reading the same article. As an example, the Mendeley readership information is displayed for the journal *Research Evaluation* in Figure 6.2.

Based on the aforementioned activities, we created the graphic for the questionnaire. We placed four articles next to each other for enabling a better comparison and straightforward representation of their data, as seen in Figure 6.1.

Figure 6.2: Screenshot (starting from left) of 1) bibliometrics information, 2) altmetric information from Altmetric.com, and 3) readership information from Mendeley.

The second part of the survey had eight questions. The first question is a drop-down box that enabled participants to select the title of the article that they decided to read first. Next, the participants are asked to answer "yes-no-uncertain" questions whether they are familiar with bibliometric information (i.e., Impact Factor, 5 years Impact Factor, etc.) on the journal level and whether bibliometrics and journal rankings are relevant for them to select an article for reading.

Similarly, the participants were asked whether they are familiar with altmetric information from Altmetric.com on the journal level. If the answer of the participants is "Yes" (assuming that these participants know about altmetrics on the journal level), they get a new question (matrix) that is related to how relevant altmetric information is (i.e., Altmetric Score, Twitter Mentions, etc.) for selecting an article for reading. This type of question enabled participants to respond based on the five-point Likert scale (i.e., "Not at all relevant," "Slightly relevant," "Moderately relevant," "Very relevant," and "Extremely relevant"), which can present enough options to participants and provide straightforward results for our study (Dawes, 2008; Chomeya, 2010). Next, if the participant is uncertain or not familiar at all with altmetrics, we provided some topic-related information to them where they can learn what altmetrics on journal level are (see Figure 6.3). A similar principle is followed for readership information from Mendeley as well. The last question of the second part of the survey is an open question that allows the participants to write any other journal or article information they use when they select an article for reading.

Altmetrics are data that track how research has been shared, discussed, and reused online. Altmetrics can help you understand:

- Who is talking about a research output (e.g., journal articles, books, slides, code)
- How often the research is discussed online
- What is said about that research

Altmetric.com is an online service that tracks a range of sources such as social media platforms, traditional media, and online reference managers, to capture mentions and citations to research outputs. For economics articles, top 5 altmetric sources are shown in the graphic above (i.e., Twitter, News, Facebook, Blogs and Policy Documents). These are the sources in which economics journal articles have been most often mentioned online.

The Altmetric Score is a weighted count of all of the mentions Altmetric.com has tracked for an individual research output, and is designed as an indicator of the amount and reach of the attention an item has received.

Altmetric information on journal-level: For each altmetric indicator (e.g., Twitter), the journal-level information represents the sum of altmetrics (e.g., the sum of all tweets) received by all individual articles published in that journal.

Figure 6.3: The topic related information presented to the participants that were uncertain and not familiar with altmetrics.

6.2.3. Third part: How useful are the metrics

With this part of the survey shown at the subsequent page of the questionnaire, we gain insights into whether participants find altmetric information on journal level as well as article level useful based on their article choice. At this part, the participants have four questions to answer, of which two are open questions, and two questions are "5-point Likert scale" questions.

Next, at this page, altmetric information and citation data on article level are presented and explained, followed by an example. With the given article level information, the participants are asked how useful they find these metrics.

By the end of the survey, the closing question is an open question that allows the participants to write any other suggestion or to expand their answers.

6.3. Survey dissemination

The survey has been distributed to roughly 15,000 economists worldwide, contacted via email addresses found within the ZBW mailing list. It is important to note that it is impossible to provide a correct number of the people that received the survey because of technical issues that took place one day after the questionnaire was online and the emails were sent. The questionnaire has been distributed starting from 04.11.2019, nonetheless, with breaks in between. On 05.11.2019, the University of Kiel (CAU) reported a Distributed Denial of Service (DDoS)[129] attack that made all the University services unavailable for legitimate users by crushing it with unsolicited traffic (Lau et al., 2000). This problem seemed to follow for more than a week, and this led to the potential to avoid the online access of the questionnaire for the participants. Meanwhile, because of the CAU problems and since ZBW is a joined[130] institute of CAU, the ZBW mailing service was also affected, which led to email delays and emails fail to send.

However, from the automated email notifications received so far from the mailing service, we have encountered 1,125 emails that failed to be sent, first because of the issues mentioned above and second because some email addresses retrieved from the mailing list were not valid. The questionnaire was online for three and a half weeks until 29.11.2019. Responses submitted were downloaded as an excel file from LimeSurvey. Based on the estimation, the overall response rate of this survey is 3.3%. The total number of responses is 496, of which 205 are partial responses and 291 are full responses.

6.4. Results

The results of this study are only based on the full responses because the 205 partial responses are either from the first page of the questionnaire, which involved accepting the privacy policy and the participants stopped filling out the survey after that, or mostly based on demographic information. Only analyzing this type of information is not relevant for this study, and therefore, partial responses are neglected for further analysis.

6.4.1. The demographics of the participants

The survey results produced 291 full responses from 23 different countries with a dominating number of males ($n = 205$) that cover 71% of the participants that ultimately submitted the survey. The average age of the participants is 48 years, with the youngest reported as 27 years and the oldest as 78 years. Three participants are 78 years old, of which two are male professors, one from Canada and the other from the Russian Federation. The last 78 years old is male with "Other" academic status from France. One of these professors points out in the open question about other journals or article information that they use, "I already have a good idea of the quality of the journals in my field." His responses and the responses of the other two participants, in general, seem to look valid, even though we assume that older people are "hard-to-reach" (Kammerer et al., 2019) because they are retired and have less interaction with research. However, based on their accurate answers, these participants are considered at the overall calculation of the results. Figure 6.4 presents the gender graphic of the participants. This

---

[129] Cyberangriffauf die Server der Uni Kiel: https://www.ndr.de/nachrichten/schleswig-holstein/Cyberangriff-auf-die-Server-der-Uni-Kiel,cyberangriff128.html
[130] ZBW as affiliated institute of CAU: https://www.zbw.eu/en/about-us/profile/history/

survey covers 71% male participants, 28% female participants and 1% with no gender information.

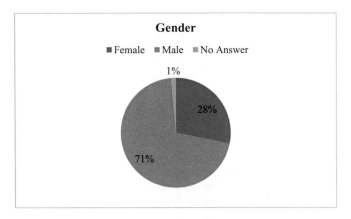

Figure 6.4: Gender information of participants.

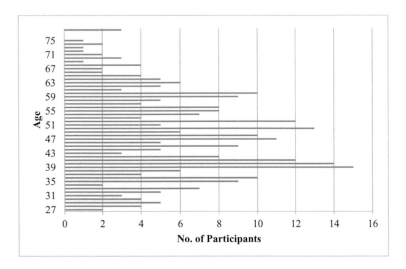

Figure 6.5: Age distribution over the number of participants.

The participant's age is shown in Figure 6.5. The mode of the participant's age is 39, which indicates the largest number of participants that filled this survey. The participant groups with ages between 27–39, 39–48, 48–57 and 57–78 years each cover 25% of the data.

The disciplines of the participants are nearly equally distributed for both economics (E) with 48% and business studies (BS) with 44% of participants. The rest (8%) are identified as "Other." The geographical heat map (Figure 6.6) with continuous coloring is used to represent the percentages of the number of participants from different countries. The heat map starts with

138

red for countries with a low percentage (starting from 0.3%) and ends with dark green for countries with a higher percentage of participants (up to 16%). The top five countries with a large number of participants that filled out the survey are Canada with 16%, Germany with 15.8%, Australia with 14%, France with 11%, and Norway with 8%. Countries depicted as white are not covered, since no participants of these countries filled the survey, either because they were not listed in the ZBW mailing list or they had no time to fill out the survey.

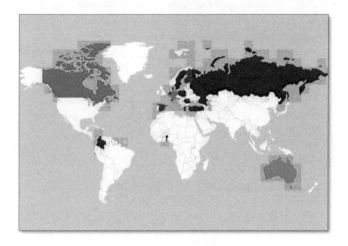

Figure 6.6: A geographic heat map representation of countries from survey responses.

Given the academic status, the highest number of participants are professors with 50%, followed by associate professors with 22% and assistant professors with 13%. Next, 5% of the participants are PhD students, 4% are Researchers, 3% are PostDocs, and 3% are Others.

In total, 84% of participants are classified as professors in general, of which 186 participants are male professors (including associate and assistant professors), and 55 are female professors (see Table 6.1). The responses from PostDocs cover five males and five females, and PhD students are ten females and six males.

Table 6.1 categorizes participants based on academic status, discipline, and gender. Since "Academic status" and "Discipline" at the questionnaire have the same category listed as "Others" (meaning the participants might have different academic status and discipline as the ones represented at the questionnaire), for distinction purposes "Discipline" is referred at Table 6.1 as "d.s." and "Academic status" as "a.s.". A high number of participants are male professors in both economics (E with $n = 87$) and business studies (BS with $n = 88$), followed by female professors ($n = 24$) in both disciplines. From "Other" discipline, 11 participants are male professors and seven are female professors. So, a vast number of participants in this survey are male professors from economics and business studies.

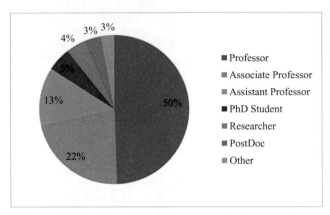

Figure 6.7: Academic status of all participants (n = 291).

Table 6.1: Categorization of participants based on academic status, gender, and discipline.

Academic status and discipline	Male	Female	No answer
Professor - BS	88	24	1
Professor - E	87	24	3
Professor d.s. = "Other"	11	7	0
PostDoc – BS	3	1	0
PostDoc – E	2	3	0
PostDoc - d.s. = "Other"	0	1	0
PhD student - BS	6	3	0
PhD student - E	0	5	0
PhD student d.s. = "Other"	0	1	0
Researcher – BS	0	0	0
Researcher – E	4	6	0
Researcher d.s. = "Other"	1	2	0
a.s. = "Other" - BS	0	1	1
a.s. = "Other" - E	2	2	0
a.s. = "Other" - d.s. = "Other"	0	2	0

6.4.2. Findings: Article selection based on the given task

Initially, the participants were asked to select one of the articles (see Figure 6.8) they found most interesting to read first based on the article's data represented at the graphic. According to the full responses from the survey, a significant number of participants (~63%) selected "Big Data in Economics" or "A4" as the article they want to read first. The article's title is, however, a fictive name, but all other information related to this article, such as author names and publication dates, is based on real data.

The article's real title is: "The relationship between workplace stressors and mortality and health costs in the United States," which was published in the *Management Science* journal. According to Altmetric.com dataset we retrieved, the real article DOI has an Altmetric Attention Score[131] of 482 and 151 Mendeley Saves. On journal level, since this article was published in the *Management Science* journal, it has an Altmetric Attention Score of 8,633 (which is the highest Altmetric Attention Score aggregated on journal level from all other articles presented in the questionnaire) and 42,177 Mendeley Saves.

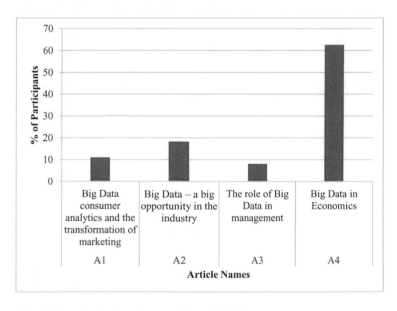

Figure 6.8: Article selection based on participant's decision.

According to the journal information provided for all four articles (see Figure 6.1), article A4 based on bibliometric indicators has the highest h-index, has the highest number of citations, and is listed at the A+ class at BWL HBI. Ranking. From altmetric indicators, the A4 has the highest Altmetric Score, highest Twitter counts, highest News counts, highest number of Facebook shares, and highest number of Blog posts in comparison with the other three journal articles. This article seems to have been mostly mentioned online in different altmetric sources compared to other articles. The A2 article is the second one that has been selected from the

---

[131] In this thesis, Altmetric Score, Altmetric Attention Score and AAS are used interchangeably.

participants, which mostly has the highest counts for bibliometric information, specifically, the highest IF and highest SCImago, but the lowest altmetrics information in comparison with the other three journal articles. We assume that the participants of this group (18%) selected an article for reading based on bibliometric information.

The article selection has also been investigated based on the participant's academic statuses (see Figure 6.9). The *y*-axis represents the percentage of votes each article accumulated, grouped by the different academic statuses. Assistant professors have the highest average for the A4 article compared to all other categories; however, according to the chart, all academic categories have the highest average for A4 compared to other articles.

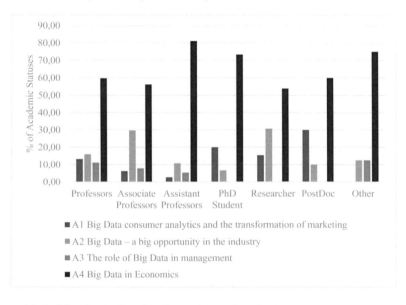

Figure 6.9: Article selection based on the participants' academic status.

6.4.3. Findings: Bibliometrics indicators and journal rankings

Participants were asked to answer whether they are familiar with traditional bibliometric indicators (see Figure 6.10). A significant number of participants (87%) are familiar with the Journal Impact Factor, 7% didn't know what Journal Impact Factor is, and 6% selected uncertain. H-index is less known (22%) compared to other metrics.

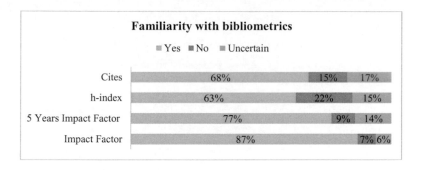

Figure 6.10: The familiarity of participants (n = 291) with traditional indicators on journal level.

The next question reports about how relevant bibliometrics are for the participants to select the article they find interesting for reading first. According to Figure 6.11, Impact Factor leads slightly with 28% for "Very relevant" responses where h-index leads with 35% for "Not at all relevant."

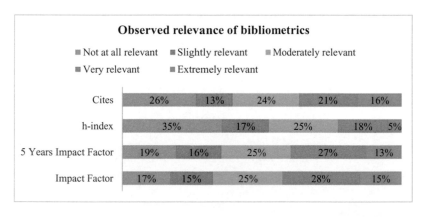

Figure 6.11: The observed relevance of bibliometrics information on the journal level.

The relevance of journal rankings (Figure 6.12) seems to be way weaker compared to traditional metrics, meaning that each of these metrics is found "not at all relevant" by more than roughly 60% of participants. For each metric, only less than 5% of the participants found the metric very relevant.

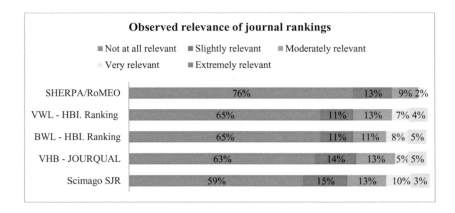

Figure 6.12: The observed relevance of journal ranking.

6.4.4. Findings: Altmetric information on journal level

The participants were also asked about the familiarity and relevance of altmetrics, similar to the questions related to traditional metrics. According to the survey answers (see Figure 6.13), around 25% ($n = 74$) of participants are familiar with Mendeley and around 21% ($n = 61$) of participants are familiar with Altmetric.com. One-third of the participants are familiar with at least one altmetric provider and two-thirds are not familiar with any of the altmetric providers at all.

However, still a high number of participants (more than half of the participants) are not familiar with these types of metrics at all.

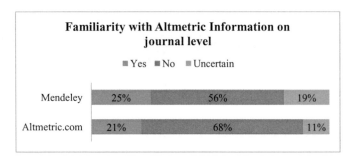

Figure 6.13: Familiarity with altmetrics on journal level from two providers from n = 291 participants.

It should be emphasized that the participants were separated into two groups based on their answers regarding their familiarity with altmetric information.

First, the group of participants that chose "Yes" (supposing that they are familiar with altmetrics from Altmetric.com or Mendeley), and second, the group of participants that selected "No" or "Uncertain" (for altmetric information from Altmetric.com and Mendeley). The group of participants that chose "Yes" had received a different question than the participants that chose "No" or "Uncertain" (see Appendix V). The question that the "Yes" group needed to answer was to scale how relevant different altmetric indicators are for choosing the article they wanted to read first.

Based on the "Yes" group, Figure 6.14 is constructed. Responses originated from the group one ($n = 61$ participants in Altmetric.com and $n = 74$ participants from Mendeley) that selected "Yes" as an answer to the question "Are you familiar with the journal information from Altmetric.com and Mendeley?" are shown. The first four altmetrics (e.g., Mendeley Discipline) belong to Mendeley and the other altmetrics below belong to Altmetric.com (e.g., Policy Documents Mentions).

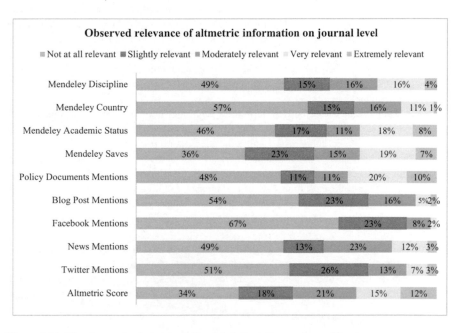

Figure 6.14: The observed relevance of altmetric information on journal level.

Mendeley's discipline, according to Figure 6.1 for each article, presents the top 5 categories of discipline retrieved from Mendeley users that read articles published in a particular journal. For example, the majority of readers of the article A1 are coming from "business, management and accounting," "social sciences," "unspecified," "psychology," and "economics, econometrics, and finance."

Mendeley's country similarly represents the countries of Mendeley users that read articles published in the journals listed in Figure 6.1. For example, for article A1, which is published in the journal *Journal of Business Research*, Mendeley readers are coming from "United States," "United Kingdom," "Spain," "Portugal," and "Indonesia."

Mendeley's academic status depicts the academic status of readers in Mendeley for a particular journal. For the article A1, the academic status of the readers of the journal *Journal of Business Research* is mostly PhDs, master students, researchers, bachelors, and unspecified. Mendeley Saves or known as counts are aggregated on journal level, which depicts the total number of users that saved articles from a particular journal in Mendeley. Mendeley counts for the article A1 present the sum of all saves each article published in the *Journal of Business Research* received.

Policy Documents in Altmetric.com are documents that provide policy and guidance from government or non-government organizations. "Policy Documents Mentions" includes references to articles in Policy Documents on journal level. For article A1, Policy Documents is shown with 26 counts, depicting the number of times articles published in this journal is mentioned in Policy Documents or posts. Blog posts represent how many times the articles published for example in *Journal of Business Research* have received blog post mentions. For article A1, 37 times articles of the above-mentioned journal are mentioned in blog posts. The same principle is followed for Facebook, News, and Twitter Mentions. Altmetric Score represents the sum of all articles published in a particular journal. For article A1, the Altmetric Score is 2,920, which is not related to the article score directly, but instead, this score is aggregated on the journal level.

The indicator "Altmetric Score" has the highest percentage of participants (12%) that selected "Extremely relevant" compared to other altmetric sources. Additionally, the indicator "Altmetric Score" in comparison with other indicators from Altmetric.com has fewer participants that chose that "Altmetric Score" is not at all relevant. "Policy Documents Mentions" has been selected as "Very relevant" from 20% of participants. Mendeley Saves are found with "Very relevant" from 19% of participants, followed by the Mendeley Academic Status of users, with 18% of participants. Mendeley Country of users was found with 1% of participants that selected "Extremely relevant" and 57% of participants that selected "Not at all relevant".

To show the relationship between the age of the participants and how they scaled the altmetric information based on relevance, we created the "Altmetric User Score" (see Figure 6.15).

The "Altmetrics User Score" is based on the average scaled answers to the question: "Which information from the graphic above was relevant for you to select the article you want to read first?."

Moreover, each Altmetric indicator (i.e., Altmetric Score, Twitter Mentions, etc.) was ranked or scaled according to the predefined options (e.g., "Slightly relevant"). In this case, each scale received a weighted number such as "Not at all relevant" gained a weight of 0, "Slightly relevant" gained a weight of 1, "Moderately relevant" received a weight of 2, "Very relevant" a weight of 3, and "Extremely relevant" a weight of 4, and they are summed up per each participant. Since the questions have six categories, the highest possible Altmetric User Score would be 24. Then, the average Altmetric User Score per age is calculated based on the scaled numbers.

Figure 6.15 represents the relationship between the age of users (x-axis) and the average Altmetrics User Score (y-axis). By following the chart below, a linear approximation is shown between these two variables. The Spearman correlation between age and average Altmetric User Score is low and negative, with ρ = -0.256.

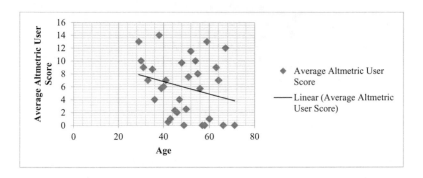

Figure 6.15: The relationship between the age of participants and their weighted scales on answering the relevance question.

According to Figure 6.15, the older the participant is, the less relevant is the altmetric information from Altmetric.com, and it is essential to note that the average Altmetric User Score drops from roughly 8 to 4, which is 50%.

Similarly, the "Mendeley User Score" is calculated for Mendeley readership information as well (i.e., Mendeley Saves, Mendeley Discipline, Country, and Academic Status) with a maximum Mendeley User Score of 16, since the participants rated 4 different altmetrics belonging Mendeley, each vote receiving a weight between 0 and 4. As shown in Figure 6.16, the participants' answers for the Mendeley readership information are almost not depending on age. Thus, the relevance of Mendeley's information appears to be roughly constant. For both Altmetric and Mendeley User Score, the variance is big, meaning the answers are spread out far from the average value. The Spearman correlation between age and average Mendeley User Score is low and negative, with ρ = -0.073.

According to the survey answers, around 56% (*n* = 162) of participants are not familiar with Mendeley and around 19% (*n* = 55) are uncertain. Around 68% (*n* = 197) of participants are not familiar with Altmetric.com and 11% (*n* = 33) are uncertain. The second group of participants that didn't know about altmetrics or were uncertain about it received information on what altmetrics are. After showing the respective information about altmetric information, this group of participants was asked to select which of these altmetric information would have been useful for them to choose the article they wanted to read first.

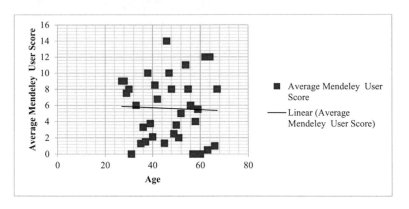

Figure 6.16: The relationship between the age of participants and their weighted scales on readership information from Mendeley on answering the relevance question.

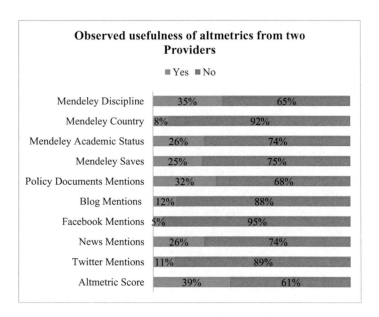

Figure 6.17: Group two of participants that were not aware of altmetrics information.

Altmetric Score on journal level from Altmetric.com has been selected from 39% of participants as a useful indicator (see Figure 6.17) when it comes to choosing an article for reading. Additionally, Mendeley user discipline has been selected as a useful indicator from 35% of participants. On average, the Mendeley readership information was selected as useful from 23.5% of participants, and Altmetric.com altmetrics were selected as useful from 20.8% of participants.

148

The results of this study match the findings of the study of Aung et al. (2017). The authors presented that the academic members of faculties (i.e., professors) are less aware of altmetrics compared to the non-faculty staff members. Based on our results (see Figure 6.18), PhD students are less aware of altmetrics from Altmetric.com; nevertheless, both professors and assistant professors are more aware of altmetrics compared to other academic statuses, despite the "Other."

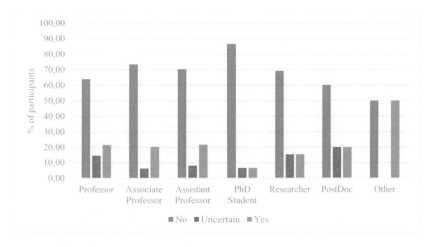

Figure 6.18: Familiarity with altmetrics from Altmetric.com based on academic status.

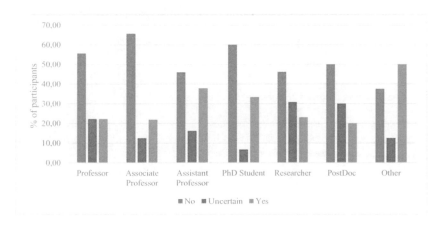

Figure 6.19: Familiarity with readership information from Mendeley based on academic status.

Similarly, the familiarity with Mendeley readership information for each academic status of participants is shown in Figure 6.19. Associate professors represent the highest number of participants that are not aware of Mendeley readership information on journal level. Although Mendeley information is familiar in the "Other" group, the number of these participants is too low (n = 8) compared to the other academic statutes, and therefore, the results shown for "Other" should not be generalized.

6.4.5. Findings: General opinions on the usefulness of indicators

The participants were asked to answer the question, "How useful do you find journal level information to select an article you want to read first?." Based on the responses (see Figure 6.20), traditional rankings are chosen as either "Very useful" or "Extremely useful" from 43% of participants, whereas Altmetric data are chosen as "Very useful" or "Extremely useful" with 14%.

These findings are in line with the survey-based findings of the study of Lemke et al. (2019), which highlighted that traditional metrics are more useful than altmetrics, especially for social scientists.

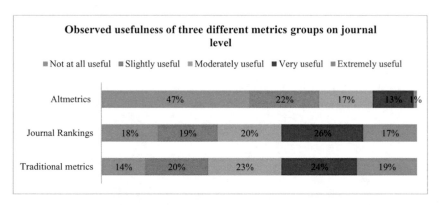

Figure 6.20: How useful do they find journal level information.

The participants were also asked to answer the question, "How useful do you find article level information to select an article you want to read first?" Forty percent of participants selected "Not at all useful" for article level information for both Mendeley Saves and Altmetric Scores (see Figure 6.21).

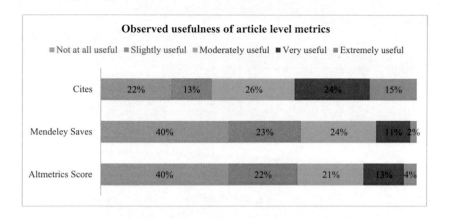

Figure 6.21: How useful are article level metrics.

We calculated the relationship between the discipline of the participants and the scaled answers to the question "How useful do you find journal level information to select an article you want to read first?" (Figure 6.20). Moreover, each journal information group (i.e., bibliometrics, journal ranking, and altmetrics) was ranked or scaled according to the predefined options (e.g., "Slightly useful").

In this case, each scale received a weighted number such as "Not at all useful" a weight of 0, "Slightly useful" gained a weight of 1, "Moderately useful" received a weight of 2, "Very useful" gained a weight of 3, and "Extremely useful" gained a weight of 4, and they are summed up per each participant. Then, the average for each discipline based on the scaled numbers is calculated.

The results presented in Figure 6.22 do not show a big difference between the disciplines of the participants and their scaled answers for the given metrics. The journal ranking group is chosen as the most useful compared to the other metric categories. In contrast, altmetric information is selected as the least useful group from all disciplines.

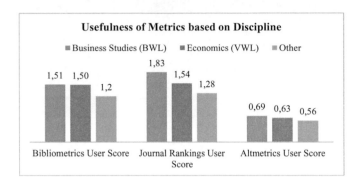

Figure 6.22: The relationship between discipline and the answers to the question "How useful do you find journal level information to select an article you want to read first?."

Similarly, we calculated the relationship between the academic status of participants and the scaled answers to the question "How useful do you find journal level information to select an article you want to read first?" (see Figure 6.23). Professors find bibliometrics and journal rankings metrics more useful. However, professors shared lower usefulness scores for the Altmetrics group. Assistant professors and PhD students mostly find journal rankings useful. On the altmetric group, participants with "Other" academic status and PhD students find altmetrics more beneficial compared to other educational statuses.

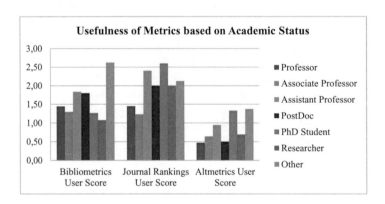

Figure 6.23: The relationship between academic status and the answers to the question "How useful do you find journal level information to select an article you want to read first?."

Similarly, we calculated the relationship between gender and the scaled answers to the question "How useful do you find journal level information to select an article you want to read first?." Female participants share higher values of usefulness than male participants.

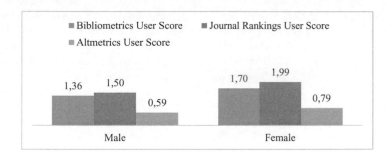

Figure 6.24: The usefulness of metrics based on gender.

We also evaluated the behavior of participants based on their academic status and the usefulness of altmetric sources (i.e., Twitter, Blogs, News, Policy Documents, Facebook) from Altmetric.com, based on the question "Given the above information on altmetrics related to Altmetric.com which information would have been useful to you to select the article you want to read first?." Participants, had to choose "Yes" or "No" answers. A large number of participants with academic status "Professor," "Associate Professor," and "Assistant Professor" chose "News" and "Policy Documents" as a useful source when they make decision to select an article for reading. Professors additionally selected Blogs and Twitter as a useful source for this purpose. Facebook as a source was not selected as useful from three types of participants "Assistant Professor", "Other," and "PostDoc."

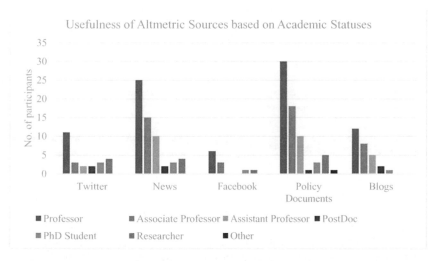

Figure 6.25: Usefulness of altmetric sources from Altmetric.com based on academic statuses.

Based on the survey question, "Which information from the graphic (i.e., altmetric sources from Altmetric.com or Mendeley readership information) above was relevant for you to select the article you want to read first?," we calculated the relevancy and showed the top three sources for each provider. The responses of this questions are weighted similarly as mentioned before, each answer type received a weighted number such as "Not at all relevant" received a weight of 0, "Slightly relevant" gained a weight of 1, "Moderately relevant" received a weight of 2, "Very relevant" weight of 3, and "Extremely relevant" with a weight of 4, and they are summed up per each participant. Only the responses from the group of participants that answered "Yes" to the question of whether they are familiar with Altmetric.com are observed.

The top three altmetric sources from Altmetric.com that on average have been selected as most relevant are as follows:

1. Altmetric Score with an average score of 1.51
2. Policy Document Mentions with an average score of 1.33
3. News Mentions with an average score of 1.07.

Facebook Mentions have been found less relevant (0.44) compared to other altmetric sources. Similarly, for Mendeley, the top three readership information that on average have been selected as relevant is as follows:

1. Mendeley Saves with 1.36
2. Mendeley Academic Status with 1.24
3. Mendeley Discipline with 1.12

Mendeley user country is found less relevant (0.85) in contrast to other Mendeley readership information.

6.4.6 Findings: Open questions

The entire questionnaire has four open questions as listed below.

1. Do you use any other journal or article information on a daily basis that is not listed in this graphic that might have helped you to select an article for reading?
2. Why would you be unlikely to use Altmetric information on the journal level?
3. Why would you be unlikely to use Altmetric information on article level?
4. If you have any suggestions about the survey or want to expand on any of your answers, please leave a comment below.

We walked through all the answers to the open questions and aggregated similar answers manually based on the context. For example, for question 1) we counted how many times participants mentioned: "JEL Classifications as another indicator that helped them to select a journal or article" (see Table 6.2). Based on participant's answers about not knowing what altmetrics are, around 50% of participants answered that altmetrics, in general, are not useful at all when it comes to selecting an article for reading first.

For the first question, the total number of participants that answered this question is 142 of which 36 answers were given simply with "no." The rest of the answers were related to indicators that are highlighted at the graphic and the rest is shown in Table 6.2. Twenty "other indicators" are suggested from economists that were not shown at the graphic for this study.

According to the Table 6.2, "articles title" was mostly mentioned from this group as an important indicator, followed by "author names" and the "journal name".

Table 6.2: Other evaluation indicators not listed in the questionnaire graphic, however, used by economists.

	Other evaluation indicators suggested by economists	No. of participants mentioned this indicator (n)
1	Articles title	31
2	Author names	23
3	Journal name	16
4	Abstract	12
5	Publication year of the article	10
6	Google Scholar citations	8
7	The reputation of the authors	6
8	Keywords	5
9	ABS Ranking	4
10	SSCI (Web of Science)	4
11	JEL Classifications	3
12	Author's affiliations	3
13	Direct emails/Word of mouth	3
14	SSRN	2
15	ResearchGate	2
16	CNRS Ranking	2
17	Australian Business Deans Council Journal Ranking	2
18	Table of Contents	1
19	EconLit	1
20	The Danish bibliometric research indicator	1
21	CEPR Weekly	1
22	References	1
23	Scopus	1
24	The UK Association of Business Schools Journal Rankings	1

The answers from question 2) are shown in Table 6.3. The answers to these questions are manually aggregated based on the contextual meanings. For example, the participants that wrote "I don't know about this indicator" are aggregated to "Not familiar indicator". A large number of participants (21) explicitly mentioned that they are not aware of altmetrics in general. For example, a participant answered, "Altmetrics are not unlikely, just new for me," and other participants mentioned, "I never occupied myself with this kind of information. I have certain journals that I scan and take a look at the articles that sound interesting." Or "Departments and field of research have long-time established quality of journals. For example, finance journal ranking is stable in the last decade. No need for any intermediary to confirm that or to change that ranking." The answers to questions 3) are similar to the answers from questions 2); therefore, both questions' results are shown in one table.

Also, the participants ($n = 12$) were confused about what altmetrics do show when evaluating research articles by simply writing "altmetrics do not reflect the scientific impact of the article", of which 2 participants mentioned that "altmetrics are noisy signals". The participants either copied and pasted the answers from 2) to 3) or wrote "as above" or "similar reason."

Table 6.3: Aggregated reasons for not likely to use altmetrics in journal and article level.

	Reasons for not likely to use altmetrics	No. of participants (n)
1	Not a familiar indicator	21
2	Altmetrics does not reflect the academic opinion/scientific impact	12
3	I am not interested	8
4	Journal rankings/cites/bibliometrics are more important	8
5	Based on media exposure/popularity	4
6	Do not understand the value of altmetrics	3
7	Never used it before	3
8	Article level is most relevant than journal level	3
9	I don't care about rankings	3
10	Noisy signal	2
11	No as a reader, yes as an editorial board, readership are important	1
12	Can be manipulated	1
13	Seems ad hoc	1
14	Difficult to find	1
15	I use a little of everything	1
16	The scope is too large	1
17	It is not a commonly accepted indicator at my institution	1

In question 4), some participants extended their comments, which we will present some of the comments in the following that might be of further help to this research. It was apparent that displaying information such as Altmetric Score and Mendeley Saves would question the range (the start and endpoint) the altmetric values have. Participants were not sure whether an Altmetric Score of 16 is represented as high or low. One participant tackled this issue "When not knowing the Altmetric Score, one doesn't have a reference whether such a score of 16 is large or not..." Another important insight is that participants found the presence of all these indicators overwhelming by writing "Was quite complex having all those numbers" or "I would present less information. It's too hard to keep track of all those things...".

Given the results of this survey, generally, economists usually prefer to look at the title of the article, author names, journal names, year of publication, and article abstract. All four open questions responses retrieved from this study are shown in Appendix VI.

6.5. Discussion and conclusion

According to the results of this survey, a significant number of economists (academics) are not aware of altmetrics. Altmetric information from Altmetric.com is not known by 68% of the participants and from Mendeley is not known by 56% of the participants. In contrast, a substantial number of participants (87%) are familiar with the Journal Impact Factor. PhD students are less aware of altmetrics from Altmetric.com compared to other career stages, even though in general, all academic statuses show low awareness of altmetrics. Associate professors represent the highest number of participants that are not aware of Mendeley readership information on the journal level. The academic status "Others" represents the highest number of participants that are aware of readership information from Mendeley. "Others" are participants that do not fit in the provided list of academic statuses. "Others" can represent, for example, "librarians," "senior lecturer," or further groups that are either differently termed in various countries or are not listed at all in our survey. However, we do not have detailed information about who "others" are in this survey.

Top three altmetric sources from Altmetric.com that on average have been selected as most relevant are as follows:
1. Altmetric Score with an average score of 1.51
2. Policy Document Mentions with an average score of 1.33
3. News Mentions with an average score of 1.07.

Top three readership information from Mendeley that on average has been selected as relevant are as follows:
1. Mendeley Saves with 1.36
2. Mendeley Academic Status with 1.24
3. Mendeley Discipline with 1.12

Next, we also investigated whether economists with the same academic status will be interested in reading the same article. The findings show that a high number of participants from all academic statuses selected the same article, by making academic status in this case not important when it comes to the selection of an article. However, it is essential to mention that academic status does normally play a role when selecting an article for reading, given the case when experienced researchers (i.e., professors) choose another article for reading compared to PhD students. But because of the given information for the articles and their individual features presented in this experimental setting, the article is perceived as too superior from all career stages.

We also found out that the older the participant is, the less relevant the altmetric information from Altmetric.com is. Nevertheless, the Mendeley readership information is found relevant independently of the participants' age.

Given the article selection responses, 63% of participants selected one single article, "Big data in Economics" or identified as A4 (see Section 6.4.2). This article is published in the "Journal of Management Science". Even though the article's name is fictive, the other related data are real. The Journal of Management Science has the highest h-index (from the bibliometric data section) in comparison with other journals; additionally, it has the highest Altmetric Score with

8,633, compared to the other listed journals as well as the highest score on Twitter, News, Facebook, and Blogs. Hence if we had the chance to filter one article out of four articles presented on the graph based on the highest Altmetric Score on journal level, the A4 article would be automatically first suggested on the list for reading. Nonetheless, we are not sure which of these indicators the participants have used when making the decision about the article selection.

With the results mentioned above, we conclude that economists do not very well know altmetric indicators from both providers. Given their answers, economists mostly use a set of journals they know according to some rankings, or they make their own intellectual judgments for articles they want to read according to its abstract, title, authors, or publication year. We assume that altmetric indicators from both providers generally are not necessarily seen by economists as relevant and useful indicators that can filter an article for reading first.

The first limitation of this study lies in the static articles suggested to participants for selection. Participants were not able to perform self-searches according to their field of interest. Second, the responses of this survey are mostly related to highly experienced researchers (i.e., professors). Third, the representation of journal level information is limited. For example, related information for each article is based on three different metric groups represented on the graph, of which these metrics include sources that support the Open Access movement by making their data freely available as well as sources that track mostly E and BS literature. Altmetric information and its usefulness, in this case, is based only on two altmetric, providers: Altmetric.com and Mendeley.

Chapter 7

Discussion, conclusion and future work

Altmetrics for Digital Libraries explored and discussed the use of altmetrics as new filters and early indicators for online impact of scientific articles, and therefore as complementary indicators to citations, especially for the journals such as *Economic and Business Studies*. Moreover, it contributes to suggesting altmetric information that can be used by library portals with an economic focus and its methodologies can be generalized to libraries for other disciplines. This approach, among others (e.g., citations), will also hold the promise of assisting researchers in coping with information overload.

Given the exponential rise of journal articles in different disciplines, and the evident problem of researchers who cannot read everything, several evaluation techniques for identifying impact (i.e., citations) and evaluating scientific output have emerged and been adopted. These indicators are seen as helpful tools for researchers to narrow the amount of scientific literature and filter relevant journals or articles based on their scientific impact (e.g., reading highly cited articles or finding journals of high impact to publish their own work). They are also helpful indicators for libraries that aim to select journals of high impact and to index their collection with the intention to show their users the highest impact and, therefore, most useful and relevant literature. However, citations and other related traditional metrics (e.g., JIF) have been broadly criticized because of their methods and limitations (e.g., they take a long time to appear), and are therefore suggested to be carefully used depending on the purpose.

Research literature has claimed that in the disciplines of E and BS, citations of scientific articles are found to be rather sparse, which indicates that not all articles published in highly cited journals have received citations or are highly cited. Some articles did not accumulate citations, which does not mean that they are not influential. Considering the case when a researcher filters for highly cited articles or articles that have at least few citations, recently published articles without citations are simply neglected, even though they might be relevant for the researchers' needs. They are not shown in the retrieval list from library systems when using citation counts as filtering tools, either because they are newly published or simply not cited. As we already know, citations usually take time to accumulate. According to the research literature, the peak of citation rate in E and BS is reached around the fifth year after the publication. This citation characteristic makes it difficult to retrieve articles that are cited or highly cited and recently published.

Due to the disadvantages of these traditional indicators, mainly when using citations as sources for determining the early scientific impact of articles, new filters, or complements to traditional filters, known as altmetrics, came into the picture. Altmetrics go beyond citations and according to the literature, most altmetrics identify another type of impact, that is, the online attention or "societal impact" of scientific outputs (e.g., articles). Moreover, the online attention of scientific articles captures attention not only from researchers, but also from more diverse audiences using different social media sources, and it appears as soon as the article is published online.

At present, with the introduction and benefits of altmetrics (e.g., those appear sooner than citations), libraries have different possibilities to integrate these information, especially based on the build-in-tools that are offered by the altmetric providers in the market, for example, by embedding the altmetric badges. However, previous studies indicate that the presence of altmetrics is different from one discipline to the other. Moreover, there is a difference between the coverage of altmetrics, the correlations between citations and altmetrics, and the social media sources on disciplines. Altmetrics data are extensively investigated for their coverage in different disciplines, but many studies have not tackled the investigation of altmetrics for a large scale of the journals such as *Economic and Business Studies* and especially put an emphasis on analyzing these data in terms of the library with an economic focus. The insights of such studies can be helpful for libraries with an economic focus, which will be aware about other possible strategies and can precisely aid the integration of altmetrics; for example, which aggregation levels of altmetrics make sense to use (because altmetrics are still sparse) or which social media sources are preferable where the articles in that particular discipline are found with the most online attention.

Therefore, this gap has been covered by this thesis based on the following factors:

1. investigated extensively altmetrics data for the disciplines such as *Economics and Business Studies*,
2. evaluated economic researchers about the usefulness of altmetrics to select scientific articles,
3. contributed on principles of Leiden Manifesto, especially when the methodology applied in this research can be broadly applicable for other disciplines and libraries.

Given the insights retrieved from the contribution, this thesis will suggest use case scenarios within a proof-of-concept based on the characteristics that the altmetric data are present for these disciplines and applicable in library portals with an economic focus. This approach, among others, will also hold the promise of assisting libraries and researchers in coping with information overload.

In the following section, we will discuss the findings of this thesis based on a different level of contribution (e.g., altmetrics for journal articles or evaluation of economists based on the use of altmetrics). Following the conclusion from the findings, we will present the implications of the study in real-world applications (i.e., library portals) and limitations, and finally we will highlight several insights for possible future studies that can further contribute when using altmetrics in library systems.

7.1. Lessons learned from the main findings

In the following sections, we will present the insights gained within this thesis based on four research questions. The findings and the insights can contribute to the implication of this thesis, suggesting the use of altmetric information to libraries with an economic focus (see Section 7.2). Generally, altmetrics (e.g., Mendeley counts) are considered as useful indicators for research evaluation, first because they can be easily accessible (i.e., articles that have received altmetrics can be simply identified by DOIs). Second, particular altmetric indicators seem to be correlated with citations by showing a "scientific impact" of the articles to an extent. Third, altmetrics can be collected within a shorter time frame than, for example, citations.

Within this thesis, we first investigated the top 1,000 E and BS journals (more than a half-million articles) in two altmetric providers: Mendeley and Altmetric.com. According to the literature (Nuredini & Peters, 2016; Costas et al., 2015), since altmetric information are present for a bigger share of articles published in recent years, more specifically, from the publication year 2011, this extended research investigated altmetrics for articles published between 2011 and 2018. Second, we received 291 full responses from economic researchers about the usefulness of altmetrics, and third, we analyzed three use cases with respect to altmetrics.

Our analysis from Chapter 5 reveals that altmetric information for journals in *Economics and Business Studies* in both Mendeley and Altmetric.com are still sparse, even when considering many journals and articles for investigation. The sparsity of altmetrics is also being confirmed for other disciplines (Thelwall, 2020).

From the top 1,000 journals, in Mendeley, 72% of journals with article publication years 2011–2018 are found, of which around 48% of articles have at least one Mendeley reader. BS journals are more findable in Mendeley compared with E, in which similar results are also found in the study by Nuredini & Peters (2015), with the top 30 journals. In Altmetric.com, 91.3% of E and BS journals are found and we discovered moderate shares of articles (around 44%) for publication years 2011–2018. Since journals within this investigation are covered with both providers and articles only moderately, when using altmetrics for library portals, especially those with an economic focus, we suggested journal level aggregations. In this way, for each library record, altmetric information could be shown. These findings relate and confirm the findings of the earlier results of Nuredini & Peters (2016).

Additionally, we revealed that the publication year 2011 includes full-scale Almetric.com data from July 2011 and onward; therefore, when considering a full-scale altmetrics for libraries, altmetrics from the publication year 2012 are suggested for use instead (Thelwall et al., 2013). We found out that altmetric information in these disciplines are not as immediate as expected. For the publication year 2018,[132] the altmetric information was found rather low. For example, the coverage of newly published articles is high in Mendeley (72%) and the reader counts for these articles are low compared with other articles published earlier than 2018. In 2018, articles received 33% less Mendeley counts than in 2017. However, this does not necessarily mean that altmetrics are not early impact indicators; this means that altmetrics in E and BS discipline still need some time to appear. Altmetrics might have better coverage, for example, a year after the publication has been published, which, when compared with citation counts for these disciplines that generate few citations in the early years after article publications and have the peak of citation in 5 years, seems to appear faster than them.

RQ 1: To what extent are readership information from Mendeley and Altmetric Attention Sources from Altmetric.com present for *Economic and Business Studies* journals?

Within this research study, the behavior of Mendeley readers can be correctly determined because the results of this research are based on all Mendeley readership information for each article. We learned that Mendeley API currently provides full data and the results are not limited to only the top 3 categories of each readership, as shown by previous studies in altmetrics. Mendeley readership information such as discipline, academic status, and country tend to show the reading behavior of Mendeley users for both E and BS journal articles. Mendeley readership information are based on what readers have saved on their Mendeley profiles. These fields are

---

[132] The publication year of articles "2018" for our study depicts the recently published articles in E and BS since the altmetric data for articles are retrieved in the beginning of 2019.

not mandatory. Based on the insights retrieved from this research, we concluded that E and BS journals generally have similar Mendeley user patterns independently of the journals' position in the Handelsblatt ranking.

1.1. Which category of readership information from Mendeley (i.e., academic status, country, and discipline) is mostly used for *Economic and Business Studies* literature?

Mendeley users who read or save E and BS articles within their Mendeley library have added their "discipline" information on their profiles only in 25.8% of the cases, which is still more compared with the other readership information. The second most covered information is the "academic status" with 22.6% of users. The least represented readership information is country, where only 4.4% of all users (who have saved at least one of the top 1,000 journal articles from E or BS) have provided country information in their Mendeley profile. The most common discipline of Mendeley users (30% of users) who read BS articles is "Business, Management and Accounting" and for E journals is "Economics, Econometrics, and Finance" with 18% of users. In the study of Nuredini and Peters (2015), most of the readers of the top 30 journal articles for both disciplines are coming from business administration. However, this discipline seems to be recently updated in Mendeley and replaced with "Business, Management and Accounting."

We found out that PhD students tend to be the core Mendeley users of E and BS journal articles, which in fact is confirmed within this study and in the study of Nuredini and Peters (2015) that investigated Mendeley only for the top 30 journals. Given this case, Mendeley can be suggested as a good altmetric source to find research articles in E and BS journals for economists with the academic status PhD. Even though the country information is not favorably represented for all users of E and BS articles, this readership information can still play an important role for readers. It has been investigated that readers of Mendeley tend to read articles that are authored from their own country. This insight can further help readers of E and BS articles to check for country information an article has, based on Mendeley users, which might indicate which specialism their country is interested in (Thelwall & Maflahi, 2015).

1.2. Concerning Altmetric Attention Sources provided by Altmetric.com, for example, Twitter, Facebook, blogs, etc., which sources have higher coverages of *Economic and Business Studies* journals/articles?

Nineteen different Altmetric Attention Sources are identified while exploring Altmetric.com data for 1,000 journals in E and BS (see Table 5.12). We explored the DOIs of E and BS found in Altmetric.com that accumulated attention in each of the sources. By studying top 1,000 journals for altmetrics, we have learned that the most prominent sources found from Altmetric.com for articles in E and BS journals are Mendeley, Twitter, News, Facebook, Blogs, and Policy Documents. Mendeley (in this case tracked by Altmetric.com) is the source that provides most altmetric counts for E and BS articles. In E, 97.7% of articles are retrieved with altmetrics. In BS journals, 98% of articles have Mendeley saves (or altmetrics). Nevertheless, besides that Mendeley accumulates more metrics, journal articles in BS are also found on Twitter (56.6% of articles) followed by Facebook that covers 11% of articles and blogs with 8.9%. For E journals, Twitter has the highest coverage of articles with 58% followed by

Facebook with 11% and Policy Posts with 9.6%. In E and BS, indicators derived from engagement with Mendeley and Twitter may serve as valuable additional metrics to traditional metrics.

RQ 2: Are journal level information useful for authors of scientific articles to help them decide which journal to send their work to, and therefore useful indicators for libraries as well?

We calculated Spearman correlation on journal level between citation counts from Dimensions, Altmetric Attention Scores (AAS), Twitter, and Mendeley readership counts. For BS journals, we spotted a strong correlation $\rho = 0.732$ between citations and the AAS (see Table 5.21). For E journals, this correlation is higher than for BS journals with a value of $\rho = 0.814$ (see Table 5.22). AAS and Dimension citations are strongly correlated with journal level rather than with article level, meaning that journals with high citation counts are also receiving substantial attention online. We also calculated the correlation between tweets and citations from Dimensions on journal level resulting in a strong correlation for BS journals with $\rho = 0.666$ and $\rho = 0.739$ for E journals. Another strong correlation is found between the Mendeley counts and Dimension citations. For journals in BS, the correlation is $\rho = 0.958$ and for E journals it is $\rho = 0.970$, denoting that highly saved journals in Mendeley also seem to be highly cited. Spearman correlation between Blogs and citations for BS journals is found with $\rho = 0.618$, which shows a positive correlation; however, this value is lower compared with other sources (e.g., Mendeley). News is identified with a Spearman correlation $\rho = 0.694$ for BS journals and $\rho = 0.762$ for E journals, showing a strong and significant correlation, especially for E journals. The correlations found in this thesis between different indicators are generally stronger on journal level than on article level.

We identified that journal level altmetrics are strongly correlated with citation counts, suggesting these indicators as potential sources, similarly as citations (e.g., journal rankings that use citations), which can assist (alternatively to citations) economic researchers or authors of articles decide which journal to send their work to. The highest Spearman correlation on journal level is identified between citations and Mendeley counts. Therefore, we suggested Mendeley counts as alternative indicators to traditional metrics. Journal level altmetrics can be useful indicators to libraries, first because, they can be used as impact indicators to evaluate journals for indexing (alternatively to citations) and second, because they will ensure that for most of the records, altmetric information could be displayed. Altmetrics on journal level can be beneficial in the "Journal Map" application, in which its aim is to help researchers to compare journals with each other and assist in selecting the appropriate journal to publish their work. Given the fact that journal level information (e.g., Journal Impact Factor) cannot identify the impact of individual articles, Altmetric.com, in accordance with Leiden Manifesto, has suggested possible ways that journal level altmetrics can be useful in the right way to "judge" the (online) impact of single articles within that journal. For instance, when using journal level altmetrics, the median of the AAS per article should also be considered along with the articles' online attention, suggesting principles and practices for better research evaluation guidance.

RQ 3: What Altmetric Attention Sources from Altmetric.com are mostly used by which group of economists (based on Mendeley readership information)?

We have selected only those articles from top 1,000 journals in E and BS that are mentioned only in one particular social media source that Altmetric.com tracks. We selected only those articles that have received online attention from one of the top 5 altmetric sources (see Table 5.15), for example, only mentioned on Twitter. These articles are then investigated within the dataset that we retrieved from Mendeley and in this way we could determine the user group of these articles based on Mendeley readership (i.e., the academic status).

For BS journal articles, PhD students are the core readers of articles that are at most mentioned in one of the altmetric sources (e.g., Twitter, Facebook, etc.). BS articles that have been mentioned only in sources such as "News" and "Blogs" are not found with Mendeley readership information such as academic status. These articles, for example, so far, seem to have been not attracted to users of Mendeley but rather they received an online attention from Altmetric.com sources. For E journal articles, PhD students are the core readers of articles that are at most mentioned in one of the altmetric sources (e.g., Twitter, Facebook, etc.). Articles mentioned in Blogs and News are mostly covered in Mendeley with academic status of users PhD (36%) followed by professors with 18%. In this case, Twitter tracked by Altmetric.com was found with a large number of E and BS journal articles, therefore we encouraged economic researchers to check for tweets, which can make it easier for them to find recently published articles for reading. Twitter, besides, is believed to show a societal impact (i.e., online attention) of scholarly articles (Eysenbach, 2011) as well as predict highly cited articles right after their publication. Therefore, we also encouraged economists who are authors to share their articles by promoting them on social media, especially on Twitter, which is supposed to increase the number of citations (Ortega, 2016). Determining the group of economist through Mendeley readership academic status led us to the insight that most of the readers of articles found in Altmetric Sources are PhDs. This limitation comes from the fact that the core readers in Mendeley are usually PhD students.

RQ 4: Do altmetric information on a journal level (as new filters) generally help economists to select the most interesting article to read first?

According to the survey results, economists are generally not aware of altmetrics, which first makes it difficult to fully understand whether altmetrics can be helpful sources for them to select an article for reading first. Altmetric information from Altmetric.com are not known by 68% of the participants and Mendeley from 56% of participants. This thesis reveals that traditional metrics (e.g., citations, JIF) are seen from economists as more useful indicators compared with altmetrics.

However, given the article selection responses, 63% of participants selected one single article, "Big Data in Economics" or identified as A4 (see Section 6.4.2). This article is published in the *Journal of Management Science*. Even though the article's name is fictive, the other related data are real. The *Journal of Management Science* has the highest *h*-index (from the bibliometric data section), and it has the highest Altmetric score with 8,633, as well as the highest score on Twitter, News, Facebook, and Blogs. Hence if we had the chance to filter one article out of four articles presented on the graph based on the highest Altmetric score on journal level, the A4 article would be automatically suggested first on the list for reading. Nonetheless, we were not sure which of these indicators the participants have used when making the decision about the article selection. Even though economists generally are not aware of the use of altmetrics, according to the article selection already provided at the survey, we could take into consideration that altmetrics might have helped them to select the most interesting article to read first.

Despite that economists were not generally familiarized with altmetrics, they still participated and answered questions that were related to the usefulness of altmetrics. For example, we found out that participants with academic status "Professors," "Associate Professors," and "Assistant Professors" selected "News" and "Policy Documents" as beneficial altmetric information when selecting an article to read first. "Professors" also chose "Blogs" and "Twitter" as useful sources for this purpose (see Figure 6.25).

7.2. Implication of this thesis

Libraries play an important role when it comes to representing new metric information in their collections and making them accessible to library users since this step needs many education efforts (e.g., educate its users for the new tools). Moreover, the use of altmetrics in libraries must be carefully implemented, based on the principles (Coombs & Peters, 2017), because libraries must consider useful representation forms for altmetrics so that the users can understand the role that altmetrics play for a particular scientific output. Since this thesis is performed within the environment of ZBW, which offers the EconBiz portal for *Economic and Business Studies* literature, the contribution of this research is mostly related to EconBiz and can be applied to other libraries with an economic focus. Libraries adopting altmetric information will enable economic researchers to deal with new alternative ways of filtering scientific articles and journals.

However, the methodology presented within this thesis could be applied and suggested to other libraries with a different focus interested in adopting the use of altmetrics. This part supports the broad benefit that can be used all over the library community. Other libraries can be educated on the methods, technology, and issues that were present during this research. First, they can be informed about the crawling process, for example, which data sources and altmetric providers can be used to retrieve altmetrics and in what way; additionally, where the data cleaning is needed and how the data can be organized and stored. They will get insights into how a large scale of data is being analyzed within this discipline and which time frame they should take into consideration to perform such data analysis for altmetric information. Second, the interested libraries might like to incorporate the opinion of researchers using the survey to understand their behavior when using altmetrics. Third, they might want to incorporate personas from their library portals, which using their characteristics can find useful scenarios for presenting altmetrics. And with the insights from these methodologies, they can suggest altmetric presentation scenarios for their library portals, first as a proof-of-concept and further develop those with real data.

Proof-of-concept

Based on the results of Chapters 5 and 6, as well as the requirements of ZBW personas, several implications of this thesis are proposed to libraries with an economic focus. Some of the parts might be useful to libraries with a focus on other disciplines as well.

First of all, when adopting and integrating altmetrics, Mendeley can be suggested as an advantage provider compared with Altmetric.com, because so far it offers freely available data when accessing via their API. So, libraries that actually are supporting the Open Access strategy might want to consider Mendeley as a possible solution and adopt their information without the need to place any fee.

Second, since altmetrics signify a counting number attached to library records, for example, an article has been 100 times tweeted or 50 times shared. These numbers might not be directly comparable in terms of impact with other related articles. Therefore, libraries that want to adopt altmetrics should contextualize this number by providing a range or percentage that allows ranking of similar articles in the same collection. For example, Altmetric.com provides "the Score tab" function, where the users of Altmetric Explorer can view contextual information for a particular article (Altmetric Support, 2019a). The Score tab presents percentiles, verbal descriptions, and rankings that can help to understand the performance of the article. It allows a comparison of a particular article with other articles in the same journal, with articles of a similar age, and with all articles saved in Altmetric.com. In the following section, several implications of altmetrics are suggested to libraries as a proof-of-concept, which are derived from the findings listed in this thesis:

1. According to the coverage of altmetric information for E and BS journals (Chapter 5), one suggestion for presenting altmetrics data in real-world applications (e.g., in libraries) would be to consider higher aggregation levels, such as on a journal level. Figure 7.1, for example, displays one possible representation of *journal level altmetrics* (from both providers) for the journal "Research Evaluation" in EconBiz (marked in red). These journal level altmetrics are already attached to some articles within EconBiz. For example, Figure 7.1 shows journal level altmetrics for the article name "Assessment, evaluation, and definitions of research impact: a review" published in the *Research Evaluation* journal.

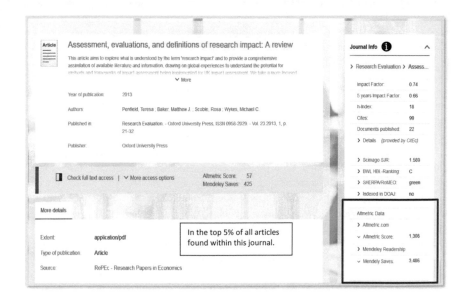

Figure 7.1: Suggested altmetric information on journal level in EconBiz.

However, when presenting altmetrics journal level information for evaluating individual articles, libraries should consider three important steps:

(i) Since journal level indicators (e.g., JIF) do not have the ability to fully represent the articles' impact, when considering altmetric journal level information for each record (i.e., article), libraries should notify users of the system to consider the flaws (e.g., they cannot identify the quality of a single article) that journal level information carries. By letting users being aware of this flaw, it will assist them in making careful decisions when using journal level indicators, in this case, altmetrics, for selecting an article for reading. One possible way to represent this type of information is using an infobox (see Figure 7.1), right after the journal information section, depicted as an info icon.

(ii) Journal level altmetrics should be transparent according to the DORA[133] declaration on research assessment by providing information hint boxes describing how they are calculated, which will help users and other interested parties to understand the rigor and quality these indicators bring (Coombs & Peters, 2017).

(iii) When presenting journal level altmetrics, based on data from Altmetric.com,[134] libraries that adopt and researchers that develop such metrics should additionally consider the presentation of using coverage percentiles, for example, the percent of articles with an AAS in a journal, or the median mentions per article. This step can be considered as useful to better

---

[133] DORA declaration: https://sfdora.org/read/
[134] Resources to help develop journal level altmetrics:
https://help.altmetric.com/support/solutions/articles/6000228801-using-altmetric-data-to-develop-journal-level-metrics

understand the journal level influence and, therefore, as good practice for adopting journal level information. For example, one workable solution for representing the attention of articles despite the journal level information is to highlight the percentage of articles within an AAS in a journal similar to those in Altmetric.com and ImpactStory. The articles' online attention (see Figure 7.1) is found within the top 5% of all research output published in that particular journal. Journal level altmetrics can additionally be applied as indicators to filter journals that are popular on social media sources or to identify journals that are highly mentioned online. Presenting altmetric information on a journal level will support the second persona use-case (i.e., interested in journal ranking). One possible option of implementing and adopting altmetrics on journal level is an application called "Journal Map," currently being developed by ZBW. The aim of Journal Map is to help different users (e.g., researchers and librarians) to compare journals with each other based on various indicators. Moreover, the users of "Journal Map" have the possibility to compare journals based on altmetrics, which with the advantages that altmetrics carry (e.g., they are more timely, come from different audiences, and more), will assist researchers in deciding where to read or publish.

2. Beside journal level altmetrics, *article level altmetrics* (see Figure 7.1; implemented in EconBiz for some articles) can also play an important role for libraries. Given the case that libraries implement article level altmetrics to represent the online impact of individual articles, users will be able to filter, for example, highly mentioned articles from Altmetric.com or highly saved articles from Mendeley. Mendeley, specifically for E and BS journal articles, shows a positive and strong correlation with Dimensions citations, meaning these counts show the scientific impact of articles to a certain extent. Moreover, Mendeley counts can be presented on an article level, as they can be attached to the pages containing articles' details. However, one should consider the fact that not each article can have Mendeley counts attached to them.

Considering the availability of altmetrics and the coverage of E and BS journal articles in altmetric providers, Mendeley counts and AASs are recommended as indicators or popularity factors that might help provide a better *ranking of search results* for library services. Moreover, a suggestion is advocated for the LibRank project, which explored citation counts for ranking results of the user search query, to consider altmetric information as additional indicators to citations. Using altmetrics, the relevance model of LibRank might perform better for retrieving relevant articles not only because the results will retrieve older articles that have accumulated citations and therefore are highly ranked, but also because this ranking will be influenced by presenting articles that are recently published and have also gathered high online attention. LibRank's ranking model with citations has been tested in the EconBiz portal within the relevance feature (see Figure 7.2, marked in red) and is suggested as a useful feature (Plassmeier et al., 2015). However, according to their study, Plassmeier et al. (2015) were liable to trying out other helpful methods that might make the relevance model perform even better.

Using altmetrics in this model, the normalization of altmetrics mainly based on articles' topics, should be considered for correcting the biases of altmetrics. Haunschild and Bornmann (2016) proposed the Mean Normalized Reader Score (MNRS), which is established from the method of normalization for citation counts and examines the calculation of the average number of Mendeley readers per article for each topic category. The authors suggested that this normalization procedure can also be used for other types of altmetrics (e.g., AAS, tweets, and more).

With that being said, a more feasible method is needed to observe the user behavior within the library portal environment to determine whether this scenario works for a better representation of the relevance model.

Figure 7.2: Altmetric information influencing relevance in EconBiz.

3. Article level or journal level altmetrics can be limited to the sources that are most used by economists for E and BS journal articles. Given the results from Chapters 5 and 6, we identified several *Altmetric Attention Sources* (e.g., Twitter) where E and BS journal articles are found with more altmetric mentions compared with other sources tracked by Altmetric.com. With this insight, we suggested a presentation of the top 5 Altmetric Attention Sources on library portals attached to each article that have accumulated altmetrics. For libraries with economic focus, the top 5 sources where most of E and BS journal articles are discussed are Twitter, News, Facebook, Blogs, and Policy Documents. The reasons for suggesting only the top 5 Altmetric Attention Sources for each article are (1) because only these sources cover a great number of E and BS journals and (2) to avoid user frustration when presenting too much information. Similarly, in Mendeley, the readership information, academic status, and discipline are present for a greater number of articles in E and BS compared with the country information. When evaluating the user behavior in Chapter 6, one participant claimed that the representation of altmetrics for each article "Was quite complex having all those numbers" or "I would present less information. It's too hard to keep track of all those things." Therefore, presenting only the relevant sources and readership information for E and BS journals will help to avoid user frustration and the inability to understand all the indicators at the same time. Presenting the main sources where E and BS journal articles are found can support the third persona.

4. According to the first persona use case (see Chapter 1), which was interested in trendy topics and since altmetrics are known as the best early indicators for impact, compared with citations, they are suggested as tools to filter recently published articles with high online attention.

Moreover, we recommended the AAS, Mendeley counts, tweets, blogs, and news as *new indicators that libraries can adopt in the* sort by *function*. For example, libraries can enable the user of library portals to sort their results based on articles published in the current year with a high AAS or Mendeley counts. This feature will show trendy articles based on social media mentions and users of the system can get insights into which topics are most discussed on a real-time basis. However, we mentioned that, in E and BS, altmetric information are not as immediate as expected and are still sparse. Alternatively, if we consider only showing a small set of articles that are trendy and that are recently published, the library portal might provide an additional informational tab highlighted as *Trending on Altmetric/Mendeley*, depicting only the articles that are recently published (e.g., on July 2020) and have received the highest online attention compared with the other articles in that dataset. For example, when the user of the portal will click on the tab "Trending on Altmetric" this click will initiate the event of showing top 3 articles with the highest Altmetric score in E and BS disciplines published in the previous 5 months. Alternatively, according to the proof-of-concept (see Chapter 5), there is a possibility to identify trendy topics for articles in E and BS, especially those that are recently published and show the topics that have received the most online attention based on the dataset. This feature should be further discussed about the methodology how to represent such data.

5. When libraries decide to adopt the use of altmetrics on either article level or journal level, they should provide *guides to train librarians as well as researchers* to inform them how and for what purposes to use these indicators. Moreover, researchers should be educated on the inherent limitations of each altmetric provider and consider whether these indicators fit their purpose for which they are intended.

The aforementioned implications can be useful for libraries with an economic focus because they can assist users in filtering relevant articles, as well as rank literature retrieved from their search. The insights under 1, 2, 4, and 5 can be applied and also considered for libraries with other focus. The implication listed under 3 "Top 5 Altmetric Attention Sources" should be utilized only in libraries with an economic emphasis. Each discipline has its own social media sources where their articles are mentioned and the recommendations found in this thesis might not be as relevant as for libraries with an economic focus. For example, articles published in psychology and clinical disciplines have more F1000 and News mentions (Htoo & Na, 2017) and these sources should be used as their primary source instead.

7.3. Limitations of the findings

The research explored in this thesis is confined by two essential limitations: (1) the selection of journals based on a specific discipline and (2) limitations related to altmetric providers (Altmetric.com and Mendeley).

Moreover, the research analysis and results of this thesis considers only the top 1,000 journals in E and BS disciplines and do not take into account the entire list of journals in the Handelsblatt ranking ($n = 3,664$). The limitation of journals to 1,000 is based on several data retrieval issues, which are mentioned in Chapter 4. These issues (e.g., not every article published in one of the 3,664 journals had a DOI) made it challenging to include all journals for this research.

The altmetric information are retrieved and analyzed for articles that are published only in scientific journals. Other types of articles, such as preprints, should be considered and evaluated separately. Besides DOIs, preprints, in economics, known as "working papers" have other identifiers (e.g., handle), and different coverage levels of altmetrics can be identified for these types of articles (Nuredini & Peters, 2019).

The altmetric information suggested in this thesis are dependent on the lifetime of the two altmetric providers. Fang et al. (2020) claimed that the presence of altmetrics is obviously increasing, but the authors are encouraging researchers to share their articles within social media, which will promote the development and application of altmetrics. This action might help to keep alive altmetric providers.

Altmetric information are also limited due to the fact that Altmetric.com tracks only certain sources and neglects other social media sources or attention sources that might be useful and relevant for readers of E and BS journal articles. For example, Altmetric.com has permission to track data from Wikipedia but not from other encyclopedias such as Britannica. This limitation misrepresents the online attention gained by the scientific articles since there is a bias toward the included sources, whereas missing sources are neglected (Gumpenberger et al., 2016). Finally, although this thesis has used the suggested technique for better Mendeley retrieval and quality results, one should still mention that Mendeley's information generally suffers from missing and incorrect values in the metadata. For example, if an article saved in Mendeley has incorrect DOIs or other missing metadata, it makes retrieving the appropriate article information and, therefore, the whole crawling process remains challenging (Nuredini & Peters, 2015). In addition, the data that are retrieved from Mendeley are based only on the users who practice Mendeley.

The statement that economists are not familiar with most of the altmetrics is based on several academic statuses this survey has captured from the mailing list of which bachelor students, however, are not covered. Therefore, a larger group of economists should be involved to draw a precise statement by also considering bachelor students. By capturing all academic statuses, libraries will know what the relevant altmetric sources for different academic statuses are.

7.4. Future work

By investigating altmetrics for E and BS journals, this thesis answers the questions raised from the beginning of this research, yet, during the investigation, new research questions came into the picture, which are suggested for future studies:

1. What is the most appropriate way to crawl and present real-time altmetric information in library systems? For this research, altmetric information from both providers are crawled once and the data are stored in a database for the purpose of analysis. But in real-world applications, such as library systems, altmetrics should be updated regularly since they are generated in real time. If library systems do apply the use of altmetrics, they should be able to update this information on a real-time basis. Questions like "how often should libraries update altmetrics" and "what is the best framework of crawling altmetric providers and, therefore, staying updated" should be answered.

2. The use of altmetrics for ranking search results in library systems (e.g., EconBiz) and identifying trendy articles should be evaluated with real users so that more precise conclusions can be drawn from the evaluations. One possible way to perform this evaluation is to implement altmetric information for all journal articles found in library portal records and use A/B testing for tracking the user's behavior when they face this information in library systems. A/B testing is a valuable method that offers two or more variants of the system to the users and determines which of the variations had a better performance (Dixon et al., 2011).

3. Finally, Mendeley and Altmetric.com should be investigated for their level of immediacy for BS and E journals. It is anticipated that altmetrics, in general, appear faster than citations or as soon as the article is published online; however, how soon altmetrics are presented right after the article's publication is unknown, especially for E and BS articles. The correct immediacy of altmetrics can play an important role since we can identify the early impact indicators more precisely and therefore use this precise insight as an advantage component (e.g., how often should libraries update altmetrics for E and BS journals) for future implications in library systems.

References

Abelson, P. H. (1980). Scientific communication. *Science*, *209*(4452), 60–62.

Abramo, G., Cicero, T., & D'Angelo, C. A. (2011). Assessing the varying level of impact measurement accuracy as a function of the citation window length. *Journal of Informetrics*, *5*(4), 659–667.

Aistleitner, M., Kapeller, J., & Steinerberger, S. (2018). The power of scientometrics and the development of economics. *Journal of Economic Issues*, *52*(3), 816–834.

Aleixandre-Benavent, R., Navarro-Molina, C., Aguilar-Moya, R., Melero-Fuentes, D., & Zurián, J. C. (2017). Trends in scientific research in Online Information Review. Part 1. Production, impact and research collaboration. *arXiv, abs/1709.07810*.

Altmetric Engineering. (2017). Biodiversity Heritage Library. Altmetric. Journal contribution. Retrieved from https://doi.org/10.6084/m9.figshare.5271919.v1 [Accessed April 10, 2020].

Altmetric Support. (2019a, July 26). Putting the Altmetric Attention Score in context. Retrieved from https://help.altmetric.com/support/solutions/articles/6000060970-putting-the-altmetric-attention-score-in-context [Accessed March 1, 2020].

Altmetric Support. (2019b, October 28). Using Altmetric data to develop journal level metrics. Retrieved from https://help.altmetric.com/support/solutions/articles/6000228801-using-altmetric-data-to-develop-journal-level-metrics [Accessed March 4, 2020].

Aung, H. H., Erdt, M., & Theng, Y. L. (2017). Awareness and usage of altmetrics: A user survey. *Proceedings of the Association for Information Science and Technology*, *54*(1), 18–26.

Baird, L. M., & Oppenheim, C. (1994). Do citations matter? *Journal of Information Science*, *20*(1), 2–15.

Bakkalbasi, N., Bauer, K., Glover, J., & Wang, L. (2006). Three options for citation tracking: Google Scholar, Scopus and Web of Science. *Biomedical Digital Libraries*, *3*(1), 7.

Bar-Ilan, J. (2010). Citations to the "Introduction to informetrics" indexed by WOS, Scopus and Google Scholar. *Scientometrics*, *82*(3), 495–506.

Bar-Ilan, J. (2012, June). JASIST@ Mendeley. In *ACM Web Science Conference 2012 workshop*. Retrieved from http://altmetrics.org/altmetrics12/bar-ilan/[Accessed February 17, 2019].

Bar-Ilan, J., Haustein, S., Peters, I., Priem, J., Shema, H., & Terliesner, J. (2012). Beyond citations: Scholars' visibility on the social Web. In *Proceedings of the 17th International Conference on Science and Technology Indicators* (pp. 98–109). Montréal, Canada.

Batrinca, B., & Treleaven, P. C. (2015). Social media analytics: A survey of techniques, tools and platforms. *Ai & Society, 30*(1), 89–116.

Bali, R., Sarkar, D., & Sharma, T. (2017). *Learning social media analytics with R*. Birmingham, UK: Packt Publishing Ltd.

Bernstam, E. V., Herskovic, J. R., Aphinyanaphongs, Y., Aliferis, C. F., Sriram, M. G., & Hersh, W. R. (2006). Using citation data to improve retrieval from MEDLINE. *Journal of the American Medical Informatics Association, 13*(1), 96–105.

Bian, J., Morid, M. A., Jonnalagadda, S., Luo, G., & Del Fiol, G. (2017). Automatic identification of high impact articles in PubMed to support clinical decision making. *Journal of Biomedical Informatics, 73*, 95–103.

Birkle, C., Pendlebury, D. A., Schnell, J., & Adams, J. (2020). Web of Science as a data source for research on scientific and scholarly activity. *Quantitative Science Studies, 1*(1), 363–376.

Blazquez, D., & Domenech, J. (2018). Big Data sources and methods for social and economic analyses. *Technological Forecasting and Social Change, 130*, 99–113.

Blei, D. M., Ng, A. Y., & Jordan, M. I. (2003). Latent Dirichlet allocation. *Journal of Machine Learning Research, 3*(Jan), 993–1022.

Blummer, B., & Kenton, J. M. (2014). Reducing patron information overload in academic libraries. *College & Undergraduate Libraries, 21*(2), 115–135.

Bolelli, L., Ertekin, S., Zhou, D., & Giles, C. L. (2009). Finding topic trends in digital libraries. In *Proceedings of the 9th ACM/IEEE-CS Joint Conference on Digital Libraries* (pp. 69–72). https://doi.org/10.1145/1555400.1555411

Bollen, J., Van de Sompel, H., Hagberg, A., & Chute, R. (2009). A principal component analysis of 39 scientific impact measures. *PLoS ONE, 4*(6), e6022. http://dx.doi.org/10.1371/journal.pone.0006022

Borgman, C. L. (1989). Bibliometrics and scholarly communication: Editor's introduction. *Communication Research, 16*(5), 583–599. http://doi.org/10.1177/009365089016005002.

Borgman, C. L. (2000). Digital libraries and the continuum of scholarly communication. *Journal of Documentation, 56*(4), 412–430. http://doi.org/10.1108/EUM0000000007121

Borgman, C. L., & Furner, J. (2002). Scholarly communication and bibliometrics. *Annual Review of Information Science and Technology, 36*(1), 1–53. https://doi.org/10.1002/aris.1440360102

Bornmann, L. (2011). Scientific peer review. *Annual Review of Information Science and Technology, 45*(1), 197–245.

Bornmann, L. (2014a). Do altmetrics point to the broader impact of research? An overview of benefits and disadvantages of altmetrics. *Journal of Informetrics, Elsevier, 8*(4), 895–903.

Bornmann, L. (2014b). Validity of altmetrics data for measuring societal impact: A study using data from Altmetric and F1000Prime. *Journal of Informetrics, 8*(4), 935–950.

Bornmann, L. (2015a). Alternative metrics in scientometrics: A meta-analysis of research into three altmetrics. *Scientometrics, 103*(3), 1123–1144.

Bornmann, L. (2015b). Usefulness of altmetrics for measuring the broader impact of research: A case study using data from PLOS and F1000Prime. *Aslib Journal of Information Management, 67*(3), 305–319.

Bornmann, L., Butz, A., & Wohlrabe, K. (2018). What are the top five journals in economics? A new meta-ranking. *Applied Economics, 50*(6), 659–675.

Bornmann, L., & Daniel, H. D. (2007). What do we know about the h index? *Journal of the American Society for Information Science and Technology, 58*(9), 1381–1385.

Bornmann, L., Haunschild, R., & Adams, J. (2019). Do altmetrics assess societal impact in a comparable way to case studies? An empirical test of the convergent validity of altmetrics based on data from the UK research excellence framework (REF). *Journal of Informetrics*, *13*(1), 325–340.

Bornmann, L., & Mutz, R. (2015). Growth rates of modern science: A bibliometric analysis based on the number of publications and cited references. *Journal of the Association for Information Science and Technology*, *66*(11), 2215–2222.

Bornmann, L. (2017). Measuring impact in research evaluations: a thorough discussion of methods for, effects of and problems with impact measurements. *Higher Education*, *73*(5), 775-787.

Bornmann, L., & Wohlrabe, K. (2019). Normalization of citation impact in economics. *Scientometrics*, *120*(2), 841–884

Borgman, L. Ch. (1999). What are digital libraries? Competing visions. *Information Processing and Management: An International Journal*, *35*(3), 227–243. http://doi.org/10.1016/S0306-4573(98)00059-4

Bowman, T. D. (2015). *Investigating the use of affordances and framing techniques by scholars to manage personal and professional impressions on Twitter.* Doctoral dissertation, Indiana University. Retrieved from http://www.tdbowman.com/pdf/2015_07_TDBowman_Dissertation.pdf [Accessed June 01, 2020].

Boyd, D., & Crawford, K. (2012). Critical questions for big data: Provocations for a cultural, technological, and scholarly phenomenon. *Information, Communication & Society*, *15*(5), 662–679.

Brody, T., Harnad, S., & Carr, L. (2006). Earlier web usage statistics as predictors of later citation impact. *Journal of the American Society for Information Science and Technology*, *57*(8), 1060–1072.

Chan, K. C., Chang, C. L., & McAleer, M. (2016). Quality weighted citations versus total citations in the sciences and social sciences, with an application to finance and accounting. *Managerial Finance*, *42*(4), 324-337.

Chomeya, R. (2010). Quality of psychology test between Likert scale 5 and 6 points. *Journal of Social Sciences*, *6*(3), 399–403.

Clermont, M., & Dyckhoff, H. (2012). Coverage of business administration literature in Google Scholar: Analysis and comparison with EconBiz, Scopus and Web of science. *Bibliometrie-Praxis und Forschung*, *1*(1).

Coats, A. W. (1960). The first two decades of the American Economic Association. *The American Economic Review*, *50*(4), 556–574.

Coombs, S. K., & Peters, I. (2017). The Leiden Manifesto under review: What libraries can learn from it. *Digital Library Perspectives*, *33*(4), 324-338. https://doi.org/10.1108/DLP-01-2017-0004

Cope, B., & Phillips, A. (2014). *The future of the academic journal* (2nd ed.). Oxford, UK: Chandos Publishing.

Costas, R., Zahedi, Z., & Wouters, P. (2015). Do "altmetrics" correlate with citations? Extensive comparison of altmetric indicators with citations from a multidisciplinary perspective. *Journal of the Association for Information Science and Technology*, *66*(10), 2003–2019. https://doi.org/10.1002/asi.2330

Dahl, T. (2009). Author identity in economics and linguistics abstracts. In Cross-linguistics and Cross-cultural perspectives on Academic Discourse (Eds.), (pp. 123–134). John Benjamins Publishing Company, Amsterdam.

Damarell, R. A., May, N., Hammond, S., Sladek, R. M., & Tieman, J. J. (2019). Topic search filters: A systematic scoping review. *Health Information & Libraries Journal*, *36*(1), 4–40.

Dawes, J. (2008). Do data characteristics change according to the number of scale points used? An experiment using 5-point, 7-point and 10-point scales. *International Journal of Market Research*, *50*(1), 61–104.

De Filippo, D., & Sanz-Casado, E. (2018). Bibliometric and altmetric analysis of three social science disciplines. *Frontiers in Research Metrics and Analytics*, *3*, 34. https://doi.org/10.3389/frma.2018.00034

Diamond, A. M. (1989). The core journals of economics. *Current Contents*, *21*(1), 4–11.

Diebold, F. X. (2012). On the Origin(s) and Development of the Term 'Big Data'. PIER (Working Paper No. 12-037). Retrieved from http://dx.doi.org/10.2139/ssrn.2152421 [Accessed March 25, 2019].

Dixon, E., Enos, E., & Brodmerkle, S. (2011). U.S. Patent No. 7,975,000. Washington, DC: U.S. Patent and Trademark Office.

Dobreva, M., Hinze, A., & Žumer, M. (Eds.). (2018). *Maturity and Innovation in Digital Libraries: 20th International Conference on Asia-Pacific Digital Libraries, ICADL 2018, Hamilton, New Zealand, November 19-22, 2018, Proceedings* (Vol. 11279). Springer.

Drongstrup, D., Malik, S., & Hassan, S.-U. (2019). Altmetrics study of economics. In G. Catalano, C. Daraio, M. Gregori, H. F. Moed, & G. Ruocco (Eds.), *17th International Conference on Scientometrics and Informetrics, ISSI 2019—Proceedings* (pp. 984–989), Rome, Italy.

EconBiz (2012, July 12). How does the EconBiz relevancy ranking works? Retrieved from https://www.econbiz.de/eb/fileadmin/images/hilfetexte/relevancy_ranking_EconBiz_about_02.pdf [Accessed July 05, 2020].

Eisend, M. (2011). Is VHB-JOURQUAL2 a good measure of scientific quality? Assessing the validity of the major business journal ranking in German-speaking countries. Business Research, 4(2), 241–274. http://dx.doi.org/10.1007/bf03342756

Elliott, D. B. (2014). The impact factor: A useful indicator of journal quality or fatally flawed? *Ophthalmic and Physiological Optics*, *34*(1), 4–7.

Elmore, S. A. (2018). The Altmetric Attention Score: What does it mean and why should I care? *Toxicologic Pathology*, *46*(3), 252–255. https://doi.org/10.1177/0192623318758294

Elston, D. M. (2019). Mendeley. *Journal of the American Academy of Dermatology*, *81*(5), 1071.

Eysenbach, G. (2006). Citation advantage of open access articles. *PLoS Biology*, *4*(5), e157.

Eysenbach, G. (2011). Can tweets predict citations? Metrics of social impact based on Twitter and correlation with traditional metrics of scientific impact. *Journal of Medical Internet Research*, *13*(4), e123.

Fang, Z., & Costas, R. (2020). Studying the accumulation velocity of altmetric data tracked by Altmetric.com. *Scientometrics*, *123*(2),— 1077-1101. https://doi.org/10.1007/s11192-020-03405-9

Fang, Z., Costas, R., Tian, W., Wang, X., & Wouters, P. (2020). An extensive analysis of the presence of altmetric data for Web of Science publications across subject fields and research topics. *Scientometrics*, *124*(3), 2519–2549.

Farin, F. (1976). *Evaluative bibliometrics: The use of publication and citation analysis in the evaluation of scientific activity.* Cherry Hill, NJ: Computer Horizons.

Fenner, M. (2014). Altmetrics and other novel measures for scientific impact. In *Opening science* (pp. 179–189). Cham: Springer. https://doi.org/10.1007/978-3-319-00026-8_12

Finardi, U. (2013). Correlation between journal impact factor and citation performance: An experimental study. *Journal of Informetrics*, *7*(2), 357–370.

Fink, A. (2003). *The survey handbook.* California: Sage Publications.

Forschungsmonitoring. (2017). VWL-Ranking: Journal Weights List Description (pdf). Retrieved from https://www.forschungsmonitoring.org/Description_VWL_Main_Journal_weights.pdf [Accessed March 14, 2019].

Forschungsmonitoring. (2018). BWL-Ranking: Journal Weights List Description (pdf). Retrieved from https://www.forschungsmonitoring.org/Description_BWL_Main_Journal_weights.pdf [Accessed March 14, 2019].

Fraser, N., Momeni, F., Mayr, P., & Peters, I. (2019). Altmetrics and open access: Exploring drivers and effects. PLoS ALM Workshop, San Francisco.

Frey, B., & Rost, K. (2010). Do rankings reflect research quality? *Journal of Applied Economics, 13*(1), 1–38. http://dx.doi.org/10.1016/s1514-0326(10)60002-5

Fujita, K., Kajikawa, Y., Mori, J., & Sakata, I. (2014). Detecting research fronts using different types of weighted citation networks. *Journal of Engineering and Technology Management*, *32*, 129–146.

Garfield, E. (1964). Citation indexing: A natural science literature retrieval system for the social sciences. *American Behavioral Scientist*, *7*(10), 58–61.

Garfield, E. (1972). Citation analysis as a tool in journal evaluation. *Science 178*, 471–479. http://doi.org/10.1126/science.178.4060.471

Garfield, E. (2006). Citation indexes for science. A new dimension in documentation through association of ideas. *International Journal of Epidemiology*, *35*(5), 1123–1127.

Glänzel, W. (2006a). On the h-index—A mathematical approach to a new measure of publication activity and citation impact. *Scientometrics*, *67*(2), 315–321.

Glänzel, W. (2006b). On the opportunities and limitations of the H-index, *Science Focus, 1*, 10–11.

Glänzel, W., & Gorraiz, J. (2015). Usage metrics versus altmetrics: Confusing terminology? *Scientometrics*, *102*(3), 2161–2164.

Glänzel, W., & Schubert, A. (2003). A new classification scheme of science fields and subfields designed for scientometric evaluation purposes. *Scientometrics*, *56*(3), 357–367.

Goldschmidt, N., & Szmrecsanyi, B. (2007). What do economists talk about? A linguistic analysis of published writing in economic journals. *American Journal of Economics and Sociology*, *66*(2), 335–378.

Gordon, M. D. (1982). Citation ranking versus subjective evaluation in the determination of journal hierarchies in the social sciences. *Journal of the Association for Information Science and Technology*, *33*(1), 55–57.

Griffiths, T. L., & Steyvers, M. (2004). Finding scientific topics. *Proceedings of the National Academy of Sciences*, *101*(suppl 1), 5228–5235.

Gumpenberger, C., Glänzel, W., & Gorraiz, J. (2016). The ecstasy and the agony of the altmetric score. *Scientometrics*, *108*(2), 977–982.

Gunn, W. (2013). Social signals reflect academic impact: What it means when a scholar adds a paper to Mendeley. *Information Standards Quarterly*, *25*(2), 33–39.

Hajra, A., & Tochtermann, K. (2017). Linking science: Approaches for linking scientific publications across different LOD repositories. *International Journal of Metadata, Semantics and Ontologies*, *12*(2–3), 124–141. https://doi.org/10.1504/IJMSO.2017.090778

Hall, C. M. (2011). Publish and perish? Bibliometric analysis, journal ranking and the assessment of research quality in tourism. *Tourism Management, 32*(1), 16–27. http://dx.doi.org/10.1016/j.tourman.2010.07.001

Hamermesh, D. S. (2018). Citations in economics: measurement, uses, and impacts. *Journal of Economic Literature*, *56*(1), 115–156.

Harzing, A., & van der Wal, R. (2009). A Google Scholar h-index for journals: An alternative metric to measure journal impact in economics and business. *Journal of the American Society for Information Science and Technology, 60*(1), 41–46. http://dx.doi.org/10.1002/asi.20953

Hassan, S. U., Imran, M., Gillani, U., Aljohani, N. R., Bowman, T. D., & Didegah, F. (2017). Measuring social media activity of scientific literature: An exhaustive comparison of Scopus and novel altmetrics big data. *Scientometrics*, *113*(2), 1037–1057.

Haunschild, R., & Bornmann, L. (2015). F1000Prime: An analysis of discipline-specific reader data from Mendeley. *F1000Research*, *4*(41), 41.

Haunschild, R., & Bornmann, L. (2016). Normalization of Mendeley reader counts for impact assessment. *Journal of Informetrics*, *10*(1), 62–73.

Haunschild, R., Bornmann, L., & Leydesdorff, L. (2015a). Networks of reader and country status: An analysis of Mendeley reader statistics. *PeerJ Computer Science*, *1*, e32.

Haunschild, R., Stefaner, M., & Bornmann, L. (2015b). Who Publishes, Reads, and Cites Papers? An Analysis of Country Information. In *ISSI*.

Haustein, S. (2012). *Multidimensional journal evaluation: Analyzing scientific periodicals beyond the impact factor*. Berlin: Walter de Gruyter.

Haustein, S. (2016). Grand challenges in altmetrics: Heterogeneity, data quality and dependencies. *Scientometrics*, *108*(1), 413–423. http://doi.org/10.1007/s11192-016-1910-9.

Haustein, S., Bowman, T. D., Costas, R., & Comesana, R. (2016). Interpreting "altmetrics": Viewing acts on social media through the lens of citation and social theories. In C. R. Sugimoto (Ed.), *Theories of informetrics: A Festschrift in Honor of Blaise Cronin* (pp. 372–405). Berlin, Boston: De Gruyter Saur. https://doi.org/10.1515/9783110308464-022

Haustein, S., Costas, R., & Larivière, V. (2015). Characterizing social media metrics of scholarly papers: The effect of document properties and collaboration patterns. *PLoS One*, *10*(3), e0120495.

Haustein, S., & Larivière, V. (2014). Mendeley as the source of global readership by students and postdocs? Evaluating Article Usage by Academic Status. In *IATUL Conference*, Espoo, Finland, June 2–5 2014. Retrieved from http://docs.lib.purdue.edu/cgi/viewcontent.cgi?article=2033&context=iatul [Accessed May 15, 2020].

Haustein, S., Peters, I., Sugimoto, C. R., Thelwall, M., & Larivière, V. (2014). Tweeting biomedicine: An analysis of tweets and citations in the biomedical literature. *Journal of the Association for Information Science and Technology*, *65*(4), 656–669.

He, Q., Chen, B., Pei, J., Qiu, B., Mitra, P., & Giles, L. (2009). Detecting topic evolution in scientific literature: how can citations help? In *Proceedings of the 18th ACM Conference on Information and Knowledge Management* (pp. 957–966). Association for Computing Machinery, New York, USA. https://doi.org/10.1145/1645953.1646076

Hirsch, J. E. (2005). An index to quantify an individual's scientific research output. *Proceedings of the National academy of Sciences*, *102*(46), 16569–16572.

Holmberg, K., & Park, H. W. (2018). An altmetric investigation of the online visibility of South Korea-based scientific journals. *Scientometrics*, *117*(1), 603–613.

Holmberg, K., & Thelwall, M. (2014). Disciplinary differences in Twitter scholarly communication. *Scientometrics*, *101*(2), 1027–1042.

Holmberg, K. J. (2015). *Altmetrics for information professionals: Past, present and future*. Waltham, MA: Chandos Publishing.

Hopkins, R. L. (1995). Countering information overload: The role of the librarian. *The Reference Librarian*, *23*(49–50), 305–333.

Htoo, T. H. H., & Na, J. C. (2017). Disciplinary differences in altmetrics for social sciences. *Online Information Review*, *41*(2), 235-251.

Jacsó, P. (2005). Google Scholar: The pros and the cons. *Online Information Review, 29*(2), 208–214. http://doi.org/10.1108/14684520510598066

Janßen, A.L. (2018). *Journal Map für die Ökonomie*. Master thesis, Christian-Albrechts-Universität zu Kiel, Kiel, Germany.

Kammerer, K., Falk, K., Herzog, A., & Fuchs, J. (2019). How to reach 'hard-to-reach' older people for research: The TIBaR model of recruitment. Retrieved from https://surveyinsights.org/?p=11822 [Accessed August 08, 2020].

Kapeller, J., Aistleitner, M., & Steinerberger, S. (2017). *Citation patterns in economics and beyond: Assessing the peculiarities of economics from two scientometric perspectives* (ICAE Working Paper Series No. 60). Retrieved from https://www.econstor.eu/bitstream/10419/171435/1/icae-wp60.pdf [Accessed March 25, 2020].

Kaplan, A. M., & Haenlein, M. (2010). Users of the world, unite! The challenges and opportunities of social media. *Business Horizons*, *53*(1), 59–68.

Kaufmann, M. (2019). Big data management canvas: A reference model for value creation from data. *Big Data and Cognitive Computing*, *3*(1), 19.

Kjellberg, S. (2010). I am a blogging researcher: Motivations for blogging in a scholarly context. *First Monday, 15*(8).

Konkiel, S., Dalmau, M., & Scherer, D. (2015). Altmetrics and analytics for digital special collections and institutional repositories. Retrieved from https://figshare.com/articles/preprint/Altmetrics_and_analytics_for_digital_special_c ollections_and_institutional_repositories/1392140 [Accessed April 15, 2019].

Kotsiantis, S. B., Kanellopoulos, D., & Pintelas, P. E. (2006). Data preprocessing for supervised leaning. *International Journal of Computer Science, 1*(2), 111–117.

Krapf, M. (2010). Research evaluation and journal quality weights. *Zeitschrift Für Betriebswirtschaft, 81*(1), 5–27. http://dx.doi.org/10.1007/s11573-010-0424-9

Kronick, D.A. (1976). A History of Scientific and Technical Periodicals: The Origins and Development of the Scientific and Technological Press, 1665– 1790 (2nd edition). Metuchen, NJ: Scarecrow Press.

Krueger, N. (2017). What Google Scholar can('t) do: Comparison of the Scholarly Search in Google Scholar and EconBiz. Retrieved from https://www.econbiz.de/eb/fileadmin/user_upload/pdfs/2017_EconBiz_oder_Google _ENGLISCH_v2.pdf [Accessed August 07, 2020].

Lammey, R. (2015). CrossRef text and data mining services. *Science Editing, 2*(1), 22–27.

Lammey, R. (2016). Using the Crossref Metadata API to explore publisher content. *Science Editing, 3*(2), 109–111.

Lapinski, S., Piwowar, H., & Priem, J. (2013). Riding the crest of the altmetrics wave: How librarians can help prepare faculty for the next generation of research impact metrics. *arXiv preprint arXiv:1305.3328.*

Larivière, V., & Sugimoto, C. R. (2019). The journal impact factor: A brief history, critique, and discussion of adverse effects. In W. Glänzel, H. F. Moed, U. Schmoch, & M. Thelwall (Eds.), *Springer handbook of science and technology indicators* (pp. 3–24). Cham: Springer.

Larsen, B. (2002). Exploiting citation overlaps for information retrieval: Generating a boomerang effect from the network of scientific papers. *Scientometrics, 54*(2), 155–178.

Lau, F., Rubin, S. H., Smith, M. H., & Trajkovic, L. (2000, October). Distributed denial of service attacks. In *SMC 2000 Conference Proceedings. 2000 IEEE International Conference on Systems, Man and Cybernetics. Cybernetics Evolving to Systems, Humans, Organizations, and Their Complex Interactions (cat. no. 0)* (Vol. 3, pp. 2275–2280). IEEE.

Lawrence, S., Giles, C. L., & Bollacker, K. (1999). Digital libraries and autonomous citation indexing. *Computer, 32*(6), 67–71. http://doi.org/10.1109/2.769447

Lemke, S., Mehrazar, M., Mazarakis, A., & Peters, I. (2019). "When You Use Social Media You Are Not Working": Barriers for the use of metrics in social sciences. *Frontiers in Research Metrics and Analytics, 3*, 39.

Lemke, S., Mehrazar, M., Peters, I., & Mazarakis, A. (2017). Evaluating altmetrics acts through their creators -How to advance. In *Proceedings of the Workshop Altmetrics* (Vol. 17), Toronto, Canada.

Leydesdorff, L. (2008, September). Journals as retention mechanisms of scientific growth. [Blog post]. Retrieved from https://www.researchtrends.com/issue7-september-

2008/journals-as-retention-mechanisms-of-scientific-growth/ [Accessed July 20, 2020].

Leydesdorff, L., & Bornmann, L. (2011). How fractional counting of citations affects the impact factor: Normalization in terms of differences in citation potentials among fields of science. *Journal of the American Society for Information Science and Technology*, *62*(2), 217–229.

Li, S., Jiao, F., Zhang, Y., & Xu, X. (2019). Problems and changes in digital libraries in the age of big data from the perspective of user services. *The Journal of Academic Librarianship*, *45*(1), 22–30.

Li, X., Thelwall, M., & Giustini, D. (2012). Validating online reference managers for scholarly impact measurement. *Scientometrics*, *91*(2), 461–471.

Linhart, A. S. (2015). Query Understanding in EconBiz. Wie suchen die Nutzer von EconBiz? Eine Analyse der Suchlogs des Suchportals der Zentralbibliothek für Wirtschaftswissenschaften. Hochschule für Angewandte Wissenschaften Hamburg. Retrieved from http://www.librank.info/wp-content/uploads/2016/07/Linhart-2015-Query-Understanding-in-EconBiz.-Wie-suchen-die-Nutzer-von-EconBiz-Eine-Analyse-der-Suchlogs-des-Suchportals-der-Zentral.pdf [Accessed April 29, 2020].

Liu, J., & Adie, E. (2013). Five challenges in altmetrics: A toolmaker's perspective. *Bulletin of the American Society for Information Science and Technology*, *39*(4), 31–34.

Loach, T. V., & Evans, T. S. (2015). Ranking journals using altmetrics. In *Proceedings of the 15th International Society of Scientometrics and Informetrics Conference* (pp. 89–94). Istanbul, Turkey.

Lorenz, D., & Löffler, A. (2015). Robustness of personal rankings: The Handelsblatt example. *Business Research*, *8*(2), 189–212.

Lossau, N. (2004, June). Search engine technology and digital libraries—Libraries need to discover the academic internet. *D-Lib Magazine, 10*(6). Retrieved from http://www.dlib.org/dlib/june04/lossau/06lossau.html [Accessed May 8, 2020].

MacRoberts, M. H., & MacRoberts, B. R. (1989). Problems of citation analysis: A critical review. *Journal of the American Society for information Science*, *40*(5), 342–349.

MacRoberts, M. H., & MacRoberts, B. R. (2010). Problems of citation analysis: A study of uncited and seldom-cited influences. *Journal of the American Society for Information Science and Technology*, *61*(1), 1–12.

Maflahi, N., & Thelwall, M. (2016). When are readership counts as useful as citation counts? Scopus versus Mendeley for LIS journals. *Journal of the Association for Information Science and Technology*, *67*(1), 191–199.

Maflahi, N., & Thelwall, M. (2018). How quickly do publications get read? The evolution of Mendeley reader counts for new articles. *Journal of the Association for Information Science and Technology*, *69*(1), 158–167.

Manning, C. D., Raghavan, P., & Schütze, H. (2008). An Introduction to Information Retrieval. —*Online Ed, Cambridge UP*. Retrieved from https://nlp.stanford.edu/IR-book/pdf/irbookonlinereading.pdf [Accessed April, 2, 2019]

Mayer-Schönberger, V., & Cukier, K. (2013). *Big data: A revolution that will transform how we live, work, and think*. London: John Murray.

McCabe, M. J., & Snyder, C. M. (2015). Does online availability increase citations? Theory and evidence from a panel of economics and business journals. *Review of Economics and Statistics*, *97*(1), 144–165.

McKinnon, A. C. (2013). Starry-eyed: Journal rankings and the future of logistics research. *International Journal of Physical Distribution & Logistics Management, 43*(1), 6–17. http://dx.doi.org/10.1108/09600031311293228

McKinnon, A. C. (2017). Starry-eyed II: the logistics journal ranking debate revisited. *International Journal of Physical Distribution & Logistics Management*, *47*(6), 431-446. https://doi.org/10.1108/IJPDLM-02-2017-0097

Mehrazar, M., Kling, C. C., Lemke, S., Mazarakis, A., & Peters, I. (2018). Can we count on social media metrics? First insights into the active scholarly use of social media. *arXiv preprint arXiv:1804.02751*.

Mohammadi, E., & Thelwall, M. (2014). Mendeley readership altmetrics for the social sciences and humanities: Research evaluation and knowledge flows. *Journal of the Association for Information Science and Technology*, *65*(8), 1627–1638.

Mohammadi, E., Thelwall, M., Haustein, S., & Larivière, V. (2015). Who reads research articles? An altmetrics analysis of Mendeley user categories. *Journal of the Association for Information Science and Technology*, *66*(9), 1832–1846.

Mohammadi, E., Thelwall, M., & Kousha, K. (2016). Can Mendeley bookmarks reflect readership? A survey of user motivations. *Journal of the Association for Information Science and Technology*, *67*(5), 1198–1209.

Naaman, M., Becker, H., & Gravano, L. (2011). Hip and trendy: Characterizing emerging trends on Twitter. *Journal of the American Society for Information Science and Technology*, *62*(5), 902–918.

Neylon, C., & Wu, S. (2009). Article-level metrics and the evolution of scientific impact. *PLoS Biology*, *7*(11), e1000242. https://doi.org/10.1371/journal.pbio.1000242

Norris, M., Oppenheim, C., & Rowland, F. (2008). The citation advantage of open-access articles. *Journal of the American Society for Information Science and Technology*, *59*(12), 1963–1972.

Nuredini, K., Lemke, S., & Peters, I. (2020). Social media and altmetrics. In R. Ball (Ed.), *Handbook bibliometrics* (pp. 201-214). Berlin, Boston: De Gruyter Saur. https://doi.org/10.1515/9783110646610-021

Nuredini, K., & Peters, I. (2015). Economic and business studies journals and readership information from Mendeley. In *Re: inventing Information Science in the Networked Society, Proceedings of the 14th International Symposium on Information Science, Zadar/Croatia, 19th—21st May 2015 (ISI 2015)* (pp. 380–392). Glückstadt: vwh Verlag Werner Hülsbusch.

Nuredini, K., & Peters, I. (2016). Enriching the knowledge of altmetrics studies by exploring social media metrics for *Economic and Business Studies* journals. In *Proceedings of the 21st International Conference on Science and Technology Indicators (STI Conference 2016), València (Spain), September 14–16, 2016*. Berlin: European Network of Indicator Designers (ENID).

Nuredini, K., Latif, A., & Peters, I. (2017). Case study on open access journals in economic and business studies and their engagement on the web. The 2017 Altmetrics Workshop, Toronto, Canada, September 26.

Nuredini, K., & Peters, I. (2019). The presence and issues of altmetrics and citation data from Crossref for working papers with different identifiers from Econstor and RePEc in the discipline of *Economic and Business Studies*. In *Proceedings of the 17th International Conference on Scientometrics & Informetrics (ISSI 2019)*, Rome, Italy.

Nuredini, K. (2021). Investigating altmetric information for the top 1,000 journals from Handelsblatt ranking in Economic and Business Studies. *Journal of Economic Surveys*. https://doi.org/10.1111/joes.12414

Odlyzko, A. (2002). The rapid evolution of scholarly communication. *Learned Publishing*, *15*(1), 7–19.

Onaifo, D., & Rasmussen, D. (2013). Increasing libraries' content findability on the web with search engine optimization. *Library Hi Tech*, *31*(1). http://doi.org/10.1108/07378831311303958

Orduña-Malea, E., & López-Cózar, E. D. (2018). Dimensions: Re-discovering the ecosystem of scientific information. *arXiv preprint arXiv:1804.05365*.

Ortega, J. L. (2016). To be or not to be on Twitter, and its relationship with the tweeting and citation of research papers. *Scientometrics*, *109*(2), 1353–1364.

Ortega, J. L. (2018a). Disciplinary differences of the impact of altmetric. *FEMS Microbiology Letters*, *365*(7), fny049.

Ortega, J. L. (2018b). Reliability and accuracy of altmetric providers: A comparison among Altmetric. com, PlumX and Crossref Event Data. *Scientometrics*, *116*(3), 2123–2138.

Ortega, J. L. (2018c). The life cycle of altmetric impact: A longitudinal study of six metrics from PlumX. *Journal of Informetrics*, *12*(3), 579–589.

Ozler, B. (2011, June 30). Working Papers are NOT working. [Blog post]. Retrieved from http://blogs.worldbank.org/impactevaluations/working-papers-are-not-working [Accessed November 17, 2019].

Pao, M. L. (1975). A quality filtering system for medical literature. *Journal of Medical Education, 50*(4), 353–359.

Patrizio, A. (2018, December 3). IDC: Expect 175 zettabytes of data worldwide by 2025. *Network World*. [Blog post]. https://www.networkworld.com/article/3325397/idc-expect-175-zettabytes-of-data-worldwide-by-2025.html [Accessed September 29, 2020]

Pentz, E. (2001). CrossRef: A collaborative linking network. *Issues in Science and Technology Librarianship*, *10*. Retrieved from http://istl.org/01-winter/article1.html [Accessed January 18, 2020].

Peters, I., Jobmann, A., Eppelin, A., Hoffmann, C. P., Künne, S., & Wollnik-Korn, G. (2014). Altmetrics for large, multidisciplinary research groups: A case study of the Leibniz Association. *Libraries in the Digital Age* (pp. 245–254). Croatia: Zadar.

Peters, I., Scherp, A., & Tochtermann, K. (2015). Science 2.0 and Libraries: Convergence of two sides of the same coin at ZBW Leibniz Information Centre for Economics. *IEEE STCSN E-Letter on Science*, *2*(3), 1.

Pianos, T. (2010). EconBiz-Meeting user needs with new technology. *Liber Quarterly*, *20*(1).

Pianos, T., & Klemenz, A. M. (2017). EconBiz-Experiences: Creating our own discovery system for business & economics. Paper presented at the meeting of *Reference and Information Services and Information Technology Sections (IFLA, VLIC)*. Wrocław, Poland.

Pianos, T., & Siegfried, D. (2019). EconBiz: Search quality and ranking transparency in the age of Google. [Brochure]. Retrieved from https://www.econbiz.de/eb/fileadmin/user_upload/pdfs/EconBiz_info_broschure_en. pdf [Accessed March 01, 2020].

Pinski, G., & Narin, F. (1976). Citation influence for journal aggregates of scientific publications: Theory, with application to the literature of physics. *Information processing & management*, *12*(5), 297-312.

Pislyakov, V. (2009). Comparing two "thermometers": Impact factors of 20 leading economic journals according to Journal Citation Reports and Scopus. *Scientometrics*, *79*(3), 541–550.

Piwowar, H., & Priem, J. (2013). The power of altmetrics on a CV. *Bulletin of the American Society for Information Science and Technology*, *39*(4), 10–13.

Plassmeier, K., Borst, T., Behnert, C., & Lewandowski, D. (2015). Evaluating popularity data for relevance ranking in library information systems. *Proceedings of the Association for Information Science and Technology*, *52*(1), 1–4.

Prabhakaran, S. (2020, July 22). Topic Modelling with Gensim. [Blog post] https://www.machinelearningplus.com/nlp/topic-modeling-gensim-python/#17howtofindtheoptimalnumberoftopicsforlda [Accessed October 5, 2020]

Price, D. J. D. S. (1963). *Little Science, Big Science*. New York: Columbia University Press.

Price, D. J. D. S. (1965). Networks of scientific papers. *Science*, *149*(3683), 510–515.

Priem, J., & Costello, K. L. (2010). How and why scholars cite on Twitter. *Proceedings of the American Society for Information Science and Technology*, *47*(1), 1–4.

Priem, J., Piwowar, H. A., & Hemminger, B. M. (2012). Altmetrics in the wild: Using social media to explore scholarly impact. *arXiv preprint arXiv:1203.4745*.

Priem, J., Taraborelli, D., Groth, P., & Neylon, C. (2010). Altmetrics: A manifesto, October 26, 2010. Retrieved from http://altmetrics.org/manifesto [Accessed February 03, 2020].

Pritchard, A. (1969). Statistical bibliography or bibliometrics. *Journal of Documentation*, *25*(4), 348–349.

Procter, R., Williams, R., Stewart, J., Poschen, M., Snee, H., Voss, A., & Asgari-Targhi, M. (2010). Adoption and use of Web 2.0 in scholarly communications. *Philosophical Transactions of the Royal Society A: Mathematical, Physical and Engineering Sciences*, *368*(1926), 4039–4056.

Raamkumar, A. S., Ganesan, S., Jothiramalingam, K., Selva, M. K., Erdt, M., & Theng, Y. L. (2018). Investigating the characteristics and research impact of sentiments in tweets with links to computer science research papers. In *International Conference on Asian Digital Libraries* (pp. 71–82). Springer, Cham.

Rafols, I., Leydesdorff, L., O'Hare, A., Nightingale, P., & Stirling, A. (2012). How journal rankings can suppress interdisciplinary research: A comparison between innovation studies and business & management. *Research Policy*, *41*(7), 1262–1282.

Ratner, B. (2009). The correlation coefficient: Its values range between +1/−1, or do they? *Journal of Targeting, Measurement and Analysis for Marketing*, *17*(2), 139–142.

Ricca, F., Scanniello, G., Torchiano, M., Reggio, G., & Astesiano, E. (2010). On the effectiveness of screen mockups in requirements engineering: results from an internal replication. In *Proceedings of the 2010 ACM-IEEE International Symposium on*

Empirical Software Engineering and Measurement (p. 17). Association for Computing Machinery, New York, USA, https://doi.org/10.1145/1852786.1852809

Ritzberger, K. (2008). A ranking of journals in economics and related fields. *German Economic Review, 9*(4), 402–430.

Robinson-García, N., Torres-Salinas, D., Zahedi, Z., & Costas, R. (2014). New data, new possibilities: Exploring the insides of Altmetric.com. El Profesional de La Información, *23*(4), 359–366. http://doi.org/10.3145/epi.2014.jul.03

Roemer, R. C., & Borchardt, R. (2015). Altmetrics and the role of librarians. *Library Technology Reports, 51*(5), 31–37.

Rousseau, S., & Rousseau, R. (2017). Being metric-wise: Heterogeneity in bibliometric knowledge. *El profesional de la información (EPI), 26*(3), 480–487.

Rowlands, I., Nicholas, D., Russell, B., Canty, N., & Watkinson, A. (2011). Social media use in the research workflow. *Learned Publishing, 24*(3), 183–195.

Rudd, J., & Rudd, M. J. (1986). Coping with information load: User strategies and implications for librarians. *College and Research Libraries, 47*(4), 315–322. https://doi.org/10.5860/crl_47_04_315

Schläpfer, J. (2012). Das Handelsblatt BWL Ranking und seine Zeitschriftenliste. *Bibliometrie—Praxis und Forschung, 1*(6), 1–8. http://dx.doi.org/10.5283/bpf.167

Schober, P., Boer, C., & Schwarte, L. A. (2018). Correlation coefficients: Appropriate use and interpretation. *Anesthesia & Analgesia, 126*(5), 1763–1768.

Seglen, P. O. (1997). Citations and journal impact factors: Questionable indicators of research quality. *Allergy, 52*(11), 1050–1056.

Seglen, P. O. (1998). Why the impact factor of journals should not be used for evaluating research. *British Medical Journal, 314*(7079), 498–502.

Shema, H., Bar-Ilan, J., & Thelwall, M. (2012). Research blogs and the discussion of scholarly information. *PLoS One, 7*(5), e35869.

Shema, H., Bar-Ilan, J., & Thelwall, M. (2014, June 14). Scholarly blogs are a promising altmetric source. [Blog post]. Retrieved from https://www.researchtrends.com/issue-37-june-2014/scholarly-blogs-are-a-promising-altmetric-source/ [Accessed August 25, 2020].

Shen, C., & Björk, B. C. (2015). 'Predatory' open access: A longitudinal study of article volumes and market characteristics. *BMC Medicine, 13*(1), 230.

Shipman, M. (2012). Can news media boost citations? Examining one (old) study. [Blog post]. Retrieved from https://sciencecommunicationbreakdown.wordpress.com/2012/11/14/does-media-boost-citations/ [Accessed January 16, 2020].

Shirky, C. (2008, September 19). *It's not information overload. Its filter failure.* [Video file]. Retrieved from https://www.youtube.com/watch?v=LabqeJEOQyI [Accessed October 14, 2019].

Siegel, S. (1957). Nonparametric statistics. *The American Statistician, 11*(3), 13–19.

Siegfried, D. (2015). Was Nutzer wollen—Marktforschung in der ZBW [PowerPoint slides]. Retrieved from https://macau.uni-kiel.de/servlets/MCRFileNodeServlet/macau_derivate_00000256/VortragSiegfriedS HBibtag2015.pdf [Accessed March 22, 2020].

Smith, L. C. (1981). Citation analysis. *Library Trends, 30*(1), 83–106.

Smith, R. (2006). Peer review: A flawed process at the heart of science and journals. *Journal of the Royal Society of Medicine*, *99*(4), 178–182.

Smyth, R. (1999). A citation analysis of Australian economic journals. *Australian Academic & Research Libraries*, *30*(2), 119–133.

Spearman, C. (1987). The proof and measurement of association between two things. *The American Journal of Psychology*, *100*(3/4), 441–471.

Stern, D. I. (2013). Uncertainty measures for economics journal impact factors. *Journal of Economic Literature*, *51*(1), 173–189.

Stieglitz, S., Dang-Xuan, L., Bruns, A., & Neuberger, C. (2014). Ein interdisziplinärer Ansatz und seine Implikationen für die Wirtschaftsinformatik [Social media analytics—An interdisciplinary approach and its implications for information systems]. *Wirtschaftsinformatik*, *56*(2), 101–109.

Sturm, J. E., & Ursprung, H. W. (2017). The Handelsblatt Rankings 2.0: Research rankings for the economics profession in Austria, Germany, and Switzerland. *German Economic Review*, *18*(4), 492–515.

Sugimoto, C. R., & Larivière, V. (2018). *Measuring research: What everyone needs to know*. Oxford University Press.

Sugimoto, C. R., Work, S., Larivière, V., & Haustein, S. (2017). Scholarly use of social media and altmetrics: A review of the literature. *Journal of the Association for Information Science and Technology*, *68*(9), 2037–2062.

Swan, A. (2006). Overview of scholarly communication. In Neil, J. (Ed.) *Open access: Key strategic, technical and economic aspects* (pp. 5–11). Oxford, UK: Chandos Publishing.

Tattersall, A. (Ed.). (2016). *Altmetrics: A practical guide for librarians, researchers, and academics*. Facet Publishing, UK.

Thelwall, M. (2017a). Are Mendeley reader counts useful impact indicators in all fields? *Scientometrics*, *113*(3), 1721–1731.

Thelwall, M. (2017b). Why do papers have many Mendeley readers but few Scopus-indexed citations and vice versa? *Journal of Librarianship and Information Science*, *49*(2), 144–151.

Thelwall, M. (2018a, January). Using altmetrics to support research evaluation. In *International Workshop on Altmetrics for Research Outputs Measurements and Scholarly Information Management* (pp. 11–28). Springer, Singapore.

Thelwall, M. (2018b). Early Mendeley readers correlate with later citation counts. *Scientometrics*, *115*(3),— 1231-1240.

Thelwall, M. (2020). Measuring societal impacts of research with altmetrics? Common problems and mistakes. *Journal of Economic Surveys*. https://doi.org/10.1111/joes.12381

Thelwall, M., Haustein, S., Larivière, V., & Sugimoto, C. R. (2013). Do altmetrics work? Twitter and ten other social web services. *PLoS One*, *8*(5), e64841.

Thelwall, M., & Maflahi, N. (2015). Are scholarly articles disproportionately read in their own country? An analysis of Mendeley readers. *Journal of the Association for Information Science and Technology*, *66*(6), 1124–1135.

Todorov, R., & Glänzel, W. (1988). Journal citation measures: A concise review. *Journal of Information Science*, *14*(1), 47–56. http://doi.org/10.1177/016555158801400106

Tomajko, K. G., & Drake, M. A. (1985). The journal, scholarly communication, and the future. *The Serials Librarian*, *10*(1–2), 289–298.

Trueger, N. S., Thoma, B., Hsu, C. H., Sullivan, D., Peters, L., & Lin, M. (2015). The altmetric score: A new measure for article-level dissemination and impact. *Annals of Emergency Medicine*, *66*(5), 549–553.

UNESCO. (2015). Scholarly communication. United Nationals Educational, Scientific and Cultural Organization, France.

Van Noorden, R. (2014, May 7). Global scientific output doubles every nine years. [Blog post]. Retrieved from http://blogs.nature.com/news/2014/05/global-scientific-output-doubles-every-nine-years.html [Accessed October 2, 2019].

Van Rossum, G., & Drake, F. L. (2011). *The python language reference manual*. Network Theory Ltd.

Visser, M., & Moed, H. F. (2008). Comparing Web of Science and SCOPUS on a paper-by-paper basis. In *Excellence and emergence. A new challenge for combination of quantitative and qualitative approaches.* Paper presented at the *10th S&T International Conference* (pp. 23–25).

Vogel, R., Hattke, F., & Petersen, J. (2017). Journal rankings in management and business studies: What rules do we play by? *Research Policy*, *46*(10), 1707–1722.

Wang, Q. (2018). A bibliometric model for identifying emerging research topics. *Journal of the Association for Information Science and Technology*, *69*(2), 290–304.

Wang, J., Alotaibi, N. M., Ibrahim, G. M., Kulkarni, A. V., & Lozano, A. M. (2017). The spectrum of altmetrics in neurosurgery: the top 100 "trending" articles in neurosurgical journals. *World Neurosurgery*, *103*, 883–895. https://doi.org/10.1016/j.wneu.2017.04.157

Ware, M., & Mabe, M. (2012). The STM report. An overview of scientific and scholarly journal publishing. International Association of Scientific, Technical and Medical Publishers, The Hague, The Netherlands. Retrieved from https://www.stm-assoc.org/2012_12_11_STM_Report_2012.pdf [Accessed September 09, 2019].

Weiland, J. (2011). Econstor: A RePEc archive for Research in Germany. [Blog post]. Retrieved from https://blog.repec.org/2011/09/15/econstor-a-repec-archive-for-research-from-germany/ [Accessed August 13, 2019].

Wets, K., Weedon, D., & Velterop, J. (2003). Post-publication filtering and evaluation: Faculty of 1000. *Learned publishing*, *16*(4), 249–258.

White, K. (2019). Science and engineering publication output trends: 2017 shows us output level slightly below that of China but the United States maintains lead with highly cited publications. *National Center for Science and Engineering Statistics*. Retrieved from https://www.nsf.gov/statistics/2019/nsf19317/nsf19317.pdf [Accessed November 08, 2020].

Willmott, H. (2011). Journal list fetishism and the perversion of scholarship: Reactivity and the ABS list. *Organization*, *18*(4), 429–442.

Wohlrabe, K. (2013). Einige Anmerkungen zum Handelsblatt-Ranking 2013. *ifo Schnelldienst*, *66*(23), 79–83.

Wouters, P., & Costas, R. (2012). *Users, narcissism and control: tracking the impact of scholarly publications in the 21st century* (pp. 847–857). Utrecht: SURF Foundation.

Wouters, P., Zahedi, Z., & Costas, R. (2019). Social media metrics for new research evaluation. In *Springer handbook of science and technology indicators* (pp. 687–713). Cham: Springer.

Yao, J. T., & Yao, Y. Y. (2003). Web-based information retrieval support systems: Building research tools for scientists in the new information age. In *Proceedings IEEE/WIC International Conference on Web Intelligence (WI 2003)* (pp. 570–573). IEEE.

Yu, H., Xu, S., Xiao, T., Hemminger, B. M., & Yang, S. (2017). Global science discussed in local altmetrics: Weibo and its comparison with Twitter. *Journal of Informetrics*, *11*(2), 466–482.

Zahedi, Z., Haustein, S., & Bowman, T. (2014a, November). Exploring data quality and retrieval strategies for Mendeley reader counts. In *SIG/MET Workshop, ASIS&T 2014 Annual Meeting, Seattle.* Retrieved from: www.asis.org/SIG/SIGMET/data/uploads/sigmet2014/zahedi.pdf [Accessed April 26, 2020].

Zahedi, Z., Costas, R., & Wouters, P. (2014b). How well developed are altmetrics? A cross-disciplinary analysis of the presence of 'alternative metrics' in scientific publications. *Scientometrics*, *101*(2), 1491–1513.

Zahedi, Z., Costas, R., Wouters, P. (2015). Do Mendeley readership counts help to filter highly cited WoS publications better than average citation impact of journals (JCS)? In *15th International Conference of the International Society for Scientometrics and Informetric (ISSI2015), Istanbul, Turkey, June 29–July 3, 2015* (pp. 1–10). Istanbul: Bogazici University Press.

Zahedi, Z., Costas, R., & Wouters, P. (2017). Mendeley readership as a filtering tool to identify highly cited publications. *Journal of the Association for Information Science and Technology*, *68*(10), 2511–2521.

Zahedi, Z., & van Eck, N. J. (2018). Exploring Topics of Interest of Mendeley Users. *Journal of Altmetrics, 1*(1), 5. http://doi.org/10.29024/joa.7

ZBW—Leibniz-Informationszentrum Wirtschaft. (2012). Jahresbericht der ZBW 2012 [PDF file]. Kiel/Hamburg, Germany. Retrieved from https://www.zbw.eu/fileadmin/pdf/ueber-uns/jb-2012.pdf [Accessed April 04, 2020].

ZBW—Leibniz-Informationszentrum Wirtschaft. (2013). Jahresbericht der ZBW 2013 [PDF file]. Kiel/Hamburg, Germany. Retrieved from https://www.zbw.eu/fileadmin/pdf/ueber-uns/jb-2013.pdf [Accessed April 04, 2020].

ZBW—Leibniz-Informationszentrum Wirtschaft. (2016). Jahresbericht der ZBW 2012 [PDF file]. Kiel/Hamburg, Germany. Retrieved from https://www.zbw.eu/fileadmin/pdf/ueber-uns/jb-2016.pdf [Accessed April 04, 2020].

ZBW—Leibniz-Informationszentrum Wirtschaft. (2018). Jahresbericht der ZBW 2018 [PDF file]. Kiel/Hamburg, Germany. Retrieved from https://www.zbw.eu/fileadmin/pdf/ueber-uns/jb-2018.pdf [Accessed April 04, 2020].

Zhou, J. (2003). A history of web portals and their development in libraries. Information Technology and Libraries, 22(3), 119–128.

Appendix I: Top 500 Handelsblatt ranking journals in business studies, their classes, and altmetric data

No.	ISSN	Class	Journal Name	Articles in Crossref	Mendeley Counts	Altmetric Scores
1	0001-4273	A+	*Academy of Management Journal*	697	84,433	8,142
2	1537-260X	C	*Academy of Management Learning & Education*	502	19,911	772
3	1558-9080	B	*Academy of Management Perspectives*	339	15,991	551
4	0363-7425	A+	*Academy of Management Review*	414	40,864	1,295
5	0001-4575	C	*Accident Analysis & Prevention*	2,823	125,363	11,222
6	0001-4788	D	*Accounting and Business Research*	296	2,906	172
7	0963-9284	D	*Accounting Education*	304	0	27
8	0155-9982	D	*Accounting Forum*	239	5,160	0
9	0888-7993	D	*Accounting Horizons*	381	4,849	190
10	0951-3574	C	*Accounting, Auditing & Accountability Journal*	572	20,589	283
11	0361-3682	C	*Accounting, Organizations and Society*	385	22,201	371
12	0360-0300	C	*ACM Computing Surveys*	600	30,032	1,323
13	0362-5915	D	*ACM Transactions on Database Systems*	254	3,453	250
14	1469-7874	C	*Active Learning in Higher Education*	198	3,607	826
15	1583-9583	D	*Administratie si Management Public*	11	0	0
16	0095-3997	D	*Administration & Society*	468	3,691	769
17	0001-8392	A+	*Administrative Science Quarterly*	387	7,834	7,088
18	0731-9053	D	*Advances in econometrics*	0	0	0
19	0742-3322	D	*Advances in Strategic Management*	0	0	0

20	0001-9909	C	*African Affairs*	489	4,655	0
21	0169-5150	C	*Agricultural Economics*	574	7,521	1,100
22	0002-7642	D	*American Behavioral Scientist*	844	9,961	6,374
23	1945-7782	A+	*American Economic Journal: Applied Economics*	325	9,190	8,533
24	1945-7731	A+	*American Economic Journal: Economic Policy*	0	0	0
25	1945-7707	A+	*American Economic Journal: Macroeconomics*	283	4,377	1,514
26	1945-7669	A	*American Economic Journal: Microeconomics*	350	0	746
27	0002-8282	A+	*American Economic Review*	1,982	110,178	24,777
28	0002-9092	C	*American Journal of Agricultural Economics*	915	5,905	3,844
29	0002-9602	B	*American Journal of Sociology*	1,491	17,122	4,427
30	1465-7252	D	*American Law and Economics Review*	172	762	0
31	0003-066X	C	*American Psychologist*	106	51	0
32	0090-0036	B	*American Public Health Association*	0	0	0
33	0003-1224	A	*American Sociological Review*	395	7,939	19,795
34	0254-5330	D	*Annals of Operations Research*	2,219	6,313	582
35	0160-7383	C	*Annals of Tourism Research*	1,092	44,130	1,162
36	1941-1383	A+	*Annual Review of Economics*	191	8,187	1,519
37	1941-1367	A	*Annual Review of Financial Economics*	140	2,958	141
38	0066-4308	A+	*Annual Review of Psychology*	205	34,804	6,334
39	1941-1340	C	*Annual Review of Resource Economics*	186	2,343	589
40	0360-0572	A	*Annual Review of Sociology*	202	0	2,122
41	1467-8330	B	*Antipode*	0	0	0

42	0888-4080	D	*Applied Cognitive Psychology*	765	7,508	5,141
43	0003-6870	D	*Applied Ergonomics*	1,423	4,619	4,730
44	1175-5652	D	*Applied Health Economics and Health Policy*	527	3,193	1,528
45	0146-6216	D	*Applied Psychological Measurement*	380	1,735	307
46	0269-994X	C	*Applied Psychology*	263	5,283	932
47	1758-0846	D	*Applied Psychology: Health and Well-Being*	182	2,218	1,269
48	1524-1904	D	*Applied Stochastic Models in Business and Industry*	588	733	101
49	0004-3702	D	*Artificial Intelligence*	668	17,227	1,200
50	0217-4561	D	*Asia Pacific Journal of Management*	337	5,261	82
51	0515-0361	D	*ASTIN Bulletin*	213	314	26
52	0278-0380	C	*AUDITING: A Journal of Practice & Theory*	345	9,071	73
53	0197-3533	D	*Basic and Applied Social Psychology*	307	6,667	2,673
54	0144-929X	D	*Behaviour & Information Technology*	785	9,212	696
55	0006-3444	B	*Biometrika*	617	4,428	483
56	1472-6963	D	*BMC Health Services Research*	5,419	0	19,548
57	0141-1926	C	*British Educational Research Journal*	504	7,030	2,032
58	0007-1013	C	*British Journal of Educational Technology*	1,012	10,873	3,234
59	0007-1080	C	*British Journal of Industrial Relations*	516	2,030	745
60	1045-3172	C	*British Journal of Management*	438	6,857	1,453
61	0007-1269	C	*British Journal of Psychology*	489	0	6,690
62	0144-6665	D	*British Journal of Social Psychology*	414	6,861	3,596
63	0007-2303	A	*Brookings Papers on Economic Activity*	0	0	0
64	0961-3218	D	*Building Research & Information*	496	6,774	3,453

65	0007-4918	D	*Bulletin of Indonesian Economic Studies*	306	1,572	960
66	2363-7005	D	*Business & Information Systems Engineering*	216	759	195
67	0007-6503	C	*Business & Society*	342	3,474	2,007
68	0007-666X	D	*Business Economics*	311	948	273
69	1052-150X	D	*Business Ethics Quarterly*	461	6,556	248
70	0962-8770	D	*Business Ethics: A European Review*	275	2,815	157
71	0007-6813	C	*Business Horizons*	701	43,410	1,686
72	0964-4733	C	*Business Strategy and the Environment*	493	9,208	275
73	0008-1256	C	*California Management Review*	280	12,740	980
74	0309-166X	D	*Cambridge Journal of Economics*	544	4,539	2,355
75	1752-1378	B	*Cambridge Journal of Regions, Economy and Society*	285	2,825	794
76	0008-4085	D	*Canadian journal of economics*	0	0	0
77	1043-951X	D	*China Economic Review*	675	14,829	342
78	1469-3062	C	*Climate Policy*	547	662	4,071
79	1863-2505	D	*Cliometrica*	117	505	474
80	1435-5558	D	*Cognition, Technology & Work*	364	0	142
81	0093-6502	C	*Communication Research*	419	5,470	4,127
82	0001-0782	D	*Communications of the ACM*	2,337	48,855	3,533
83	1024-5294	D	*Competition & Change*	198	1,585	374
84	0926-6003	D	*Computational Optimization and Applications*	651	2,007	106
85	1613-9658	D	*Computational statistics*	630	1,982	201
86	0167-9473	C	*Computational Statistics & Data Analysis*	2,169	24,407	493
87	0360-8352	C	*Computers & Industrial Engineering*	2,902	60,295	310
88	0305-0548	C	*Computers & Operations Research*	2,078	43,643	389
89	0747-5632	C	*Computers in Human Behavior*	4,136	270,841	35,205

90	0166-3615	D	*Computers in Industry*	852	34,920	258
91	1063-293X	D	*Concurrent Engineering*	230	1,442	22
92	0144-6193	D	*Construction Management and Economics*	762	8,990	432
93	1025-3866	D	*Consumption Markets & Culture*	337	2,572	612
94	0823-9150	B	*Contemporary Accounting Research*	581	9,728	689
95	1465-7287	D	*Contemporary economic policy*	0	0	0
96	0277-5921	D	*Contributions to Political Economy*	66	296	53
97	1938-9655	D	*Cornell Hospitality Quarterly*	354	7,520	587
98	0964-8410	D	*Corporate Governance: An International Review*	375	0	349
99	1535-3958	C	*Corporate Social Responsibility and Environmental Management*	369	5,012	124
100	0963-1690	D	*Creativity and Innovation Management*	372	2,427	813
101	1045-2354	C	*Critical Perspectives on Accounting*	527	9,114	365
102	0261-0183	D	*Critical Social Policy*	470	3,697	1,629
103	0963-7214	A	*Current Directions in Psychological Science*	603	13,208	14,727
104	1368-3500	C	*Current Issues in Tourism*	736	15,521	1,008
105	0011-3921	D	*Current Sociology*	516	7,002	3,348
106	0011-7315	C	*Decision Sciences*	472	4,317	278
107	0167-9236	C	*Decision Support Systems*	1,278	89,261	1,267
108	0012-155X	D	*Development and Change*	565	7,123	1,636
109	0963-8288	D	*Disability and Rehabilitation*	2,749	28,423	6,652
110	0166-218X	D	*Discrete Applied Mathematics*	3,083	14,649	753
111	0924-6703	D	*Discrete Event Dynamic Systems*	177	618	20
112	0921-8009	C	*Ecological Economics*	2,257	128,242	7,198
113	0747-4938	C	*Econometric Reviews*	387	1,888	146

114	0266-4666	B	*Econometric Theory*	478	1,327	304
115	0012-9682	A+	*Econometrica*	720	9,781	2,125
116	0143-831X	D	*Economic and Industrial Democracy*	402	1,852	418
117	0013-0079	C	*Economic Development and Cultural Change*	286	5,387	1,490
118	0013-0095	B	*Economic Geography*	311	2,224	883
119	0095-2583	D	*Economic Inquiry*	776	5,121	4,573
120	0264-9993	D	*Economic Modelling*	2,723	55,033	2,011
121	1468-0327	B	*Economic Policy*	164	2,280	1,308
122	0953-5314	C	*Economic Systems Research*	221	2,141	204
123	0938-2259	B	*Economic Theory*	556	1,876	124
124	0013-0427	B	*Economica*	386	1,246	1,117
125	1570-677X	C	*Economics & Human Biology*	485	4,720	3,551
126	0954-1985	D	*Economics & Politics*	167	1,060	628
127	0165-1765	D	*Economics Letters*	3,69	45,50	3,758
128	0272-7757	C	*Economics of Education Review*	697	21,957	6,940
129	2212-0122	C	*Economics of Transportation*	123	1,908	142
130	0308-5147	D	*Economy and Society*	216	3,255	750
131	1741-1432	D	*Educational Management Administration & Leadership*	542	4,215	678
132	0261-3794	C	*Electoral Studies*	895	17,62	7,253
133	1567-4223	D	*Electronic Commerce Research and Applications*	513	17,35	193
134	1019-6781	D	*Electronic Markets*	270	3,616	642
135	1566-0141	D	*Emerging Markets Review*	354	6,437	67
136	0140-9883	C	*Energy Economics*	2,202	68,750	4,747
137	0301-4215	C	*Energy Policy*	5,469	299,551	16,851
138	0969-9988	D	*Engineering, Construction and Architectural Management*	410	9,521	41
139	0898-5626	C	*Entrepreneurship & Regional Development*	347	6,908	273
140	1042-2587	B	*Entrepreneurship Theory and Practice*	495	13,178	924

141	0308-518X	C	*Environment and Planning A: Economy and Space*	1,349	16,081	3,513
142	2399-6544	D	*Environment and Planning C: Politics and Space*	203	97	0
143	0263-7758	B	*Environment and Planning D: Society and Space*	559	7,195	2,295
144	0924-6460	D	*Environmental and Resource Economics*	837	9,15	1,432
145	0364-152X	D	*Environmental Management*	1,495	24,020	2,686
146	1462-9011	C	*Environmental Science & Policy*	1,497	39,498	6,145
147	0013-936X	B	*Environmental Science & Technology*	8,963	131,299	56,700
148	0014-0139	D	*Ergonomics*	1,269	13,268	3,965
149	1538-7216	D	*Eurasian Geography and Economics*	257	2,390	514
150	2192-4406	D	*EURO Journal on Computational Optimization*	108	74	8
151	0963-8180	D	*European Accounting Review*	321	3,573	68
152	0014-2921	C	*European Economic Review*	1,003	24,012	2,589
153	1354-7798	D	*European Financial Management*	320	1,891	148
154	0959-6801	C	*European Journal of Industrial Relations*	246	1,260	396
155	0960-085X	C	*European Journal of Information Systems*	337	15,610	251
156	0309-0566	D	*European Journal of Marketing*	801	25,925	655
157	0377-2217	B	*European Journal of Operational Research*	5,251	162,564	1,839
158	0176-2680	D	*European Journal of Political Economy*	540	9,115	1,321
159	0046-2772	C	*European Journal of Social Psychology*	689	10,881	7,622
160	1359-432X	C	*European Journal of Work and*	460	5,551	1,764

			Organizational Psychology			
161	0263-2373	C	*European Management Journal*	553	37,006	752
162	1740-4754	D	*European Management Review*	274	2,294	163
163	0965-4313	D	*European Planning Studies*	987	10,244	775
164	1016-9040	D	*European Psychologist*	306	2,587	582
165	0165-1587	D	*European Review of Agricultural Economics*	296	3,214	459
166	1361-4916	D	*European Review of Economic History*	183	888	279
167	1468-2672	B	*European Sociological Review*	582	3,966	3,479
168	1618-4742	D	*European Sport Management Quarterly*	276	2,452	602
169	0969-7764	D	*European Urban and Regional Studies*	289	2,198	400
170	1356-3890	D	*Evaluation*	345	4,124	654
171	1063-6560	D	*Evolutionary Computation*	215	2,012	171
172	1386-4157	C	*Experimental Economics*	308	9,595	925
173	0957-4174	C	*Expert Systems with Applications*	7,421	219,055	1,988
174	0014-4983	D	*Explorations in Economic History*	312	2,082	860
175	0894-4865	B	*Family Business Review*	202	4,416	996
176	1354-5701	C	*Feminist Economics*	268	1,957	948
177	0949-2984	B	*Finance and Stochastics*	221	1,539	39
178	0015-198X	D	*Financial Analysts Journal*	377	5,471	1,368
179	0046-3892	D	*Financial Management*	366	2,948	632
180	0732-8516	D	*Financial Review*	255	1,390	79
181	1936-6582	C	*Flexible Services and Manufacturing Journal*	252	2,078	14
182	0306-9192	C	*Food Policy*	929	57,158	5,790
183	1554-0642	C	*Foundation and Trends in Accounting*	31	410	12
184	1567-2395	B	*Foundation and Trends in Finance*	17	487	9
185	1551-3076	D	*Foundations and trends in econometrics*	12	0	74
186	0016-3287	C	*Futures*	853	36,415	1,933

187	1568-4539	D	*Fuzzy Optimization and Decision Making*	204	445	8
188	0165-0114	D	*Fuzzy Sets and Systems*	1,883	13,787	100
189	0899-8256	C	*Games and Economic Behavior*	1,227	7,378	813
190	0968-6673	D	*Gender, Work & Organization*	388	3,117	1,031
191	1465-6485	D	*German Economic Review*	259	1,158	334
192	0959-3780	B	*Global Environmental Change*	1,081	104,707	17,896
193	1470-2266	D	*Global Networks*	260	2,601	415
194	2042-5791	C	*Global Strategy Journal*	245	1,015	338
195	0952-1895	B	*Governance*	451	4,211	2,166
196	0740-624X	C	*Government Information Quarterly*	656	79,759	1,347
197	1059-6011	C	*Group & Organization Management*	251	4,191	1,126
198	1089-2699	D	*Group Dynamics*	164	4,496	166
199	1368-4302	D	*Group Processes & Intergroup Relations*	480	6,390	3,935
200	0361-6274	C	*Health Care Management Review*	361	2,581	1,045
201	1386-9620	D	*Health Care Management Science*	301	8,025	309
202	1057-9230	C	*Health Economics*	1,112	8,390	0
203	1744-1331	D	*Health Economics, Policy and Law*	347	2,061	901
204	1471-1842	D	*Health Information and Libraries Journal*	0	0	0
205	0168-8510	C	*Health Policy*	1,576	23,837	5,415
206	1475-6773	C	*Health Services Research*	0	0	0
207	0018-1560	C	*Higher Education*	917	17,094	3,691
208	0952-8733	D	*Higher Education Policy*	288	0	407
209	0951-5224	D	*Higher Education Quarterly*	258	1,738	383
210	0018-2702	D	*History of Political Economy*	425	1,705	333
211	0018-7208	C	*Human Factors: The Journal of the Human Factors and Ergonomics Society*	705	9,818	4,685
212	0895-9285	D	*Human Performance*	174	4,792	943

213	0018-7267	C	*Human Relations*	685	15,310	5,07
214	1044-8004	D	*Human Resource Development Quarterly*	250	2,485	403
215	0090-4848	C	*Human Resource Management*	528	5,736	1,182
216	0954-5395	D	*Human Resource Management Journal*	276	3,910	1,023
217	1053-4822	C	*Human Resource Management Review*	328	21,362	500
218	1478-4491	C	*Human Resources for Health*	559	22,983	4,456
219	0018-9391	D	*IEEE Transactions on Engineering Management*	784	12,943	77
220	1089-778X	B	*IEEE Transactions on Evolutionary Computation*	799	14,948	347
221	1524-9050	D	*IEEE Transactions on Intelligent Transportation Systems*	2,465	49,922	1,231
222	1041-4347	D	*IEEE Transactions on Knowledge and Data Engineering*	1,950	34,018	831
223	2472-5854	C	*IISE Transactions*	209	37	17
224	2041-4161	B	*IMF Economic Review*	210	1,416	571
225	0019-7939	C	*Industrial & labor relations review*	537	5,681	2,560
226	0960-6491	C	*Industrial and Corporate Change*	441	8,184	0
227	1754-9426	D	*Industrial and Organizational Psychology*	809	7,634	801
228	0263-5577	D	*Industrial Management & Data Systems*	699	28,118	203
229	0019-8501	C	*Industrial Marketing Management*	1,260	81,940	689
230	0019-8676	D	*Industrial Relations: A Journal of Economy and Society*	308	1,985	932
231	1366-2716	D	*Industry & Innovation*	315	3,880	553
232	0378-7206	C	*Information & Management*	648	52,010	0
233	1471-7727	D	*Information and Organization*	137	8,161	235

234	0306-4573	D	*Information Processing & Management*	668	23,641	603
235	0197-2243	D	*Information Society*	300	0	744
236	1350-1917	C	*Information Systems Journal*	293	4,970	529
237	1047-7047	B	*Information Systems Research*	498	1,336	1,583
238	1091-9856	C	*INFORMS Journal on Computing*	0	0	0
239	0167-6687	D	*Insurance: Mathematics and Economics*	0	0	0
240	0020-6598	B	*International Economic Review*	512	3,607	0
241	0265-0487	C	*International Journal of Advertising*	398	6,603	803
242	1815-4654	B	*International Journal of Central Banking*	0	0	0
243	0959-6119	C	*International Journal of Contemporary Hospitality Management*	830	25,403	811
244	1086-4415	C	*International Journal of Electronic Commerce*	161	4,441	49
245	0169-2070	C	*International Journal of Forecasting*	742	18,409	867
246	0308-1079	C	*International Journal of General Systems*	419	1,142	213
247	0278-4319	C	*International Journal of Hospitality Management*	1,176	48,205	992
248	0268-4012	C	*International Journal of Information Management*	855	45,253	894
249	1460-8545	B	*International Journal of Management Reviews*	271	10,133	1,032
250	0144-3577	C	*International Journal of Operations & Production Management*	574	15,457	247
251	0960-0035	C	*International Journal of Physical Distribution & Logistics Management*	400	15,801	267
252	0925-5273	B	*International Journal of Production Economics*	2,8	123,362	629
253	0020-7543	C	*International Journal of Production Research*	3,816	39,694	481

254	0263-7863	C	*International Journal of Project Management*	950	151,455	598
255	0167-8116	B	*International Journal of Research in Marketing*	454	17,639	1,015
256	1099-2340	C	*International Journal of Tourism Research*	427	3,762	625
257	0309-1317	C	*International Journal of Urban and Regional Research*	940	12,948	1,542
258	1096-7494	B	*International Public Management Journal*	253	4,118	480
259	0266-2426	C	*International Small Business Journal: Researching Entrepreneurship*	449	7,646	734
260	1751-5823	C	*International Statistical Review*	0	0	0
261	1066-2243	C	*Internet Research*	332	11,935	377
262	0021-9886	C	*JCMS: Journal of Common Market Studies*	1,141	6,406	2,869
263	0165-4101	A	*Journal of Accounting and Economics*	382	32,503	436
264	0021-8456	A	*Journal of Accounting Research*	343	9,645	856
265	0091-3367	C	*Journal of Advertising*	254	11,309	846
266	1471-0358	C	*Journal of Agrarian Change*	373	3,823	844
267	0883-7252	A	*Journal of Applied Econometrics*	499	2,531	1,390
268	0021-9010	A	*Journal of Applied Psychology*	116	0	0
269	0378-4266	C	*Journal of Banking & Finance*	2,242	96,994	1,237
270	0735-0015	B	*Journal of Business & Economic Statistics*	502	4,190	611
271	0889-3268	C	*Journal of Business and Psychology*	365	16,532	3,960
272	0167-4544	C	*Journal of Business Ethics*	3,214	74,485	6,829
273	0735-3766	C	*Journal of Business Logistics*	265	2,909	242
274	0148-2963	C	*Journal of Business Research*	3,018	220,730	2,920

275	0883-9026	A	*Journal of Business Venturing*	377	37,741	1,242
276	0959-6526	C	*Journal of Cleaner Production*	8,659	354,352	5,872
277	0021-9916	A	*Journal of Communication*	588	12,991	8,664
278	1083-6101	B	*Journal of Computer-Mediated Communication*	290	17,849	7,597
279	0022-0027	A	*Journal of Conflict Resolution*	492	4,555	5,228
280	1057-7408	B	*Journal of Consumer Psychology*	485	32,310	6,632
281	1537-5277	A	*Journal of Consumer Research*	796	44,882	18,690
282	0929-1199	C	*Journal of Corporate Finance*	938	46,277	2,148
283	0304-3878	B	*Journal of Development Economics*	761	38,424	5,063
284	0304-4076	A	*Journal of Econometrics*	1,327	16,776	1,549
285	0167-2681	C	*Journal of Economic Behavior & Organization*	1,862	37,018	7,777
286	0165-1889	C	*Journal of Economic Dynamics and Control*	1,160	14,696	822
287	1468-2710	B	*Journal of Economic Geography*	347	5,044	867
288	1381-4338	A	*Journal of Economic Growth*	100	4,526	1,052
289	0022-0515	A	*Journal of Economic Literature*	717	0	3,235
290	0895-3309	A	*Journal of Economic Perspectives*	412	28,270	24,159
291	0950-0804	C	*Journal of Economic Surveys*	378	4,352	1,09
292	0022-0531	B	*Journal of Economic Theory*	1,025	9,775	515
293	0268-0939	C	*Journal of Education Policy*	505	5,850	1,790
294	0095-0696	C	*Journal of Environmental Economics and Management*	594	10,324	2,300

295	1350-1763	B	*Journal of European Public Policy*	691	6,366	2,373
296	0022-1031	C	*Journal of Experimental Social Psychology*	1,175	24,454	21,025
297	1877-8585	C	*Journal of Family Business Strategy*	247	12,779	55
298	0022-1090	B	*Journal of Financial and Quantitative Analysis*	676	9,061	763
299	1479-8409	C	*Journal of Financial Econometrics*	216	1,484	92
300	0304-405X	A+	*Journal of Financial Economics*	1,126	101,080	2,843
301	1042-9573	C	*Journal of Financial Intermediation*	276	4,967	329
302	1386-4181	C	*Journal of Financial Markets*	272	5,883	220
303	0920-8550	C	*Journal of Financial Services Research*	204	2,133	105
304	1572-3089	C	*Journal of Financial Stability*	554	16,052	657
305	0925-5001	C	*Journal of Global Optimization*	1,067	3,551	228
306	0167-6296	B	*Journal of Health Economics*	757	13,838	9,706
307	1096-3480	C	*Journal of Hospitality & Tourism Research*	221	1,104	614
308	0022-166X	A	*Journal of Human Resources*	313	6,87	3,403
309	1088-1980	C	*Journal of Industrial Ecology*	1,087	8,949	4,977
310	0268-3962	C	*Journal of Information Technology*	218	4,883	573
311	1094-9968	B	*Journal of Interactive Marketing*	215	12,905	784
312	0047-2506	A	*Journal of International Business Studies*	485	17,309	1,054
313	0022-1996	A	*Journal of International Economics*	722	16,760	1,585
314	1075-4253	C	*Journal of International Management*	285	9,784	79
315	1069-031X	C	*Journal of International Marketing*	188	8,299	124
316	0261-5606	C	*Journal of International Money and Finance*	1,013	19,248	968

317	0734-306X	A+	*Journal of Labor Economics*	327	10,470	3,091
318	0149-2063	A	*Journal of Management*	677	21,650	12,801
319	0742-597X	C	*Journal of Management in Engineering*	621	16,445	58
320	0742-1222	B	*Journal of Management Information Systems*	375	11,492	473
321	0022-2380	A	*Journal of Management Studies*	526	20,478	2,879
322	0278-6125	C	*Journal of Manufacturing Systems*	639	19,032	93
323	0022-2429	A+	*Journal of Marketing*	422	45,990	2,804
324	0022-2437	A	*Journal of Marketing Research*	540	34,767	6,027
325	0304-3932	A	*Journal of Monetary Economics*	674	19,022	936
326	0022-2879	B	*Journal of Money, Credit and Banking*	780	5,787	735
327	0047-259X	C	*Journal of Multivariate Analysis*	1,373	4,983	248
328	0963-1798	C	*Journal of Occupational and Organizational Psychology*	332	8,777	2,494
329	1076-8998	B	*Journal of Occupational Health Psychology*	21	0	0
330	0272-6963	A	*Journal of Operations Management*	409	23,304	613
331	0894-3796	B	*Journal of Organizational Behavior*	634	12,604	4,125
332	0022-3514	A	*Journal of Personality and Social Psychology*	303	246	0
333	0276-8739	C	*Journal of Policy Analysis and Management*	554	0	4,024
334	0022-3808	A+	*Journal of Political Economy*	527	16,341	4,194
335	0933-1433	C	*Journal of Population Economics*	347	7,362	1,904
336	0737-6782	B	*Journal of Product Innovation Management*	720	14,552	1,083
337	1477-9803	A	*Journal of Public Administration Research and Theory*	516	7,593	1,707

338	0047-2727	B	*Journal of Public Economics*	999	34,493	6,925
339	0743-9156	C	*Journal of Public Policy & Marketing*	36	166	3
340	1478-4092	C	*Journal of Purchasing and Supply Management*	286	9,870	98
341	0022-4065	C	*Journal of Quality Technology*	301	1,953	23
342	0022-4146	C	*Journal of Regional Science*	654	3,612	770
343	0022-4359	B	*Journal of Retailing*	378	31,551	1,976
344	0895-5646	C	*Journal of Risk and Uncertainty*	183	2,045	550
345	0022-4405	C	*Journal of School Psychology*	366	12,436	999
346	1757-5818	C	*Journal of Service Management*	297	12,944	181
347	1094-6705	A	*Journal of Service Research*	272	6,862	758
348	0047-2778	C	*Journal of Small Business Management*	0	0	0
349	1523-2409	A	*Journal of Supply Chain Management*	275	3,702	0
350	0966-9582	C	*Journal of Sustainable Tourism*	690	12,894	2,032
351	0092-0703	A	*Journal of the Academy of Marketing Science*	368	37,625	1,800
352	1532-2882	C	*Journal of the American Society for Information Science and Technology*	0	0	0
353	0162-1459	A	*Journal of the American Statistical Association*	1,342	8,354	2,886
354	1536-9323	C	*Journal of the Association for Information Systems*	362	9,362	16
355	1542-4766	A	*Journal of the European Economic Association*	441	8,991	2,785
356	0964-1998	C	*Journal of the Royal Statistical Society: Series A (Statistics in Society)*	600	10,082	1,427
357	1369-7412	A	*Journal of the Royal Statistical Society:*	401	4,715	565

			Series B (Statistical Methodology)			
358	0035-9254	C	*Journal of the Royal Statistical Society: Series C (Applied Statistics)*	429	2,180	388
359	0143-9782	C	*Journal of Time Series Analysis*	490	1,282	404
360	0966-6923	C	*Journal of Transport Geography*	1,479	63,030	2,637
361	0047-2875	B	*Journal of Travel Research*	522	774	834
362	0094-1190	B	*Journal of Urban Economics*	425	15,564	2,301
363	0001-8791	C	*Journal of Vocational Behavior*	769	50,805	2,485
364	1090-9516	C	*Journal of World Business*	606	42,685	540
365	1930-2975	C	*Judgment and Decision Making*	0	0	0
366	0927-5371	C	*Labour Economics*	701	17,047	1,102
367	0024-6301	C	*Long Range Planning*	400	18,700	320
368	1044-5005	C	*Management Accounting Research*	256	0	110
369	0025-1909	A+	*Management Science*	1,751	42,173	8,611
370	1523-4614	A	*Manufacturing & Service Operations Management*	424	6,221	327
371	0732-2399	A	*Marketing Science*	532	15,216	2,891
372	0960-1627	B	*Mathematical Finance*	268	941	43
373	0025-5610	B	*Mathematical Programming*	905	3,937	290
374	0364-765X	C	*Mathematics of Operations Research*	466	2,348	83
375	0025-7079	C	*Medical Care*	1,673	14,463	0
376	0272-989X	C	*Medical Decision Making*	747	5,659	3,662
377	0887-378X	C	*Milbank Quarterly*	426	4,291	6,421
378	0276-7783	A	*MIS Quarterly*	447	55,490	83
379	1540-1960	C	*MIS Quarterly Executive*	0	0	0
380	0027-3171	B	*Multivariate Behavioral Research*	464	9,776	414
381	1566-113X	C	*Networks and Spatial Economics*	280	1,027	62

382	1356-3467	C	*New Political Economy*	352	3,077	1,404
383	1351-0711	C	*Occupational and Environmental Medicine*	2,372	10,978	18,291
384	0305-0483	B	*Omega*	983	32,930	224
385	0030-364X	B	*Operations Research*	893	15,154	535
386	0171-6468	C	*OR Spectrum*	307	2,438	30
387	1350-5084	C	*Organization*	558	7,252	1,660
388	1086-0266	C	*Organization & Environment*	246	3,008	616
389	1047-7039	A	*Organization Science*	713	62,003	4,398
390	0170-8406	C	*Organization Studies*	890	22,663	3,484
391	0749-5978	C	*Organizational Behavior and Human Decision Processes*	537	23,903	7,973
392	2041-3866	C	*Organizational Psychology Review*	121	3,641	355
393	1094-4281	B	*Organizational Research Methods*	247	5,817	1,017
394	0305-9049	C	*Oxford Bulletin of Economics and Statistics*	420	2,477	1,031
395	0146-1672	C	*Personality and Social Psychology Bulletin*	1,042	21,362	32,501
396	0031-5826	A	*Personnel Psychology*	459	7,439	3,614
397	1170-7690	C	*PharmacoEconomics*	879	6,643	3,256
398	0032-2687	C	*Policy Sciences*	217	4,396	1,052
399	0190-292X	C	*Policy Studies Journal*	405	7,792	2,006
400	0032-3217	C	*Political Studies*	539	3,657	3,507
401	1059-1478	B	*Production and Operations Management*	1,178	5,461	1,226
402	0953-7287	C	*Production Planning & Control*	693	5,047	166
403	0309-1325	A	*Progress in Human Geography*	637	18,870	4,989
404	0033-2909	A+	*Psychological Bulletin*	89	48	0
405	0340-0727	C	*Psychological Research*	797	6,260	1,671
406	0033-295X	A	*Psychological Review*	114	0	0
407	0956-7976	A	*Psychological Science*	1,808	15,798	149,303
408	0742-6046	C	*Psychology & Marketing*	747	8,846	1,918
409	0033-3123	B	*Psychometrika*	440	6,420	310
410	0033-3298	C	*Public Administration*	700	6,816	1,856
411	0033-3352	B	*Public Administration Review*	1,346	16,487	5,577
412	1471-9037	C	*Public Management Review*	619	4,486	1,040

413	1537-5331	C	Public Opinion Quarterly	497	3,565	3,899
414	1759-7323	A	Quantitative Economics	227	880	229
415	1570-7156	A	Quantitative Marketing and Economics	113	1,526	114
416	1747-0218	C	Quarterly Journal of Experimental Psychology	1,449	11,932	7,838
417	1554-0626	A	Quarterly Journal of Political Science	0	0	0
418	0166-0462	C	Regional Science and Urban Economics	640	5,841	1,225
419	0034-3404	C	Regional Studies	1,155	9,612	2,738
420	1748-5983	C	Regulation & Governance	312	3,307	892
421	0951-8320	C	Reliability Engineering & System Safety	1,996	54,08	560
422	0958-2029	C	Research Evaluation	284	3,486	0
423	0361-0365	C	Research in Higher Education	323	7,493	2,227
424	0191-3085	C	Research in Organizational Behavior	91	6,070	642
425	0048-7333	B	Research Policy	1,208	124,485	12,132
426	0928-7655	C	Resource and Energy Economics	392	9,276	420
427	1380-6653	B	Review of Accounting Studies	336	16,645	534
428	1094-2025	A	Review of Economic Dynamics	395	6,691	597
429	0034-6535	A	Review of Economics and Statistics	717	14,946	7,583
430	1750-6816	B	Review of Environmental Economics and Policy	213	6,021	1,276
431	1572-3097	B	Review of Finance	208	268	238
432	0893-9454	A+	Review of Financial Studies	1,051	22,678	2,002
433	0969-2290	C	Review of International Political Economy	329	3,718	1,815
434	1467-9469	C	Scandinavian Journal of Statistics	0	0	0
435	0355-3140	C	Scandinavian Journal of Work, Environment & Health	566	5,065	2,985

436	0162-2439	C	Science, Technology, & Human Values	320	2,150	3,356
437	1095-7189	C	SIAM Journal on Optimization	773	0	193
438	1532-9194	C	Sloan Management Review	0	0	0
439	0921-898X	C	Small Business Economics	774	14,846	2,043
440	1534-7605	C	Social Forces	975	0	5,775
441	0277-9536	C	Social Science & Medicine	4,029	106,339	46,189
442	0306-3127	C	Social Studies of Science	356	5,793	5,357
443	1475-1461	B	Socio-Economic Review	271	3,593	1,872
444	0038-0385	C	Sociology	915	19,267	7,998
445	1467-9566	C	Sociology of Health & Illness	0	0	0
446	1932-4391	B	Strategic Entrepreneurship Journal	221	4,041	669
447	0143-2095	A+	Strategic Management Journal	1,028	34,342	4,915
448	1476-1270	C	Strategic Organization	215	4,031	493
449	1070-5511	A	Structural Equation Modeling: A Multidisciplinary Journal	459	3,812	326
450	0307-5079	C	Studies in Higher Education	1,027	9,715	4,271
451	1359-8546	C	Supply Chain Management: An International Journal	359	23,412	282
452	0167-6911	C	Systems & Control Letters	1	7,263	50
453	0040-1625	C	Technological Forecasting and Social Change	2,142	92,758	3,021
454	0166-4972	C	Technovation	499	46,936	611
455	1941-6520	A+	The Academy of Management Annals	233	9,816	679
456	0001-4826	A	The Accounting Review	794	41,73	367
457	0275-0740	C	The American Review of Public Administration	406	3,171	972
458	0090-5364	A	The Annals of Statistics	855	13,568	906

459	0007-1315	D	*The British Journal of Sociology*	538	4,235	3,448
460	0889-4019	D	*The Career Development Quarterly*	250	3,195	155
461	0305-7410	C	*The China Quarterly*	0	0	0
462	1368-4221	B	*The Econometrics Journal*	231	1,279	217
463	0013-0117	D	*The Economic History Review*	1,326	2,232	1,387
464	0013-0133	A	*The Economic Journal*	806	10,318	10,664
465	0195-6574	D	*The Energy Journal*	546	7,305	68
466	0967-2567	D	*The European Journal of the History of Economic Thought*	366	840	230
467	0022-0507	C	*The Journal of Economic History*	769	1,417	2,072
468	0022-1082	A+	*The Journal of Finance*	866	28,904	3,604
469	0022-2186	C	*The Journal of Law and Economics*	277	3,404	2,26
470	8756-6222	C	*The Journal Of Law, Economics, and Organization*	203	1,207	561
471	0963-8687	C	*The Journal of Strategic Information Systems*	285	16,119	152
472	0892-9912	C	*The Journal of Technology Transfer*	490	5,116	883
473	1048-9843	B	*The Leadership Quarterly*	597	75,422	3,218
474	0033-5533	A+	*The Quarterly Journal of Economics*	400	19,466	16,496
475	0741-6261	B	*The RAND Journal of Economics*	321	3,924	698
476	0034-6527	A+	*The Review of Economic Studies*	433	9,267	3,137
477	0347-0520	C	*The Scandinavian Journal of Economics*	426	3,842	199
478	0038-0261	C	*The Sociological Review*	777	5,737	13,892
479	1536-867X	B	*The Stata Journal*	0	0	0
480	0257-3032	B	*The World Bank Research Observer*	126	2,509	977
481	1555-7561	A	*Theoretical Economics*	0	0	0
482	0261-5177	B	*Tourism Management*	1,620	124,216	3,173
483	0967-070X	C	*Transport Policy*	1,112	28,194	1,883
484	0144-1647	C	*Transport Reviews*	414	6,084	1,726

485	0049-4488	C	*Transportation*	641	6,468	1,508
486	0965-8564	C	*Transportation Research Part A: Policy and Practice*	1,633	67,500	4,385
487	0191-2615	B	*Transportation Research Part B: Methodological*	1,371	49,212	800
488	0968-090X	B	*Transportation Research Part C: Emerging Technologies*	1,784	74,458	1,613
489	1361-9209	C	*Transportation Research Part D: Transport and Environment*	1,391	46,435	2,321
490	1366-5545	C	*Transportation Research Part E: Logistics and Transportation Review*	1,118	41,055	332
491	0041-1655	B	*Transportation Science*	485	10,521	251
492	0042-0980	C	*Urban Studies*	1,919	18,675	7,458
493	1098-3015	C	*Value in Health*	8,807	15,738	2,060
494	0140-2382	B	*West European Politics*	728	6,840	1,845
495	0950-0170	C	*Work Employment and Society*	782	12,485	5,113
496	0730-8884	C	*Work and Occupations*	219	2,454	1,108
497	0267-8373	C	*Work and Stress*	189	4,772	1,447
498	0305-750X	C	*World Development*	2,050	65,047	12,724
499	1468-4462	B	*Information, Communication & Society*	0	0	0
500	1619-4500	D	*4OR: A Quarterly Journal of Operations Research*	242	480	90

Appendix II: Top 500 Handelsblatt ranking journals in economics, their classes, and altmetric data

No.	ISSN	Class	Journal Name	Articles in Crossref	Mendeley Counts	Altmetric Scores
1	1032-3732	E	*Accounting History*	363	1,347	171
2	1017-6772	D	*African Development Review*	407	2,020	157
3	0742-4477	D	*Agribusiness*	341	1,259	99
4	1459-6067	D	*Agricultural and Food Science*	0	0	0
5	1068-2805	E	*Agricultural and Resource Economics Review*	242	2,148	34
6	0169-5150	C	*Agricultural Economics*	574	7,521	1,100
7	0889-048X	D	*Agriculture and Human Values*	593	8,839	1,615
8	1945-7782	A+	*American Economic Journal: Applied Economics*	325	9,19	8,533
9	1945-7731	A	*American Economic Journal: Economic Policy*	0	0	0
10	1945-7707	A+	*American Economic Journal: Macroeconomics*	283	4,377	1,514
11	1945-7669	A	*American Economic Journal: Microeconomics*	350	0	746
12	0002-8282	A+	*American Economic Review*	1,982	110,178	24,777
13	0002-9092	C	*American Journal of Agricultural Economics*	915	5,905	3,844
14	1465-7252	D	*American Law and Economics Review*	172	762	682
15	0003-0554	A	*American Political Science Review*	495	16,721	7,039
16	1614-2446	D	*Annals of Finance*	163	503	21
17	1370-4788	E	*Annals of Public and Cooperative Economics*	282	1,339	140
18	1941-1383	A	*Annual Review of Economics*	191	8,187	1,519
19	1941-1367	A	*Annual Review of Financial Economics*	140	2,958	141
20	1941-1340	C	*Annual review of resource economics*	0	0	0
21	0883-024X	E	*Anthropology of Work Review*	205	262	192

22	2040-5790	D	Applied Economic Perspectives and Policy	368	2,987	1,580
23	0003-6846	D	Applied Economics	3,146	17,848	2,813
24	0143-6228	C	Applied Geography	1,505	69,801	2,388
25	1175-5652	D	Applied Health Economics and Health Policy	527	3,193	1,528
26	1350-486X	D	Applied Mathematical Finance	172	654	14
27	1365-7305	D	Aquaculture Economics & Management	185	2,616	128
28	1364-985X	D	Australian Journal of Agricultural and Resource Economics	396	2,509	638
29	0312-8962	D	Australian Journal of Management	258	1,308	299
30	1935-1704	F	B.E. Journal of Theoretical Economics	0	370	0
31	1050-4753	D	Behavioral Research in Accounting	138	1,443	69
32	2214-8469	E	Borsa Istanbul review	0	0	0
33	0007-1080	C	British Journal of Industrial Relations	516	2,03	745
34	0007-2303	B	Brookings Papers on Economic Activity	0	0	0
35	1369-5258	D	Business and Politics	138	1,382	0
36	0007-666X	D	Business Economics	311	948	273
37	1052-150X	C	Business Ethics Quarterly	461	6,556	248
38	0007-6805	D	Business History Review	935	1,681	357
39	0008-1256	C	California Management Review	280	12,740	980
40	0309-166X	D	Cambridge Journal of Economics	544	0	0
41	1752-1378	C	Cambridge Journal of Regions, Economy and Society	285	2,825	0
42	0008-3976	D	Canadian Journal of Agricultural Economics	0	0	0
43	0008-4085	D	Canadian Journal of Economics	0	0	0
44	1435-246X	D	Central European Journal of Operations Research	398	1,071	44
45	1610-241X	D	CESifo Economic Studies	226	1,406	0
46	1671-2234	D	China & World Economy	250	1,103	227
47	1043-951X	D	China Economic Review	675	14,829	342

48	0305-7410	C	*China Quarterly*	0	0	0
49	1680-2012	E	*China Review*	0	0	0
50	1469-3062	C	*Climate Policy*	547	662	4,071
51	0010-3802	D	*Community Development Journal*	487	3,432	0
52	1024-5294	D	*Competition & Change*	198	0	375
53	1619-697X	E	*Computational Management Science*	197	767	77
54	0738-8942	C	*Conflict Management and Peace Science*	282	2,193	1,715
55	1043-4062	D	*Constitutional Political Economy*	165	1,102	175
56	0823-9150	B	*Contemporary Accounting Research*	581	0	672
57	0891-3811	E	*Critical Review*	180	1,958	354
58	1545-8490	D	*Decision Analysis*	224	936	233
59	1024-2694	E	*Defence and Peace Economics*	398	1,216	323
60	0070-3370	B	*Demography*	728	11,312	9,623
61	0012-1533	F	*Developing Economies*	0	0	0
62	0012-155X	C	*Development and Change*	565	7,123	1,636
63	0950-6764	D	*Development Policy Review*	466	3,731	1,371
64	2153-0785	C	*Dynamic Games and Applications*	278	714	65
65	1212-3609	D	*E+M Ekonomie a Management*	280	2,297	1
66	0885-2006	C	*Early Childhood Research Quarterly*	562	20,193	2,335
67	0921-8009	C	*Ecological Economics*	2,257	128,242	7,198
68	0747-4938	C	*Econometric Reviews*	387	1,888	146
69	0266-4666	B	*Econometric Theory*	478	1,327	304
70	0012-9682	A+	*Econometrica*	720	9,781	2,125
71	0143-831X	D	*Economic and Industrial Democracy*	402	1,852	418
72	0012-9984	E	*Economic and Social Review*	0	0	0
73	0013-0079	C	*Economic Development and Cultural Change*	286	5,387	1,49
74	0891-2424	D	*Economic Development Quarterly*	279	1,932	1,040
75	0013-0095	B	*Economic Geography*	311	2,224	888
76	0095-2583	C	*Economic Inquiry*	776	5,121	4,573
77	0264-9993	D	*Economic Modelling*	2,723	55,033	2,011
78	0266-4658	B	*Economic Policy*	164	2,280	1,308

79	0939-3625	B	*Economic Systems*	379	7,116	195
80	0953-5314	B	*Economic Systems Research*	221	2,141	204
81	0938-2259	C	*Economic Theory*	556	1,876	124
82	0013-0427	D	*Economica*	386	1,246	1,117
83	1570-677X	C	*Economics & Human Biology*	485	4,720	3,551
84	0954-1985	D	*Economics & Politics*	167	1,060	628
85	2071-789X	D	*Economics & Sociology*	496	3,527	12
86	0266-2671	D	*Economics and Philosophy*	290	1,008	241
87	0165-1765	D	*Economics Letters*	3,708	45,500	3,758
88	0272-7757	C	*Economics of Education Review*	0	0	0
89	1043-8599	D	*Economics of Innovation and New Technology*	342	1,818	265
90	0967-0750	E	*Economics of Transition*	253	697	106
91	2212-0122	C	*Economics of Transportation*	123	1,908	142
92	0308-5147	C	*Economy and Society*	216	3,255	750
93	1557-3060	C	*Education Finance and Policy*	190	1,690	1,373
94	1566-0141	C	*Emerging Markets Review*	354	6,437	67
95	0377-7332	D	*Empirical Economics*	1,130	9,578	695
96	0360-5442	C	*Energy*	8,847	246,419	5,179
97	0140-9883	B	*Energy Economics*	2,202	68,750	4,747
98	0195-6574	C	*Energy Journal*	546	7,305	68
99	1467-2227	E	*Enterprise and Society*	876	1,442	399
100	0898-5626	C	*Entrepreneurship and Regional Development*	347	6,908	273
101	1355-770X	D	*Environment and Development Economics*	384	2,375	786
102	0308-518X	C	*Environment and Planning A: Economy and Space*	1,349	16,081	3,513
103	0263-774X	D	*Environment and Planning C: Government and Policy*	493	6,581	521
104	0924-6460	D	*Environmental and Resource Economics*	837	9,150	1,432
105	1432-847X	E	*Environmental Economics and Policy Studies*	226	2,576	113
106	0963-2719	D	*Environmental Values*	376	1,953	213
107	2190-9733	D	*European Actuarial Journal*	184	0	20
108	0955-534X	D	*European Business Review*	287	6,595	97
109	0014-2921	C	*European Economic Review*	1,003	24,012	2,589
110	1354-7798	D	*European Financial Management*	320	1,891	148

111	0959-6801	C	European journal of industrial relations	246	1,260	396
112	1354-0661	B	European Journal of International Relations	293	3,150	2,158
113	0377-2217	B	European Journal of Operational Research	5,251	162,564	1,839
114	0176-2680	D	European Journal of Political Economy	540	9,115	1,321
115	0168-6577	C	European Journal of Population	266	1,324	671
116	0165-1587	D	European Review of Agricultural Economics	296	3,214	459
117	1361-4916	D	European Review of Economic History	183	888	279
118	1386-4157	C	Experimental Economics	308	9,595	925
119	1473-7167	D	Expert Review of Pharmacoeconomics & Outcomes Research	717	5,259	2,094
120	0014-4983	C	Explorations in Economic History	312	2,082	860
121	1354-5701	D	Feminist Economics	268	1,957	948
122	0949-2984	C	Finance and Stochastics	221	1,539	39
123	0015-198X	D	Financial Analysts Journal	377	0	11
124	0046-3892	C	Financial Management	366	2,948	632
125	0732-8516	C	Financial Review	255	1,390	79
126	0015-2218	D	FinanzArchiv: Public Finance Analysis	165	658	103
127	0143-5671	D	Fiscal Studies	243	1,158	544
128	0306-9192	C	Food Policy	929	462	5,806
129	0015-7120	D	Foreign affairs	0	0	0
130	1389-9341	D	Forest Policy and Economics	1,085	31,496	1,691
131	1567-2395	A	Foundation and Trends in Finance	17	487	9
132	1554-0642	D	Foundations and Trends in Accounting	31	410	12
133	1551-3076	D	Foundations and Trends in Econometrics	12	179	0
134	1551-3114	C	Foundations and Trends in Entrepreneurship	36	0	18
135	2073-4336	D	Games	315	166	257
136	0899-8256	C	Games and Economic Behavior	1,227	7,378	813
137	1465-6485	D	German Economic Review	259	1,158	334

138	0002-1121	E	*German Journal of Agricultural Economics*	0	0	0
139	1526-3800	C	*Global Environmental Politics*	390	7,268	891
140	1044-0283	E	*Global Finance Journal*	219	4,039	27
141	1470-2266	D	*Global Networks*	260	2,601	415
142	0017-4815	D	*Growth and Change*	347	1,407	404
143	1574-0706	A	*Handbook of Economic Forecasting*	0	0	0
144	0017-8012	E	*Harvard Business Review*	0	0	0
145	1386-9620	D	*Health Care Management Science*	301	8,025	309
146	1057-9230	C	*Health Economics*	1,112	8,39	8,986
147	1744-1331	D	*Health Economics, Policy and Law*	347	2,061	901
148	0268-1080	C	*Health Policy and Planning*	968	12,330	7,962
149	0017-9124	C	*Health Services Research*	1,202	0	11,049
150	0018-2702	D	*History of Political Economy*	425	1,705	333
151	1051-1482	D	*Housing Policy Debate*	351	1,640	1,956
152	0267-3037	C	*Housing Studies*	693	5,466	1,342
153	1044-8004	D	*Human Resource Development Quarterly*	250	2,485	403
154	0019-7939	C	*Industrial & Labor Relations Review*	537	5,681	2,56
155	0960-6491	C	*Industrial and Corporate Change*	441	8,184	0
156	0019-8676	D	*Industrial Relations: A Journal of Economy and Society*	308	1,985	932
157	1366-2716	D	*Industry and Innovation*	315	0	555
158	0167-6245	D	*Information Economics and Policy*	242	0	457
159	1617-9846	E	*Information Systems and e-Business Management*	224	1,609	99
160	0167-6687	D	*Insurance: Mathematics and Economics*	1,018	6,590	221
161	0092-2102	D	*Interfaces*	467	2,501	225
162	0020-6598	A	*International Economic Review*	512	0	0
163	2110-7017	E	*International Economics*	243	3,610	123
164	1554-7191	D	*International Entrepreneurship and Management Journal*	386	5,564	202

165	1367-0271	E	*International Finance*	181	546	115
166	1815-4654	C	*International Journal of Central Banking*	0	0	0
167	2146-4553	D	*International Journal of Energy Economics and Policy*	47	0	0
168	0169-2070	C	*International Journal of Forecasting*	742	18,409	867
169	0020-7276	C	*International Journal of Game Theory*	391	2,128	62
170	2199-9023	D	*International Journal of Health Economics and Management*	101	0	0
171	0167-7187	C	*International Journal of Industrial Organization*	592	8,078	336
172	0925-5273	C	*International Journal of Production Economics*	2,800	123,362	629
173	0167-8116	C	*International Journal of Research in Marketing*	454	17,639	1,015
174	1558-6235	E	*International journal of sport finance*	0	0	0
175	0219-0249	D	*International Journal of Theoretical and Applied Finance*	460	813	50
176	0309-1317	B	*International Journal of Urban and Regional Research*	940	12,948	1,542
177	0020-7780	D	*International Labour Review*	327	1,275	403
178	0020-8183	A	*International Organization*	341	6,588	3,414
179	0160-0176	D	*International Regional Science Review*	164	1,144	101
180	0269-2171	E	*International Review of Applied Economics*	363	1,793	600
181	1051-4694	C	*International Review of Comparative Public Policy*	0	0	0
182	1059-0560	E	*International Review of Economics & Finance*	1,104	19,432	141
183	1477-3880	D	*International Review of Economics Education*	227	1,802	153
184	1932-1465	C	*International Review of Environmental and Resource Economics*	0	0	0

185	1369-412X	E	*International Review of Finance*	308	1,344	111
186	1057-5219	D	*International Review of Financial Analysis*	850	14,321	2,451
187	0927-5940	D	*International Tax and Public Finance*	355	2,041	399
188	0922-1425	E	*Japan and the World Economy*	248	2,934	93
189	0021-9886	B	*JCMS: Journal of Common Market Studies*	1,141	6,406	2,869
190	0165-4101	A	*Journal of Accounting and Economics*	382	32,503	436
191	0021-8456	A	*Journal of Accounting Research*	343	9,645	856
192	0148-558X	D	*Journal of Accounting, Auditing & Finance*	248	2,594	151
193	1522-8916	E	*Journal of African Business*	189	1,003	62
194	0963-8024	D	*Journal of African Economies*	284	2,539	1,024
195	0021-857X	C	*Journal of Agricultural Economics*	410	3,816	445
196	0883-7252	B	*Journal of Applied Econometrics*	499	2,531	1,39
197	0266-4763	E	*Journal of Applied Statistics*	1,586	7,007	561
198	1049-0078	D	*Journal of Asian Economics*	384	6,831	69
199	0378-4266	C	*Journal of Banking & Finance*	2,242	96,994	1,237
200	2214-6350	E	*Journal of Behavioral and Experimental Finance*	197	153	81
201	1387-6996	D	*Journal of Bioeconomics*	180	1,327	527
202	0735-0015	B	*Journal of Business & Economic Statistics*	502	4,19	611
203	2155-7950	F	*Journal of Business and Economics*	268	447	0
204	0306-686X	D	*Journal of Business Finance & Accounting*	418	5,731	199
205	0148-2963	C	*Journal of Business Research*	3,018	220,73	2,920
206	1476-5284	E	*Journal of Chinese economic and business studies*	0	0	0
207	0147-5967	D	*Journal of Comparative Economics*	538	6,544	698

208	0022-0027	B	*Journal of Conflict Resolution*	492	4,555	5,228
209	0022-0078	E	*Journal of Consumer Affairs*	260	1,649	835
210	0168-7034	D	*Journal of Consumer Policy*	240	2,923	480
211	0093-5301	A	*Journal of Consumer Research*	796	44,882	18,69
212	1815-5669	E	*Journal of Contemporary Accounting & Economics*	149	3,415	108
213	0944-6532	E	*Journal of convex analysis*	0	0	0
214	0929-1199	C	*Journal of Corporate Finance*	938	46,277	2,148
215	0885-2545	D	*Journal of Cultural Economics*	202	1,095	383
216	1619-4500	C	*4OR: A Quarterly Journal of Operations Research*	242	480	90
217	0304-3878	A	*Journal of Development Economics*	761	38,424	5,063
218	0022-0388	D	*Journal of Development Studies*	1,077	9,465	2,154
219	0304-4076	B	*Journal of Econometrics*	1,327	16,776	1,549
220	0167-2681	C	*Journal of Economic Behavior & Organization*	1,862	37,018	7,777
221	0165-1889	C	*Journal of Economic Dynamics and Control*	1,160	14,696	822
222	1468-2702	B	*Journal of Economic Geography*	347	5,044	870
223	1381-4338	A	*Journal of Economic Growth*	100	4,526	1,052
224	1860-711X	E	*Journal of Economic Interaction and Coordination*	157	621	71
225	0022-0515	A+	*Journal of Economic Literature*	717	0	3,235
226	0895-3309	A	*Journal of Economic Perspectives*	412	28,270	24,159
227	1748-7870	E	*Journal of Economic Policy Reform*	207	1,099	728
228	0167-4870	C	*Journal of Economic Psychology*	734	29,480	3,725
229	0144-3585	E	*Journal of Economic Studies*	419	4,857	109
230	0950-0804	C	*Journal of Economic Surveys*	378	4,352	1,09
231	0022-0531	B	*Journal of Economic Theory*	1,025	9,775	515

232	1058-6407	C	*Journal of Economics & Management Strategy*	384	3,752	747
233	0927-5398	D	*Journal of Empirical Finance*	598	12,509	276
234	0095-0696	B	*Journal of Environmental Economics and Management*	594	10,324	2,300
235	0964-0568	D	*Journal of Environmental Planning and Management*	821	5,888	957
236	1350-1763	D	*Journal of European Public Policy*	691	0	2,357
237	0936-9937	D	*Journal of Evolutionary Economics*	383	6,123	223
238	1058-0476	E	*Journal of Family and Economic Issues*	360	5,366	1,079
239	0022-1090	A	*Journal of Financial and Quantitative Analysis*	676	9,061	763
240	1479-8409	C	*Journal of Financial Econometrics*	216	1,484	92
241	0304-405X	A+	*Journal of Financial Economics*	1,126	101,08	2,843
242	1042-9573	B	*Journal of Financial Intermediation*	276	4,967	329
243	1386-4181	B	*Journal of Financial Markets*	272	5,883	220
244	0920-8550	D	*Journal of Financial Services Research*	204	2,133	105
245	1572-3089	C	*Journal of Financial Stability*	554	16,052	657
246	0277-6693	D	*Journal of Forecasting*	421	1,499	493
247	1104-6899	D	*Journal of Forest Economics*	275	2,962	192
248	0270-7314	D	*Journal of Futures Markets*	535	1,012	144
249	1435-5930	D	*Journal of Geographical Systems*	137	925	46
250	1740-0228	C	*Journal of Global History*	342	1,148	302
251	1389-4978	D	*Journal of Happiness Studies*	797	11,259	6,459
252	0167-6296	B	*Journal of Health Economics*	757	13,838	9,706
253	0361-6878	D	*Journal of Health Politics, Policy and Law*	481	6,964	4,021

254	1360-080X	D	*Journal of Higher Education Policy and Management*	448	3,507	1,160
255	1051-1377	D	*Journal of Housing Economics*	285	2,329	310
256	1932-8575	D	*Journal of Human Capital*	133	1,666	507
257	1945-2829	D	*Journal of Human Development and Capabilities*	342	886	270
258	0022-166X	A	*Journal of Human Resources*	313	6,870	3,466
259	1566-1679	E	*Journal of Industry, Competition and Trade*	192	854	106
260	1744-1374	D	*Journal of Institutional Economics*	360	1,945	750
261	0047-2506	A	*Journal of International Business Studies*	485	17,309	1,054
262	0954-1748	D	*Journal of International Development*	671	3,945	1,490
263	1369-3034	C	*Journal of International Economic Law*	337	952	730
264	0022-1996	A	*Journal of International Economics*	722	16,760	1,588
265	1570-7385	D	*Journal of International Entrepreneurship*	170	3,482	73
266	1042-4431	D	*Journal of International Financial Markets, Institutions and Money*	695	9,867	416
267	0261-5606	C	*Journal of International Money and Finance*	1,013	19,248	968
268	0910-5476	E	*Journal of International Studies*	0	0	0
269	0734-306X	A	*Journal of Labor Economics*	327	10,470	3,091
270	0195-3613	E	*Journal of labor research*	1	0	0
271	0164-0704	D	*Journal of Macroeconomics*	711	10,761	450
272	1385-3457	D	*Journal of Management & Governance*	275	6,939	137
273	1049-2127	D	*Journal of Management Accounting Research*	210	2,746	35
274	0022-2429	A	*Journal of Marketing*	422	4,599	2,804
275	0022-2437	A	*Journal of Marketing Research*	540	34,767	6,028
276	0304-4068	D	*Journal of Mathematical Economics*	714	2,744	158

277	0899-7764	E	*Journal of media economics*	0	0	0
278	0304-3932	A	*Journal of Monetary Economics*	674	19,022	936
279	0022-2879	B	*Journal of Money, Credit and Banking*	780	5,787	735
280	1042-444X	E	*Journal of Multinational Financial Management*	230	3,339	32
281	1937-321X	D	*Journal of Neuroscience, Psychology, and Economics*	28	0	0
282	0022-3433	B	*Journal of Peace Research*	510	9,962	6,492
283	1474-7472	D	*Journal of Pension Economics and Finance*	340	1,415	267
284	0276-8739	C	*Journal of Policy Analysis and Management*	554	0	4,024
285	0161-8938	D	*Journal of Policy Modeling*	667	10,537	455
286	0022-3808	A+	*Journal of Political Economy*	527	16,341	4,194
287	0933-1433	C	*Journal of Population Economics*	347	7,362	1,904
288	0160-3477	D	*Journal of post Keynesian economics*	0	0	0
289	0895-562X	D	*Journal of Productivity Analysis*	333	3,012	125
290	0959-9916	D	*Journal of Property Research*	147	727	40
291	1467-9779	D	*Journal of public economic theory*	0	0	0
292	0047-2727	B	*Journal of Public Economics*	999	34,493	6,925
293	0896-5803	D	*Journal of Real Estate Research*	0	0	0
294	0022-4146	C	*Journal of Regional Science*	654	3,612	770
295	0922-680X	D	*Journal of Regulatory Economics*	233	1,832	309
296	0022-4367	C	*Journal of Risk and Insurance*	396	2,258	187
297	0895-5646	C	*Journal of Risk and Uncertainty*	183	2,045	550
298	0047-2778	C	*Journal of Small Business Management*	0	0	0
299	1527-0025	E	*Journal of Sports Economics*	334	927	1,988
300	0162-1459	B	*Journal of the American Statistical Association*	1,342	8,354	2,886

301	1542-4766	A	*Journal of the European Economic Association*	441	8,991	2,785
302	1868-7865	D	*Journal of the Knowledge Economy*	516	0	0
303	0160-5682	D	*Journal of the Operational Research Society*	1,384	9,795	595
304	0964-1998	C	*Journal of the Royal Statistical Society: Series A (Statistics in Society)*	600	10,082	1,427
305	1369-7412	A	*Journal of the Royal Statistical Society: Series B (Statistical Methodology)*	401	4,715	565
306	0022-5193	D	*Journal of Theoretical Biology*	3,604	37,688	5,301
307	0143-9782	C	*Journal of Time Series Analysis*	490	1,282	404
308	0022-5258	D	*Journal of Transport Economics and Policy*	0	0	0
309	0047-2875	B	*Journal of Travel Research*	522	774	834
310	0735-2166	C	*Journal of Urban Affairs*	741	4,361	1,533
311	0094-1190	B	*Journal of Urban Economics*	425	15,564	2,301
312	1090-9516	C	*Journal of World Business*	606	42,685	540
313	1011-6702	D	*Journal of World Trade*	0	0	0
314	1930-2975	C	*Judgment and Decision Making*	0	0	0
315	0023-5962	D	*Kyklos*	257	1,951	1,094
316	0023-656X	E	*Labor History*	398	692	351
317	0927-5371	C	*Labour Economics*	701	17,047	1,102
318	0023-7639	C	*Land Economics*	304	5,213	479
319	1531-426X	C	*Latin American Politics and Society*	546	2,646	0
320	0023-9186	D	*Law and Contemporary Problems*	0	0	0
321	0269-0942	E	*Local Economy: The Journal of the Local Economy Policy Unit*	530	2,764	652
322	1365-1005	C	*Macroeconomic Dynamics*	849	2,138	179
323	1740-8776	D	*Management and Organization Review*	470	0	286
324	0025-1909	A	*Management Science*	1,751	42,173	8,611
325	0143-6570	E	*Managerial and Decision Economics*	477	1,767	249

326	1523-4614	A	*Manufacturing & Service Operations Management*	424	6,221	327
327	0738-1360	D	*Marine Resource Economics*	248	2,644	580
328	1479-2931	E	*Maritime Economics & Logistics*	238	1,521	62
329	0308-8839	D	*Maritime Policy & Management*	428	2,398	94
330	0732-2399	A	*Marketing Science*	532	15,216	2,891
331	0960-1627	C	*Mathematical Finance*	268	941	43
332	0165-4896	E	*Mathematical Social Sciences*	583	3,022	127
333	1862-9679	D	*Mathematics and Financial Economics*	188	720	88
334	0364-765X	D	*Mathematics of Operations Research*	466	2,348	83
335	0026-1335	D	*Metrika*	352	375	17
336	0026-1386	D	*Metroeconomica*	291	609	113
337	0026-2234	C	*Michigan Law Review*	0	0	0
338	0028-0283	C	*National Tax Journal*	329	2,598	177
339	1566-113X	C	*Networks and Spatial Economics*	280	1,027	62
340	1594-5685	D	*New Medit*	34	0	0
341	1356-3467	C	*New Political Economy*	352	3,077	1,404
342	0899-7640	D	*Nonprofit and Voluntary Sector Quarterly*	630	10,713	1,870
343	1048-6682	D	*Nonprofit Management and Leadership*	293	1,966	556
344	1092-0277	D	*North American Actuarial Journal*	223	1,008	72
345	0923-7992	D	*Open Economies Review*	311	1,688	150
346	0030-364X	B	*Operations Research*	893	15,154	535
347	0171-6468	C	*OR Spectrum*	307	2,438	30
348	1086-0266	C	*Organization & Environment*	246	3,008	616
349	0305-9049	C	*Oxford Bulletin of Economics and Statistics*	420	2,477	1,031
350	1360-0818	D	*Oxford Development Studies*	233	1,185	993
351	0030-7653	D	*Oxford Economic Papers*	453	1,402	1,409
352	0266-903X	D	*Oxford Review of Economic Policy*	288	3,179	2,911
353	1361-374X	E	*Pacific Economic Review*	356	634	226
354	0927-538X	D	*Pacific-Basin Finance Journal*	588	9,569	90

355	1056-8190	D	*Papers in Regional Science*	494	2,734	1,158
356	1170-7690	C	*PharmacoEconomics*	879	6,643	3,256
357	0032-2687	D	*Policy Sciences*	217	4,396	1,052
358	0190-292X	C	*Policy Studies Journal*	405	7,792	2,006
359	0032-3195	E	*Political Science Quarterly*	1,027	571	547
360	1470-594X	E	*Politics, Philosophy & Economics*	164	1,022	230
361	0032-4663	E	*Population*	274	270	40
362	0098-7921	C	*Population and Development Review*	686	3,915	3,169
363	0032-468X	D	*Population Bulletin*	0	0	0
364	0167-5923	D	*Population Research and Policy Review*	303	1,961	1,585
365	0032-4728	D	*Population Studies*	247	1,733	986
366	1463-1377	D	*Post-Communist Economies*	258	959	216
367	1060-586X	C	*Post-Soviet Affairs*	164	1,881	416
368	1059-1478	B	*Production and Operations Management*	1,178	5,461	1,226
369	0033-3352	B	*Public Administration Review*	1,346	16,487	5,577
370	0275-1100	D	*Public Budgeting & Finance*	278	730	201
371	0048-5829	C	*Public Choice*	819	6,835	1,658
372	1091-1421	D	*Public Finance Review*	276	844	918
373	1566-7170	E	*Public Organization Review*	274	948	71
374	1759-7323	B	*Quantitative Economics*	227	880	229
375	1469-7688	D	*Quantitative Finance*	1,275	5,838	1,175
376	1570-7156	C	*Quantitative Marketing and Economics*	113	1,526	114
377	1554-0626	B	*Quarterly journal of Political Science*	0	0	0
378	0166-0462	D	*Regional Science and Urban Economics*	640	5,841	1,225
379	0034-3404	C	*Regional Studies*	1,155	0	2,739
380	1748-5983	C	*Regulation & Governance*	312	3,307	892
381	0275-5319	D	*Research in International Business and Finance*	771	12,486	251
382	0147-9121	E	*Research in Labor Economics*	0	0	0
383	0739-8859	D	*Research in Transportation Economics*	554	11,524	644
384	0048-7333	B	*Research Policy*	1,208	124,485	12,132
385	0928-7655	C	*Resource and Energy Economics*	392	9,276	420

386	0301-4207	C	Resources Policy	778	23,981	812
387	0014-9187	D	Review (Federal Reserve Bank)	71	586	344
388	1380-6653	B	Review of Accounting Studies	336	16,645	534
389	0305-6244	D	Review of African Political Economy	434	2,732	1,220
390	1380-6645	D	Review of Derivatives Research	90	541	14
391	1363-6669	E	Review of Development Economics	534	2,599	481
392	1094-2025	B	Review of Economic Dynamics	395	6,691	597
393	0034-6535	A	Review of Economics and Statistics	717	14,946	7,583
394	1569-5239	D	Review of Economics of the Household	308	1,108	2,166
395	1750-6816	B	Review of Environmental Economics and Policy	213	6,021	1,276
396	1572-3097	A	Review of Finance	208	268	238
397	1058-3300	D	Review of Financial Economics	218	2,794	72
398	0034-6586	D	Review of Income and Wealth	518	2,103	1,363
399	0889-938X	D	Review of Industrial Organization	389	1,804	443
400	0965-7576	D	Review of International Economics	497	0	356
401	0969-2290	C	Review of International Political Economy	329	3,718	1,815
402	0260-2105	C	Review of International Studies	455	5,847	1,549
403	2049-5323	D	Review of Keynesian Economics	249	1,290	418
404	1863-6683	D	Review of Managerial Science	255	906	78
405	1446-9022	D	Review of Network Economics	135	958	3
406	0953-8259	D	Review of Political Economy	352	1,589	414
407	0924-865X	D	Review of Quantitative Finance and Accounting	539	1,937	42
408	0486-6134	E	Review of Radical Political Economics	516	1,952	462

409	0173-7600	E	*Review of Regional Research*	76	233	33
410	0034-6764	E	*Review of Social Economy*	244	1,097	349
411	1610-2878	D	*Review of World Economics*	243	1,681	220
412	1645-6726	D	*Revstat Statistical Journal*	0	0	0
413	0225-5189	E	*Revue canadienne d'études du développement*	0	0	0
414	0358-5522	D	*Scandinavian Economic History Review*	226	478	214
415	0956-5221	D	*Scandinavian Journal of Management*	377	12,038	127
416	0036-8237	D	*Science & Society*	254	955	52
417	1720-3929	D	*SCIENZE REGIONALI*	87	0	0
418	0921-898X	C	*Small Business Economics*	774	14,846	2,043
419	0176-1714	D	*Social Choice and Welfare*	623	4,320	432
420	0303-8300	D	*Social Indicators Research*	2,182	25,715	4,524
421	0038-4941	D	*Social Science Quarterly*	692	4,142	4,890
422	0037-7910	E	*Social Security Bulletin*	0	0	0
423	0037-7961	C	*Social Service Review*	0	0	0
424	0038-0121	D	*Socio-Economic Planning Sciences*	312	6,778	103
425	1475-1461	C	*Socio-Economic Review*	271	3,593	1,872
426	0038-2280	E	*South African Journal of Economics*	303	1,107	179
427	0038-4038	D	*Southern Economic Journal*	554	3,878	1,789
428	1742-1772	D	*Spatial Economic Analysis*	207	875	242
429	1973-2201	D	*Statistica*	0	0	0
430	1874-7655	D	*Statistical Journal of the IAOS*	337	1,003	85
431	1618-2510	E	*Statistical Methods & Applications*	293	650	34
432	0932-5026	C	*Statistical Papers*	682	1,93	36
433	0954-349X	D	*Structural Change and Economic Dynamics*	360	7,181	135
434	0039-3665	C	*Studies in Family Planning*	282	2,254	1,062
435	1081-1826	D	*Studies in Nonlinear Dynamics and Econometrics*	0	0	0
436	1424-7755	D	*Swiss Political Science Review*	400	866	617
437	1392-8619	D	*Technological and Economic Development of Economy*	0	0	0
438	0953-7325	D	*Technology Analysis & Strategic Management*	648	7,123	336

439	0308-5961	D	*Telecommunications Policy*	784	0	993
440	1133-0686	C	*TEST (Springer)*	389	1,208	0
441	0001-4826	B	*The Accounting Review*	794	41,73	367
442	0002-8762	D	*The American Historical Review*	5,688	4,326	0
443	0003-1305	D	*The American Statistician*	501	1,440	2,623
444	0570-1864	D	*The Annals of Regional Science*	450	2,696	445
445	0002-7162	C	*The Annals of the American Academy of Political and Social Science*	665	5,509	6,607
446	1368-4221	C	*The Econometrics Journal*	231	1,279	217
447	0013-0117	C	*The Economic History Review*	1,326	2,232	1,387
448	0013-0133	A	*The Economic Journal*	806	3,607	10,690
449	0957-8811	D	*The European Journal of Development Research*	503	2,989	820
450	1351-847X	D	*The European Journal of Finance*	507	2,238	265
451	1618-7598	D	*The European Journal of Health Economics*	718	6,015	2,587
452	0967-2567	D	*The European Journal of the History of Economic Thought*	366	840	230
453	0020-7063	D	*The International Journal of Accounting*	361	6,040	0
454	0021-9118	D	*The Journal of Asian Studies*	1,511	2,539	494
455	0022-0507	C	*The Journal of Economic History*	769	1,417	2,072
456	1569-1721	D	*The Journal of Economic Inequality*	235	2,718	984
457	0971-3557	E	*The Journal of Entrepreneurship*	150	1,133	195
458	1070-4965	F	*The Journal of Environment & Development*	156	2,348	342
459	0022-1082	A+	*The Journal of Finance*	866	28,904	3,604
460	0022-1821	C	*The Journal of Industrial Economics*	241	1,995	372
461	0022-2186	C	*The Journal of Law & Economics*	277	3,404	2,26
462	8756-6222	C	*The Journal of Law, Economics, and Organization*	203	1,207	0

463	0047-2530	C	The Journal of Legal Studies	173	862	668
464	1091-4358	D	The Journal of Mental Health Policy and Economics	0	0	0
465	0095-4918	D	The Journal of Portfolio Management	664	3,613	870
466	0895-5638	D	The Journal of Real Estate Finance and Economics	371	3,102	335
467	1083-5547	E	The Journal of Real Estate Portfolio Management	0	0	0
468	1090-4999	D	The Journal of Regional Analysis & Policy	0	0	0
469	0892-9912	C	The Journal of Technology Transfer	490	5,116	883
470	1062-9408	D	The North American Journal of Economics and Finance	600	5,763	98
471	0033-5533	A+	The Quarterly Journal of Economics	400	19,466	16,496
472	1062-9769	E	The Quarterly Review of Economics and Finance	575	10,249	192
473	0741-6261	B	The RAND Journal of Economics	321	3,924	698
474	0034-6446	E	The Review of Black Political Economy	183	1,447	444
475	0034-6527	A+	The Review of Economic Studies	433	9,267	3,137
476	0893-9454	A+	The Review of Financial Studies	1,051	22,678	2,002
477	1559-7431	B	The Review of International Organizations	236	3,835	405
478	0347-0520	C	The Scandinavian Journal of Economics	426	3,842	199
479	0258-6770	C	The World Bank Economic Review	198	265	0
480	0257-3032	C	The World Bank Research Observer	126	2,509	0
481	0378-5920	D	The World Economy	934	4,894	788
482	1555-7561	A	Theoretical Economics	0	0	0
483	0040-5833	D	Theory and Decision	432	1,995	150
484	1134-5764	D	TOP (Springer)	320	170	21
485	1354-8166	D	Tourism Economics	694	6,434	124
486	0049-4488	C	Transportation	641	6,468	1,508

487	0041-1612	E	*Transportation Journal*	247	939	72
488	0965-8564	C	*Transportation Research Part A: Policy and Practice*	1,633	67,5	4,385
489	0191-2615	B	*Transportation Research Part B: Methodological*	1,371	49,212	800
490	1361-9209	C	*Transportation Research Part D: Transport and Environment*	1,391	46,435	2,321
491	1366-5545	C	*Transportation Research Part E: Logistics and Transportation Review*	1,118	41,055	332
492	1078-0874	C	*Urban Affairs Review*	377	2,491	1,236
493	0042-0980	C	*Urban Studies*	1,919	18,675	7,458
494	0957-1787	D	*Utilities Policy*	487	11,439	572
495	1369-1066	D	*Venture Capital*	146	1,700	597
496	2212-4284	D	*Water Resources and Economics*	153	2,572	0
497	0043-1397	B	*Water Resources Research*	4,663	60,041	9,378
498	0305-750X	C	*World Development*	2,050	65,047	12,737
499	1474-7456	D	*World Trade Review*	404	1,033	259
500	0044-0094	B	*Yale Law Journal*	0	0	0

Appendix III: Correlations of Altmetric Attention Sources with citations on journal level

1. Spearman correlation between different Altmetric Attention Sources for business studies journals

			AAS	Tweets	Mendeley	Dimensions Citations	News	Blog	Facebook	Policy Documents
Spearman-Rho	AAS	Korrelationskoeffizient	1,000	,936**	,724**	,732**	,916**	,913**	,834**	,735**
		Sig. (2-seitig)		,000	,000	,000	,000	,000	,000	,000
		N	475	475	475	475	475	475	475	475
	Tweets	Korrelationskoeffizient	,936**	1,000	,656**	,666**	,773**	,829**	,824**	,668**
		Sig. (2-seitig)	,000		,000	,000	,000	,000	,000	,000
		N	475	475	475	475	475	475	475	475
	Mendeley	Korrelationskoeffizient	,724**	,656**	1,000	,958**	,706**	,586**	,693**	,540**
		Sig. (2-seitig)	,000	,000		,000	,000	,000	,000	,000
		N	475	475	475	475	475	475	475	475
	DimensionsCitations	Korrelationskoeffizient	,732**	,666**	,958**	1,000	,694**	,618**	,676**	,582**
		Sig. (2-seitig)	,000	,000	,000		,000	,000	,000	,000
		N	475	475	475	475	475	475	475	475
	News	Korrelationskoeffizient	,916**	,773**	,706**	,694**	1,000	,815**	,755**	,630**
		Sig. (2-seitig)	,000	,000	,000	,000		,000	,000	,000
		N	475	475	475	475	475	475	475	475
	Blog	Korrelationskoeffizient	,913**	,829**	,586**	,618**	,815**	1,000	,715**	,732**
		Sig. (2-seitig)	,000	,000	,000	,000	,000		,000	,000
		N	475	475	475	475	475	475	475	475
	Facebook	Korrelationskoeffizient	,834**	,824**	,693**	,676**	,755**	,715**	1,000	,552**
		Sig. (2-seitig)	,000	,000	,000	,000	,000	,000		,000
		N	475	475	475	475	475	475	475	475
	PolicyDocs	Korrelationskoeffizient	,735**	,668**	,540**	,582**	,630**	,732**	,552**	1,000
		Sig. (2-seitig)	,000	,000	,000	,000	,000	,000	,000	
		N	475	475	475	475	475	475	475	475

2. Spearman correlation between different Altmetric Attention Sources for E journals

			AAS	Tweets	Mendeley	Dimensions Citations	News	Blog	Facebook	Policy Documents
Spearman-Rho	AAS	Korrelationskoeffizient	1,000	,947**	,818**	,814**	,912**	,912**	,791**	,770**
		Sig. (2-seitig)		,000	,000	,000	,000	,000	,000	,000
		N	438	438	438	438	438	438	438	438
	Tweets	Korrelationskoeffizient	,947**	1,000	,743**	,739**	,790**	,827**	,798**	,684**
		Sig. (2-seitig)	,000		,000	,000	,000	,000	,000	,000
		N	438	438	438	438	438	438	438	438
	Mendeley	Korrelationskoeffizient	,818**	,743**	1,000	,970**	,779**	,708**	,688**	,739**
		Sig. (2-seitig)	,000	,000		,000	,000	,000	,000	,000
		N	438	438	438	438	438	438	438	438
	DimensionCitations	Korrelationskoeffizient	,814**	,739**	,970**	1,000	,762**	,710**	,668**	,765**
		Sig. (2-seitig)	,000	,000	,000		,000	,000	,000	,000
		N	438	438	438	438	438	438	438	438
	News	Korrelationskoeffizient	,912**	,790**	,779**	,762**	1,000	,815**	,681**	,700**
		Sig. (2-seitig)	,000	,000	,000	,000		,000	,000	,000
		N	438	438	438	438	438	438	438	438
	Blog	Korrelationskoeffizient	,912**	,827**	,708**	,710**	,815**	1,000	,698**	,736**
		Sig. (2-seitig)	,000	,000	,000	,000	,000		,000	,000
		N	438	438	438	438	438	438	438	438
	Facebook	Korrelationskoeffizient	,791**	,798**	,688**	,668**	,681**	,698**	1,000	,532**
		Sig. (2-seitig)	,000	,000	,000	,000	,000	,000		,000
		N	438	438	438	438	438	438	438	438
	PolicyDocuments	Korrelationskoeffizient	,770**	,684**	,739**	,765**	,700**	,736**	,532**	1,000
		Sig. (2-seitig)	,000	,000	,000	,000	,000	,000	,000	
		N	438	438	438	438	438	438	438	438

Appendix IV: Economic and business studies topics using latent Dirichlet allocation

	Topics retrieved from articles found in Altmetric.com	
Topics	Business Studies	Economics
Topic 0	['evidence', 'natural', 'assessment', 'approach', 'learning', 'model' 'social', 'board']	['security', 'network', 'monetary', 'energy', 'effect', 'policy', 'analysis']
Topic 1	['sustain', 'service', 'economic', 'land', 'change', 'analysis', 'evidence', 'development']	['international', 'study', 'growth', 'performance', 'inequality']
Topic 2	['policy', 'risk', 'analysis', 'sector', 'evidence', 'factors', 'social', 'health']	['job', 'bank', 'growth', 'income', 'long', 'measur', 'return', 'model']
Topic 3	['impact', 'assessment', 'approach', 'policy', 'health', 'analysis', 'market']	['effect', 'policy', 'impact', 'model', 'market', 'china', 'approach', 'value']
Topic 4	['industry', 'impact', 'effect', 'management', 'data']	['report', 'serie', 'economic', 'annual', ' 'econometric', 'society']
Topic 5	['economic', 'change', 'impact', 'transit', 'analysis', 'behavior', 'model']	['inequality', 'auction', 'finance', 'income', 'preference', 'method', 'high', 'investment"]
Topic 6	['energy', 'data', 'objective', 'evolutionary', 'algorithm', 'analysis', 'optimization']	['price', 'set', 'product', 'rate', 'data', 'trade', 'board']
Topic 7	['market', 'influence', 'growth', 'networks', 'social', 'implementation', 'safety', 'model']	['ecosystem', 'growth', 'performance', 'international', 'effect', 'theory', 'industry']
Topic 8	[learning', 'technology', 'performance', 'model', 'social', 'analysis']	['analys', 'finance', 'firm', 'field', 'health', 'evidence']
Topic 9	['reports', 'society', 'econometric', 'public', 'manuscript']	['capital', 'behavior', 'land', 'market', 'assessment', 'impact', 'experiment']
Topic 10	['data', 'innovation', 'approach', 'energy', 'land', 'consumption', 'project']	['value', 'outcome', 'energy', 'consumption', 'theory', 'study', 'development']
Topic 11	['firm', 'impact', 'design', 'business', 'trust', 'value',	['change', 'network', 'trade', 'gas', 'preference', 'land', 'service']

	'theory', 'online', 'financial', 'investment']	
Topic 12	['change', 'meta', 'climate', 'data', 'food', 'time', 'urban']	['price', 'risk', 'firm', 'public', 'choice', 'demand', 'market']
Topic 13	['retirement', 'innovation', 'role', 'health',]	['approach', 'dynamic', 'environment', 'application', 'growth', 'measure', 'policy', 'performance', 'economic', 'analysis']
Topic 14	['study', 'demand', 'data', 'vehicle', 'model', 'care', 'health', 'social']	['trade', 'oil', 'sector' 'investment', 'risk', 'price', 'theory']

Topics retrieved from articles found in Mendeley		
Topics	**Business Studies**	**Economics**
Topic 0	['business', 'capital', 'role', 'environment', 'firm', 'social', 'corporate', performance']	['war', 'distribution', 'data', 'estimation', 'approach', 'stochastic', 'choice', 'model']
Topic 1	['sentiment', 'research', 'effect', 'remove', 'improvement', 'america', 'moral', 'games', 'synthesis', 'organic']	['public', 'case', 'electric', ' 'vote', 'vehicle', 'place', 'provision', 'curve']
Topic 2	['screen', 'high', 'factor', 'speed', 'physical', 'patient', 'cancer', 'related', 'work', 'study']	['national', 'job', 'social', 'identity', 'tourism', 'life', 'land', 'satisfaction', 'security', 'food']
Topic 3	['predict', 'case', 'wealth', 'production', 'cost', 'material', 'water', 'global', 'analysis', 'failure']	['optimization', 'management', 'hybrid', 'electricity', 'storage', 'system', 'energy']
Topic 4	['brain', 'chronic', 'mental', 'children', 'older', 'audit', 'injury', 'young', 'adult']	['performance', 'engine', 'process', 'heat', 'thermal', 'power', 'optimization', 'experiment']
Topic 5	['linear', 'inference', 'media', 'social', 'test', 'data', 'estimation', 'time']	['review', 'chain', 'power', 'assessment', 'district', 'gas', 'future', 'analysis', 'supply']

Topic 6	['text', 'trends', 'geography', 'africa', 'introduction', 'special', 'issue', 'united', 'states']	['china', 'individual', 'social', market', 'product', 'corporate', 'income']
Topic 7	['influence', 'effect', 'mobile', 'student', 'learning', 'school', 'online', 'social', 'self']	['model', 'advantage', 'fund', 'evaluation', 'health', 'border', 'cross', 'evolution', 'performance', 'preference']
Topic 8	['program', 'model', 'approach', 'stochastic', 'problem', 'algorithm', 'multi', 'optimization']	['difference', 'finance', 'economic', 'work', 'school', 'evidence', 'gender', 'family', 'children', 'house']
Topic 9	['capacity', 'social', 'consumer', 'role', 'data', 'information', 'big', 'organization', 'technology', 'behavior']	['health', 'crisis', 'analysis', 'risk', 'information']
Topic 10	['process', 'class', 'data', 'criteria', 'analysis', 'graph', 'early', 'make', 'decision']	['internet', 'influence', 'impact', 'digital', 'new', 'data', 'study', 'management', 'forest']
Topic 11	['system', 'account', 'critical', 'board', 'creative', 'editorial', 'agenda', 'theory', 'practice', 'research']	['inequality', 'spatial', 'panel', 'productivity', 'data', 'economic', 'growth']
Topic 12	['dynamic', 'traffic', 'data', 'analysis', 'approach', 'model', 'network']	['market', 'data', 'approach', 'insurance', 'analysis', 'risk', 'regression']
Topic 13	['information', 'inequality', 'economy', 'study', 'income', 'low', 'literature', 'systematic', 'review']	['development', 'research', 'economic', 'africa', 'review', 'country']
Topic 14	['good', 'food', 'satisfaction', 'assessment', 'quality', 'sector', 'service', 'cycle', 'public', 'life']	['machine', 'climate', 'emission', 'structur', 'class', 'diffusion', 'people']
Topic 15	['randomize', 'study', 'manage', 'trial', 'collective', 'entrepreneurial', 'resilience', 'social', 'entrepreneurship', 'networks']	['nonprofit', 'technological', 'role', 'leadership', 'international', 'fertility', 'innovation', 'ownership', 'strategic', 'entrepreneurship']

Topic 16	computing', 'medium', 'cloud', 'regression', 'identification', 'career', 'analysis', 'data']	['international', 'approach', 'inflation', 'rate', 'exchange', 'trade']
Topic 17	['event', 'maintenance', 'process', 'production', 'integrated', 'manufacture', 'performance', 'plan', 'control', 'system']	['governance', 'cross', 'country', 'firm', 'capital', 'china', 'impact', 'bank', 'risk']
Topic 18	['detection', 'time', 'drive', 'real', 'fuzzy', 'data']	['journal', 'finance', 'money', 'global', 'health', 'knowledge', 'international', 'institution']
Topic 19	['international', 'chain', 'price', 'oil', 'market', 'supply']	['analysis', 'forecast', 'equity', 'return', 'market', 'price', 'oil', 'volatility', 'stock']
Topic 20	['employee', 'team', 'perceive', 'difference', 'leadership', 'job', 'work', 'gender', 'role', 'effect']	['social', 'world', 'issue', 'special', 'account', 'public', 'political', 'economy', 'economic']
Topic 21	['environmental', 'consumption', 'analysis', 'study', 'emission', 'carbon', 'urban', 'china', 'energy']	['welfare', 'history', 'time', 'crisis', 'optimal', 'direct', 'foreign', 'investment']
Topic 22	['border', 'institution', 'country', 'study', 'cultur', 'nation', 'high', 'cross', 'education']	['organization', , 'performance', 'environment', 'sustain', 'small', 'early', 'innovation', 'development']
Topic 23	['public', 'patient', 'study', 'impact', 'term', 'service', 'care', 'health']	['scale', 'cost', 'water', 'organic', 'waste', 'recovery', 'heat', 'analysis', 'cycle']
Topic 24	['preference', 'heterogeneity', 'road', 'labor', 'economic', 'engineer', 'choice', 'growth', 'tourism']	['study', 'resource', 'effect', 'resource', 'approach', 'capital', 'human']
Topic 25	['monetary', 'credit', 'debt', 'bank', 'politic', 'crisis', 'finance', 'policy', 'risk']	['trade', 'flow', 'good', 'affect', 'united', 'matter', 'states', 'tax']
Topic 26	['stroke', 'set', 'parallel', 'classification', 'machine', 'learn']	['commodity', 'market', 'future', 'monetary', 'credit', 'evidence', 'policy']
Topic 27	['implementation', 'organization', 'development', 'union', 'waste', 'project', 'private', 'sustainable', 'public', 'european']	['size', 'study', 'performance', 'run', 'short', 'firm', 'term']

Topic 28	['utility', 'environment', 'equality', 'branch', 'land', 'adaptation', 'project', 'climate']	['central', 'america', 'social', 'development', 'africa', 'study', 'case', 'south', 'environment']
Topic 29	['product', 'development', 'research', 'social', 'framework', 'knowledge', 'innovation', 'management']	['outcome', 'impact', 'hospital', 'characteristic', 'management', 'analysis', 'performance']

Appendix V: Questionnaire

A study on article selection behavior

Dear participant,

I am Kaltrina Nuredini, a doctoral candidate and researcher at ZBW—Leibniz Information Centre for Economics, Kiel, Germany. I would first like to thank you for accepting to take part in this survey. This survey is being conducted as part of my doctoral research with the intention to investigate how information related to journal articles is used and which information is most useful.

This survey should take approximately 15 minutes to complete. Please always use the survey navigation button "Next" and do not use your browser "Back" button to return to or edit a previous page.

If you have any questions about the survey, please email me at XXXXXXXXXXX.

Thank you for your time and I really appreciate your input!

There are 23 questions in this survey

Privacy Policy

You have received this survey because your email address is pointed out in the ZBW mailing list. Your participation in this survey is voluntary and you can leave this survey at any time. The survey responses are completely anonymous and treated confidentially. The responses will be stored on a server that is maintained by the University of Kiel—Germany. The questionnaire, the mock-up, and the experimental data received from this survey will subsequently be published on Zenodo (an open-access repository operated by CERN) to support the open science movement.*

○ I acknowledge that I have read and hereby agree with the above explained procedure.

Personal Information

Your Age*

Only an integer value may be entered in this field.

[   ]

Your Discipline*

○ Economics (VWL)
○ Business Studies (BWL)
○ Other

Your Country*
○ Albania

○ Algeria
○ Andorra
○ Angola
○ Antigua and Barbuda
○ Argentina
○ Armenia
○ Australia
○ Austria

[196 countries]

Your Gender*

○ Female
○ Male
○ No Answer

Your Academic Status*

○ Bachelor Student
○ Master Student
○ PhD Student
○ Researcher
○ PostDoc
○ Assistant Professor
○ Professor
○ Associate Professor
○ Other

Part I

Dear participant,

Below is a task on which the questions in this survey are based. Please take some time to read through the task and ensure you have understood it before proceeding.

Task: Imagine that you work as a researcher in an economics department and your colleague sent you the four articles given below that you might be interested to read for your research. (Note: these articles are entirely fictitious).

Please take some time to look at the articles' details and associated data from the graphic below. At the graphic, three types of journal information are presented: *traditional bibliometrics* (i.e., Impact Factor, h-index, 5 years Impact Factor, and Cites—all information is retrieved from CitEc), *journal rankings* (e.g., Scimago SRJ), and *altmetric information* (i.e., Altmetric.com and Mendeley).

240

Based on these data, please select the article that you would find the most interesting to read first. All article data are visible. Based on your selection, please answer the following questions.

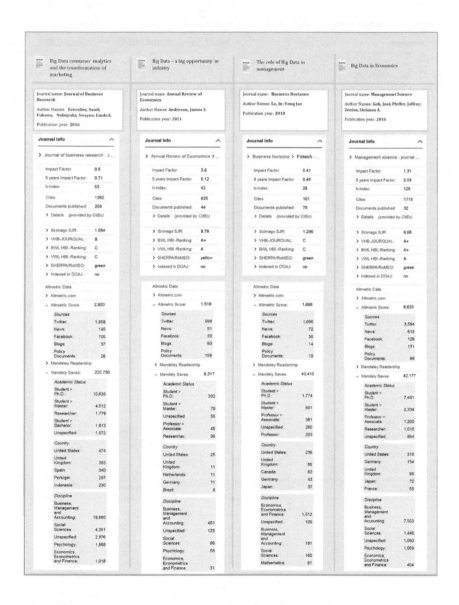

Which article have you selected?***

O Big Data consumer analytics and the transformation of marketing

○ Big Data—a big opportunity in industry
○ The role of Big Data in Management
○ Big Data in Economics

Are you familiar with the journal information such as:*

	Yes	Uncertain	No
Impact Factor	○	○	○
5 years Impact Factor	○	○	○
_h_-index	○	○	○
Cites (citation data provided by CitEc)	○	○	○

Which information from the graphic above was relevant for you to select the article you want to read first?*

	Extremely relevant	Very relevant	Moderately relevant	Slightly relevant	Not at all relevant
Impact Factor	○	○	○	○	○
5 Years Impact Factor	○	○	○	○	○
_h_-index	○	○	○	○	○
Cites (citation data provided by CitEc)	○	○	○	○	○
Scimago SJR	○	○	○	○	○
VHB-JOURQUAL	○	○	○	○	○
BWL HBI.-Ranking	○	○	○	○	○
VWL HBI.-Ranking	○	○	○	○	○
SHERPA/RoMEO	○	○	○	○	○

Are you familiar with the journal information such as:*

	Yes	Uncertain	No
Altmetrics from Altmetric.com	○	○	○

Which information from the graphic above was relevant for you to select the article you want to read first?*

Only answer this question if the following conditions are met:

Answer was "Yes" at question "10 [F6]" (Are you familiar with the journal information such as: (Altmetrics from Altmetric.com))

	Extremely relevant	Very relevant	Moderately relevant	Slightly relevant	Not at all relevant
Altmetric score	○	○	○	○	○
Twitter mentions	○	○	○	○	○
News mentions	○	○	○	○	○
Facebook mentions	○	○	○	○	○
Blog post mentions	○	○	○	○	○
Policy document mentions	○	○	○	○	○

Altmetrics are data that track how research has been shared, discussed, and reused online. Altmetrics can help you understand:
- Who is talking about a research output (e.g., journal articles, books, slides, code)
- How often the research is discussed online
- What is said about that research

Altmetric.com is an online service that tracks a range of sources, such as social media platforms, traditional media, and online reference managers, to capture mentions and citations to research outputs. For economics articles, top 5 altmetric sources are shown in the graphic above (i.e., Twitter, News, Facebook , Blogs, and Policy Documents). These are the sources in which economics journal articles have been most often mentioned online.

The Altmetric score is a weighted count of all of the mentions. Altmetric.com has tracked for an individual research output, and is designed as an indicator of the amount and reach of the attention an item has received.

Altmetric information on journal-level: For each altmetric indicator (e.g., Twitter), the journal-level information represents the sum of altmetrics (e.g., the sum of all tweets) received by all individual articles published in that journal.

Only answer this question if the following conditions are met:

Answer was "No" or "Uncertain" at question "10 [F6]" (Are you familiar with the journal information such as: (Altmetrics from Altmetric.com))

Given the above information on altmetrics related to Altmetric.com which information would have been useful to you to select the article you want to read first?

Please choose **all** that apply:
- ☐ Altmetric score
- ☐ Twitter mentions
- ☐ News mentions
- ☐ Facebook mentions
- ☐ Blog post mentions
- ☐ Policy document mentions

Are you familiar with the journal information such as:*

	Yes	Uncertain	No
Readership information from Mendeley	○	○	○

Which information from the graphic above was relevant for you to select the article you want to read first?*

Only answer this question if the following conditions are met:

Answer was "Yes" at question "14 [F10]" (Are you familiar with the journal information such as: (Readership information from Mendeley))

	Extremely relevant	Very relevant	Moderately relevant	Slightly relevant	Not at all relevant
Mendeley Saves	○	○	○	○	○
Academic status of users in Mendeley	○	○	○	○	○

	Extremely relevant	Very relevant	Moderately relevant	Slightly relevant	Not at all relevant
Country of users in Mendeley	O	O	O	O	O
Discipline of users in Mendeley	O	O	O	O	O

Mendeley is a desktop and web program operated by Elsevier, and it is used for managing and sharing research papers, discovering research data, and collaborating online. Mendeley Readership is a number known as "count" showing how many times an article has been saved to users' libraries in Mendeley. Mendeley categorizes the articles based on their users' information, such as the users' discipline, academic status, and country of origin.

Mendeley readership information on journal level represents the sum of all users' information category counts (e.g., the sum of all article saves on users' libraries with specified academic statuses) and all individual articles have been published in that journal.

Given the above information on readership data related to Mendeley which information would have been useful to you to select the article you want to read first?
Please choose **all** that apply:

☐ Mendeley Saves
☐ Academic status of users in Mendeley
☐ Country of users in Mendeley
☐ Discipline of users in Mendeley

Do you use any other journal or article information on a daily basis, which is not listed in this graphic and which might have helped you to select an article for reading?

Part II

If you need to see the graphic of articles and their journal information again, then please click here: visit graphic

How useful do you find journal-level information to select an article you want to read first?*

	Extremely useful	Very useful	Somewhat useful	Slightly useful	Not at all useful
Bibliometrics Information (e.g., Impact Factor, 5 years Impact Factor, *h*-index, Cites)	○	○	○	○	○
Journal Rankings (e.g., Scimago SRJ, BWL–HBI Ranking, VWL–HBI Ranking, SHERPA/RoMEO)	○	○	○	○	○
Altmetrics (e.g., Altmetric.com, Mendeley)	○	○	○	○	○

Why would you be unlikely to use Altmetric information on the journal level?*

Only answer this question if the following conditions are met:

Answer was "Somewhat useful" or "Slightly useful" at question "19 [p22]" (How useful do you find journal-level information to select an article you want to read first? [Altmetrics (e.g., Altmetric.com, Mendeley)])

Article-level information is the number of times an individual article is mentioned online or cited in other publications. For example, article-level information for the article "Big Data consumer analytics and the transformation of marketing" is shown in the graphic below from three different providers: Altmetric score from Altmetric.com, Mendeley Saves from Mendeley, and Cites from CitEc.

How useful do you find article-level information to select an article you want to read first?*

	Extremely useful	Very useful	Somewhat useful	Slightly useful	Not at all useful
Altmetric score	○	○	○	○	○
Mendeley Saves	○	○	○	○	○
Cites (citation data provided by CitEc)	○	○	○	○	○

Why would you be unlikely to use Altmetric information on article level?∗

Only answer this question if the following conditions are met:
Answer was "Somewhat useful," "Slightly useful," "Somewhat useful," or "Slightly useful" at question "21 [p24]"

If you have any suggestions about the survey or want to expand on any of your answers, please leave a comment below.

Thank you for completing this survey.

Appendix VI: Survey open questions responses

1. Do you use any other journal or article information on a daily basis, which is not listed in this graphic and which might have helped you to select an article for reading?

A predefined, internal to my institution but consistent with general academic perception, list of top journals, second tier journal, etc.
ABS
ABS ranking
ABS Ranking list
Abstract
Abstract, key words are relevant
Abstract, key words, references, authors affiliations
Accounting Accountability and Auditing Journal *Accounting Forum* *Journal of Business Ethics*
Actually, I rarely use this information. I go on the title, the key words, and the date of the article. I selected this one because it was the most recent and most focused.
Affiliation of researchers
Article Influence Score from Web of Knowledge
Authorship of the articles. If I know a person in the field, I am more likely to read his/her work.
Citation count in Google Scholar, Web of Science citation counts
Citations by others/relevant sources
Citations in relevant articles
CNRS ranking of the journal in which the article is published.
Direct emails from journal contents; word of mouth; searches in Google Scholar for topics that are of interest
Even though I do not look at the journal *Management Science* that much, I do know that it is a very high quality journal and that was the reason I selected it first.
Familiarity with the journal (I follow a number of journals that are specific to my field), author, topic of the article—regardless of impact factor
General reputation of the journal. Topic of the article.
Google Scholar
Google Scholar
Google Scholar citations
Google Scholar citations, journal title, authors
Google Scholar Cites
Google Scholar search ranking
Google Scholar, SSRN, CEPR Weekly working paper email
I actually found the publication date very relevant, the more current the more interesting for me to read.
I almost exclusively use the title and the abstract.

I would not base my choice on the information above. The system forced me to make a choice, but please take this as invalid.
I am based in Australia, where we have an Australian Business Deans Council journal ranking which would feature strongly in my decision-making.
I and everyone I know uses a metric correlated with these measures: journal name. We all know which journals are good/bad and going up/down. The year of publication is important as well.
I do not rely on any of these metrics but focus on the journals in my specialization that are both established and highly ranked. Since I'm in business, most of the highly ranked journals are captured in the FT45 list. When I search for articles to read, I use Scopus and search terms *i.e., key words) that are relevant to my particular research project.
I have a good idea of journal status in the discipline. I usually rely on that for known journals. Article age was a factor in my choice. Given that these are real journals, I glanced at the metrics out with curiosity, but went with title, journal, and age of article.
I have a list of journals in my discipline and I am more likely to read if it is one among them.
I just know the top journals in my field and prioritize readings in these journals.
I know journal rankings in my field and related fields (ABS, Financial Times) pretty much by heart and these are the only ones that matter at my university. So I don't really care about any metrics, nor do I consider them highly relevant as they are subject to randomness, fads, and manipulation.
I know which journals are most relevant for me. Also, I base my readings on the topic mostly.
I look at the title of an article and its abstract. Journal title and other metrics matter a little.
I only used the title to select the article and ignored everything else.
I receive the contents of the new issues of a selection of journals.
I select articles to read overwhelmingly based on my own prior knowledge of the authors and the journals. This also applies to the example, where I selected the only article (allegedly) written by an economist I know and published in an economics journal I know, as opposed to the other three management journals.
First of all, I select based on the title. Article Nos. 2 and 4 are highly qualified but No. 4 is economics-oriented and No. 2 is too general.
I selected the most recent one. I would not rely on bibliometric indices without having some knowledge of the journals at all (it would be a blind choice to me).
I selected the paper because it was published in *Management Science*, and this is my main choice. Out of the other three, I looked at the tittle, one was in marketing, which I am not interested in. Between the remaining two, I chose the one in *Annual Review of Economics*, as it seemed like an overall better journal, although the title again would make me hesitate, it seems to be about the profession. I think I may have ended reading the other one in *Business Horizons*.

I simply go by the journal name oftentimes. There is surely a strong effect of "branding," also among scientific journals.
I used the title alone to make my decision.
I would select it on the basis of reputation and relevance to my own research.
I would typically select based mainly on the title and abstract.
Impact factor excludes citations in the same journal. Some journals use these to manipulate their impact factor.
In an ideal world, I'd have data on document citations per year. That'd be the single best indicator of publication quality in my view.
In my country, there is an official tier list of journals, ranking some of them as more important than others (two tiers). If uncertain, I would probably pick an article from a journal at the top tier. In some cases, I also look at whether the journal is in the (Social) Science Citation Index/Web of Science, alternatively Scopus, as I see this as an indication of quality.
In selecting a journal article, the following come into play: 1. Relevance of specific article to my current research activities. 2. From a known journal that is either one I publish in (or aim to), or that is well-regarded by the community of scholars associated with the journal that I am intending to publish in. 3. Overall citation count. It would be remiss not to pay attention to an already highly cited article, both because it is more likely to have something useful to my current research and because it is likely to be well known by reviewers. It is also likely to be mentioned in other papers I am reading on the topic so it gives me more context. 4. Name recognition of the authors if appropriate (since this can signal not only quality, but also knowing their backgrounds, I know how well the work will methodologically or philosophically fit into my own work).
Information contained in graphic but relevant to selection: year of publication, specificity of title
JEL-Classifications
Journal evaluation by universities. I will read whatever is considered as an A journal or is part of the FT-50
Journal name
Journal quality lists
Journal rankings, or better whether the journal belongs or not to the top 5–10 journals in my field, title, and abstract.
Journals are largely irrelevant these days. Researchers no longer read journals in the sense of regularly going to a library and looking over recent journal publications. Researchers look for articles, not journals. When publishing, authors are highly driven by visibility. It is no longer "publish or perish" it's "get visible or vanish." For instance, journals that no longer have issues, but publish papers as they get through the vetting process are preferable, as this focuses attention on the paper, not on the journal. Journal ranking information is mainly used by academic management to demonstrate the quality of their research. Many such managements reject the

strategy of publishing new research in few more focused journals, using them to build into a major article in a higher ranked journal. They want all research in these higher ranked journals, which is unrealistic.
Knowledge of quality of the journal itself
Mailing lists, TOC
Mendeley's suggestions: Others have read the following article. I don't know whether this is the focus of your study, but content of the article, e.g., key words
My primary source of information about journals is my own knowledge of journal reputation and my experience with the journal.
N/A
No
No
No
No
No
No
No
No
No
No
No
No
No
No
No
No
No
No
No
No
No
No
No
No
No—I use the journal publisher's name, the authorship of the article, the article title, and key words to determine which article to read. Sometimes I check to see if a journal is on the predatory publications list.
No honestly I use little of this information I read anything I find over the topic of my interest.
No none. You have asked me to imagine that I am working in an economics department—I have selected the paper that appears most obviously related to my position as someone working in economics. If I worked in a marketing department, I

252

would have selected the first paper. Each paper seems intended for a different audience. I picked the one that seems more relevant to me.

No, I never use metrics to guide my choices. Most often I know of authors in my field already, or discover new work cited in work of authors I track.

No

No

No. I search in ECONLIT for an article. I read the abstract and decide if I should proceed. I seldom use other information other than whether the publication is in a peer-reviewed article.

No. I tend to focus primarily on A+ journals and then follow the citation trail. All large journal databases allow searches by journal name. All academics know which journals to search for.

No.
I know the journals that are interested to me and pay no attention to social media.

No. Article was selected as it was the most recent. Nothing to do with journal rankings.

No. I choose papers by topic and by relation (citation) to other papers/authors that I know already.

Number of the citations/*h*-index for the article itself.

Old-fashioned clues: key words, date of publication, formulation of the title, intro. I find all the metrics complicated to understand and mostly related to the popularity of papers. Often I'm looking for "niche" papers that are not that popular but key to my research. In this case, the metrics are not useful.

Paper topics are far more important to my reading than any of the statistical services mentioned above. I consult New Economic Papers (daily to weekly online paper summaries by field, emailed to subscribers) from nep.repec.org; SSRN journals (similar to NEP), and table of contents for both general interest (e.g., *American Economic Review*, *Journal of Political Economy*, and *Econometrica*) and specialist interests in my fields.

Prior knowledge of the journal

Rankings from other countries such as the United States, Australia

Rankings of economic journals, especially those published in my home country

Relevance to my research

Reputation

ResearchGate

Simply the title of the paper. I am more interested in management and industry than economics or marketing.

SSRN, ResearchGate

Tables of contents sent by journals, publishers, and others

The abstract!

The abstract.

The article title and abstract are by far the most relevant info. I do not care about the number of cites or impact factor or any other article-specific metric and I only have a secondary interest in journal quality, but I will pick the article (based on title and

abstract) that seems the most relevant for my research, and will likely pick all articles that are reasonably relevant.
The classification of academic journals in economics provided by the CNRS (Centre National de la Recherche Scientifique).
The content is what matters to me. The metrics is a poor approximation of the relevance of the content to what I am doing.
The Danish Bibliometric Research Indicator, and my department's list of preferred journals.
The headline
The journal name familiarity and the topic of an article paper itself.
The journal title and the familiarity with the journal.
The main factor for me was the journal name. Of the four journals, *Management Science* is the only one that I am familiar with, and it is a very good and reputed journal.
The most important factor for me is the title of the article. It gives me an indication of whether the subject matter of the article is of interest to me.
The name of the journal is the most important information. I follow certain top journals (regardless of their recent numerical performance in the above metrics).
The perceived importance of the journal
The relevance of the article is the most important thing.
The title of the article and the journal name (I know that this isn't what your study is about, but this was a big part of my decision).
The title of the journal and the author
The UK Association of Business Schools journal rankings
The year of publication (!), the reputation of the authors
There is a selection of maybe 30 well-known journals that are relevant and trustworthy in my field, I would hesitate from citing any article that is not published here. I do not relay on the peer-reviewed process in other journals, there is just too many scam journals out there.
There is internal field rankings for all journals, and I would go with that. Therefore, no other information needed to compare journals. *Management Science* article strictly dominates all other journals and no other measure of impact changes that.
Title/topic of research
Title of the article, year of publication (i.e., is the article new given that this field is changing rapidly)
Title, JEL classification, author(s), author('s) affiliation
Title/topic Abstract JEL key words
To be quite honest, I don't really look at all of the above information on a daily basis. What I look at is: (1) does the topic fit with the information I am looking for (so I look at the abstract) and (2) is it published in a good journal (i.e., does it have an impact factor, not so much what impact factor does it have or how high is it).

Top 5 journals in my field, the author I know, my research field will attract my attention.
Topic of the article. The decision was difficult because I am not that much interested in marketing, finance, or economics. The one article that seemed topical for me (e.g., Big Data in Management and *Business Horizons*) was then apparently the most interest to scholars in economics and finance. Plus, it was in a very low impact journal. So I wasn't very enthusiastic about it. The Pfeffer article was interesting because of Pfeffer but otherwise it appeared to be an econ article. The information generally conflicted. The category that might have helped was confounded, i.e., "Business Management and Accounting." It seemed like there were no articles that were relevant to OB, and when they seemed to be the other data suggested they were more relevant to econ, finance, or accounting. So all in all, I didn't much care to read any of these, sorry. I chose the Big Data in Economics but, from the title, I have little to no interest in this article. However, the data suggested that readers in my field might be interested in it, Pfeffer is not an econ scholar, and *Management Science* is not an econ journal. So I have a hope that the title is misleading.
Year of publication
Year of publication: the reason I chose the article "Big Data in Economics" was a combination of journal ranking and year of publication.
Year published
Yes
Yes, I look at relevance of the article topic to my current research, its potential to impact business "in the real world," and whether I have found other interesting articles in the same journal.
Yes, my universities journal rankings system (Quintiles) and the Australian Council of Deans of Business journal ranking. I use Q1 & 2, and A*, A, B*, B rankings as prestige factors.
Yes, the SSCI (Web of Science, Thompson Reuters) provides a quantile ranking of all journals within SSCI field categories based on impact factors. This is highly relevant for me.

2. Why would you be unlikely to use Altmetric information on the journal level?

–
–
1. Not very familiar with altmetric. 2) According to me, Facebook and Twitter are not very relevant for scientific information.
Adds no substantial information.
Altmetric information is interesting, but does not (in my opinion) provide any additional information on journals/articles that is relevant to how I select articles to read.
Altmetric is less familiar to me.

As mentioned before, nothing is better than checking the content of the article. So the presence of key words in the abstract is the indicator I use.
Because for me what matters more is the topic of the article.
Because I can find it at the article level and I find the journal Altmetric score not a good judge of journal quality.
Because I often search for "niche" papers that are by definition not popular enough to have high metrics' scores.
Because it is heavily based on media exposure.
Because it is not a commonly accepted indicator of prestige/impact at my institution.
Because it may give misleading information when you are comparing journals in different disciplines (economics, accounting, business, and management). I would use it to compare journals within the same discipline.
Because journal rankings are still more important as metrics in the scientific sphere.
Because sometimes highly ranked journals publish weak articles and vice versa. I can judge for myself whether the article is solid.
Because the decision is whether I find the article interesting and this is based on article quality. I do not see such a strong connection between Twitter and policy reports and article quality. I find Mendeley information based on semantic content interesting.
Because they do not measure scientific impact.
Bibliometric data and journal rankings are more relevant to me in terms of quality of the research and for publication of my own research.
Departments and field of research have long-time established quality of journals. For example, finance journal ranking is stable in the last decade. No need for any intermediary to confirm that or to change that ranking. Most of these platforms are redundant.
Don't fit into my search routines; online signal-to-noise ratio is too low.
Feels to be more practitioner-relevant.
General problem of altmetrics: not related to quality, short-time orientation.
Generalization not enough yet.
I already have a good idea of the quality of the journals in my field.
I am more interested in the content than the measures of quality (which can be misleading).
I am not familiar with it and don't really trust those crowd-based measures.
I am not so familiar with it.
I am not.
I am skeptical about metrics. It might originate in institutional dynamics rather than academic merits. Metrics can be useful against a backdrop of inflationary publication but nothing replaces title and abstract reading, to the least.
I assume that the Altmetric score depends a lot on the hype around a certain topic. For my research, I care little about how many people have already read a specific article. Only the quality of the article in terms of rigor is important. Rigor does not necessarily need to correlate with readership, unfortunately.
I believe that article-level information is most relevant, because it provides more specific information about the article I am considering. Moreover, journal-level metrics may not always reflect the quality of an article. Great articles could be published in lower ranked journals.

256

I combine all the information, being the topic, the author, and the cites, as the most important source to decide what to read.
I do not know it.
I do not need it.
I do not need more information.
I do not really understand the evaluation of altmetric.
I do not think it is that relevant to me, probably because I also do not yet fully understand it's potential.
I do use little of everything.
I don't care a lot about rankings. I look at abstracts first to see if the paper can interest me.
I don't know Altmetric very well.
I don't know it.
I don't see the value for my decision-making.
I don't think the quantities are relevant for most of my searches—I look for the fit to what I want to read about.
I may consider it to find out where to submit but would rather select the papers I read or cite based on the reputation of the journal that published them.
I never occupied myself with this kind of information. I have certain journals that I scan and take a look at the articles that sound interesting.
I read articles not journals.
I select papers mostly based on key words match/abstract. I am familiar with some top journals in my and relevant fields. Metrics in general are on limited marginal value.
I think I need to become more familiar with it, before I can evaluate its importance for me.
I think we should primarily select by content (topic, etc.) and all journal information should be secondary to that. Given good content, we should also select from reputable journals but we should not be driven by reputation as it is not the primary aspect of academic inquiry and social value.
I want to make my own judgment.
I wasn't aware of it until now so I will start paying more attention to it.
If I understand correctly, mentioning in the news or equivalent is on the level of the article not the journal. My hypothesis would be that this "mentioning" is based on the interest of topics rather than journals.
I'm not that interested in those measures, and academic management has no interest in altmetrics.
In my field of research (real estate), there are only a few journals. They are known quite well, thus bibliographic information is less useful than in other fields. Furthermore, I personally distrust the above mentioned rankings, metrics, etc. I choose between articles mainly on the basis of abstract, title, authors, reputation of authors, and some heuristics (e.g., the more an article relies on data from the United States, the less likely it is that I read it; reason: real estate markets are very different and findings cannot easily adapted to other international markets).
Indicates talk more than status, I guess. Anyway, new concept for me.

Initially I select articles based on topic/content and those I know to be thought/ranked highly from an accounting/social accounting perspective. Unlikely is possibly not the best word but not first choice. Equally there is an alternate ranking system in Australia.
It does not seem that relevant to my career as an academic.
It feels like a more popular perception of a journal rather on a scientific ground.
It is not always relevant; some articles are more basic research and will be less likely to be picked up by popular press. Papers with "fancy" insights might make it to mainstream media but this may not always be the best research. It may also encourage sloppy research as people will be looking for surprising results without being thorough.
It seems after the fact. Usually when I read articles they are relevant to my topic of research. I don't have time to read much outside of what I need to, sadly. I am unfamiliar with altmetrics—the possibility that the article was read by other researchers was interesting, but useful only in more recent articles. I don't really have time to dig out that kind of data and tend to go by topic, cites, journals, authors, and if I can see at a glance quality of methods.
It seems more like a popularity, not like an academic impact score.
It's difficult to find.
Lack of familiarity; personal network of information pointing to relevant authors, subjects, media.
Look for content of paper and relevance for my use rather than impact score.
N/A
N/A
Nearly pure quantitative figure. Does only provide limited addition information if compared with other rankings.
Never used it before.
No
No clear information about the underlying data.
No enough info on
No need, the top journals in my field is a common knowledge (based on long-term impact factor).
Not a big impact
Not a familiar indicator for me
Not aware
Not convinced it is impartial; can be manipulated more than impact factors, etc.
Not familiar with
Not important
Not necessarily quality that makes it to the media, social media, etc.
Not necessarily what the reader is looking for is in a high-ranked journal. Other variables include who are the authors (e.g., I have my favorite researchers and I read they work anywhere they publish) and the methodology/topic (e.g., you might be researching something which is eschewed by top journals).
Not so familiar with it.
Not sufficiently benchmarked, still signaling something subjective, as far as I am concerned.

Not sure if colleagues value this kind of information.
Not sure that citations come from peers, academic people, or scholars who are competent in that particular research area.
Not that useful in selecting interesting and high quality articles. Measures something else (public interest on the paper which is not equal to quality).
Not unlikely, just new for me.
One has to make sense of altmetric mentions, and there may be cases when the papers are essentially cited because they just feed the ego of the authors (and their "fan" club) while in other cases it may be legitimately relevant because of appropriate mentions by concerned citizens.
Other criteria are more important.
Other measures including IF are informative enough and I already know what top journals are in economics.
Probably not my common habit.
Quality of info?
Relevance of the article is the key thing. Journal metrics are often not a good indicator of article quality, and high-ranking journals can be reluctant to publish work challenging conventional paradigms.
Retired
See below
Seems ad hoc
That is not what I said. Altmetric information has to grow in breadth and scope before it is relevant to choose papers, although I always look at the information and consider it to some extent.
The altmetrics don't necessarily reflect informed academic opinion.
The general public is not a good judge of complex scientific content.
The primary reason to select which article to read first is its content expressed in title, abstract, key words.
The scope is too large.
There are too many rankings available. Altmetric is simply one among many and if a project is being discussed on Facebook is not necessarily a good criteria for its relevance. It simply lets you know that you have found a topic that people find interesting.
These do not reflect the impact in the scientific community.
This information could be biased.
Twitter/social media popularity is not a valid indicator of scientific rigor and scientific contribution and highly dependent on "sexiness of research topic."
Uncertain
Unclear origin
Where did I say that I was unlikely to use that? I am less likely to look at this because I do feel that it is a noisy signal.
Yes
Yes, as a reader No, as member of an editorial board, readership is important.
Yes

3. Why would you be unlikely to use Altmetric information on article level?

–
–
?
1. Not very familiar with altmetric.
2. According to me, Facebook and Twitter are not very relevant for scientific information.
Altmetric is less familiar to me.
As above
As above, general public may not be a good judge.
Attention does not equal quality, so journal rankings are still (more) important to me. If you cite literature in papers, the journals usually play a greater role for reviewers and editors because you can quickly see that it is a "good" or "bad" article in terms of journal ranking, while Altmetric scores do not appear in reference sections.
Because for me what matters more is the topic of the article.
Because I cannot be sure that the discussion is an academic discussion or other type of research dissemination.
Because I care more about content than anything else.
Because I choose my article based on the topic of interest, not because it is talked about.
Because it is not clear what it actually means.
Because the article can be interesting for me even if it is not interesting for other people.
cf. above reply.
Cites are more relevant to me than a metric encompassing more diverse forms of publication.
Depends. For own area of expertise, key issues are topic, journal + author. For areas outside own expertise, journal ranking, number of cites (age-corrected).
Difficult to see whether this is part of the scientific discourse.
Do not know what it is.
Do not really need it.
Don't have a good feel for what the metric means, whereas I can directly relate to citation counts.
Don't understand.
Easy to manipulate myself. Would make researchers invest a lot of time on marketing their articles on social media to manage impact. Similar to downloads at SSRN that can also be manipulated.
For my day-to-day work, content of the article is more important than popularity.
For new articles, article-level information does not provide much relevant information. For old articles, all I need to know is in the title/abstract + journal and author name.
General problem of altmetrics: not related to quality, short-time orientation.
Get that information from other sources.

I am not enough familiar with this index, I cannot appreciate whether it is relevant for me or not.
I am not so familiar with it.
I am not.
I am reluctant to take social media mentions as a measure of article quality.
I assume that the Altmetric score depends a lot on the hype around a certain topic. For my research, I care little about how many people have already read a specific article. Only the quality of the article in terms of rigor is important. Rigor does not necessarily need to correlate with readership, unfortunately.
I do not know it.
I do not know the altmetric.
I do not need more information.
I do not think it is that relevant to me, probably because I also do not yet fully understand it is potential.
I don't expect very technical articles to be highly ranked according to altmetrics, even if they are top papers.
I don't follow altmetric.
I don't know enough about it.
I don't think the mere quantities included are helpful.
I have other sources such as Social Sciences Citation Index.
I never occupied myself with this kind of information. I have certain journals that I scan and take a look at the articles that sound interesting.
I read for topics and content rather than field impact and similar statistics for readership (especially on social media).
I think I need to become more familiar with it, before I can evaluate its importance for me.
I wasn't aware of it until now so I will start paying more attention to it.
I would also look if the journal is within my discipline (economics), if it is well ranked and cited journal, and if the author is familiar to me (James Anderson is in this case).
If my understanding of this metric is correct, as well as your question, then see my previous comment.
If the article is on an important journal ranking list that my university uses, or is in a commonly recognized prestigious journal, but does not yet have many saves, etc.
If you search an article on a certain topic which is scarce, then I don't have the luxury to keep these scores into account.
I'm not sure who the people are who are downloading and mentioning the article.
I'm not that much interested in those measures, and academic management has no interest in altmetrics.
In reading articles to support my own research activity, I don't see social media exposure as relevant.
It does not measure scientific impact.
It is as before. All information is useful, but primarily we should select by content and then follow by assessing that the journal has value.

Given two articles of equal value in terms of content, then in order to prioritize one might choose the journal of greatest impact and/or the paper of greatest citations, but content must lead.

The scholar's own mind and interests must be the key arbiter of what to read and therefore all information about the journal and paper should be secondary.

It is no less probable than the other.
It seems more like a popularity, not like an academic impact score.
It is difficult to find.
Just one of the factors to consider.
N/A
N/A
Never used it before.
No
No enough info on.
No time, and not useful for screening of papers.
Not aware.
Not important.
Not so familiar with it.
Not sure if colleagues value this kind of information.
Not sure that citations come from peers, academic people, or scholars who are competent in that particular research area.
Not that useful in selecting interesting and high quality articles. Measures something else (public interest on the paper which is not equal to quality).
Not very intuitive nor essential.
Once again: The topic is "big data"—every article older than 2 years is too old. The metrics (all) are related to recent years.
Online presence doesn't guarantee the quality of the article.
Other criteria are more important.
Probably not my common habit.
Provides only limited information on whether other reader have similar intention when dealing with this topic.
Quality?
Reliability and validity of social media analysis.
Researchers do not use articles based on some scores, but in the light of the questions they examine.
Retired
s.o.
Same as above. Citation is enough as a measure of importance and if not I can also read the abstract to see whether it is interesting enough.
Same reason as above: many papers are cited because they have to be so. Citations are often short, allusive, and superficial. Citation nurtures further citation precisely owing to the logic of metrics. It says little of academic quality.
Same reasons; not impartial.
See above.

See answer above.
See below.
See below.
Similar reason. I have a good idea of those topics I wish to keep up with.
Simply because I did not know about it and thus I am not used to looking for this information.
Simply not interested.
Still in its infancy.
The fact that many discuss an article could be an expression of "herdentrieb."
The scientific content proxied by the impact factor of the journal is more important.
This information could be biased.
Too complicated information vis-a-vis value added.
Too general index.
Too little information/knowledge about it.
Too much focus on social media.
Topic not useful.
Unclear origin.
Unlikely to factor into my decision-making about the quality of the journal.
Why should I consider relevant an article based on how many people discuss it? This type of comparisons works within a popular field, but not for narrow and technical fields/subfields. In particular, it depends on the number of readers, authors, practitioners working in that field. The issue extends to the number of reads, citations, etc. I might start to use altmetric or other information if it will be proven informative about the quality of research. For the moment, I doubt it!
Yes

4. If you have any suggestions about the survey, or want to expand on any of your answers please leave a comment below.

–
–
–
Check my previous comments regarding year of publication, who are the authors, and method/topic.
Check the different perception of the importance of bibliometrics by discipline.
Create a better mobile view!
Don't start your survey by asking for personal information; that should come at the end of your survey and you should always allow respondents the option to opt out of certain answers (e.g., age). Speaking of age, how is that relevant to your study? Would it not be better to ask for years of experience in a particular field? On that note, I'm guessing that more senior scholars do not rely on these ranking indices as they are well aware of the high quality journals in their respective fields. Furthermore, we also tend to know who is working in particular areas and would focus on specific authors in our search for relevant articles for our research.

When making decisions for promotions and tenure, for example, we use citations provided by either Scopus or Google Scholar at my institution. Some of these indices may be useful when preparing a comparative list of acceptable journals across different disciplines; however, I would not use them to develop a reading list.

For journals I did not already know, I might be influenced by journal rankings, etc. But I would probably be more influenced by my article-level indicators such as cites. If it is within my discipline, I don't look at journal metrics, because I already know all the strong journals, and so not knowing the journal means it's weak. If I have to choose among articles in weak journals, it doesn't really matter which is the strongest of a weak bunch; in that case I'd look at citations (everybody use G. Scholar for that), article age, etc.

Good luck with your research!

Good luck.

Having been in the academic profession for now just over 30 years, I have a good sense of which journals are of high quality and which are not. To me, it is the reputation of the journal among the profession which is the decisive factor and how difficult it is to get an acceptance in that journal.

I am much less interested in metrics of the paper, and much more in its qualitative substance and originality. So, I have to read the abstract first to determine its intellectual merits. The rest for me is just a white noise perpetuated by the algorithmic management of publicity and superficial visibility.

I am not sure whether I understood the questions well. Found journal- and article-level information confusing. I generally search with search strings, or backward/forward snowballing from existing articles, then I consider the fit of the article based on title and abstract information. Then I check journal quality and start reading the full article.

I am of an age that remembers when the focus of business research was to have an impact on business "in the real world." None of these measures show this factor. They show the impact of an article on other academics, which should not be the primary purpose of doing research in an applied area such as business and management. If an impact factor of some sort could be developed that indicated how business people were affected by someone's research, then I might be more interested in using it to determine some of my reading. However, even then I would be extremely wary of simply using some factor to identify/screen my personal review of literature as no factor is perfect and missing out on an insight based on the excuse that it did not show up on someone's factor list is, in my mind, inexcusable.

I guess that the desired information cannot be obtained via a survey questionnaire. It might be more feasible to observe real user behavior on bibliographic catalogs/databases.

I have my set of journals that I follow + arxiv new publications + publications/news of a network of researchers that I know or worked with so I am not so much interested in objective measures like altmetric. I do not discard them, my approach may simply be related to the fact that I have been in this scientific business for quite some time. For new researchers and in new fields, it may be instruments.
Very nice survey, btw.

I look at the authors, the recency, and the title/abstract. I don't care too much about bibliometrics when choosing something to read on a topic.

I look at the researcher's academic affiliation.

I make very moderate use of bibliometrics because I choose articles that I wish to read on the basis of the topic, the author, the abstract, and the reputation of the journal according to common knowledge and my own experience.
I read papers linked with my subject. I do not have so much importance to the journal that publish them. If they had been cited by an interesting author, they can be useful for me. Be careful with the pact that my computer that there were a risk of virus when I open your survey. Maybe people will hesitate to answer you.
I select the papers to read based on the topic of my own interest.
I think people follow metrics on their own articles, but are less interested in journal-level metrics (they just follow some journals they think are worth following).
I think that you need to differentiate between three issues: 1. Selecting journal/article for reading (to increase my knowledge related to an issue) 2. Selecting a journal to submit my paper 3. Selecting journal/article for citing. Item 1: I select an article based on my need and my own professional judgment. Put it simply, I first skim over a paper to find out its relevance to my topic of interest, and its usefulness, and quality. To do so, I do not usually care about bibliometrics information, journal ranking, or altmetric. I will pay attention to bibliometrics information, journal ranking, or altmetric only in cases in which I cannot judge the relevance, usefulness, and quality. Item 2: I am in tenure track and the tenure track system is usually based on ABS or other well-known rankings. In my university, the tenure criteria are based on ABS ranking. So, I will follow it and I do not pay attention to bibliometrics information, journal ranking, or altmetric. Item 3: Ibid. However, for citing usually I also need to think about which journal I am submitting the paper. For instance, if I am submitting the paper to AMJ, I will cite more paper from AMJ. Best wishes.
I think the first question is flawed as in practice I would have read the abstracts and introduction of all four articles before deciding on which one to read in detail and focus on first.
I think you are conducting a potentially interesting study, but as I said above, academics tend to know the specific journals to look at without needing to look at impact factor, etc. You might want to take that into account, if you are not already doing so. Good luck!
I usually base my choices on the content of articles.
I was puzzled by the title of the last paper, suggesting that the article is more related to economics than to management.
I would avoid showing actual journal names as the individual images people have of them create uncontrollable variance. Maybe an attention check will help you to filter out those that didn't really read all the detailed information). Good luck!
If an article is relevant to me and high quality, I am usually directly familiar with the journal and its publication standards, or with the author themselves. I only use journal metrics when assessing publications in other subfields for purpose of tenure/promotion/salary review.

If I were to run this experiment, I would standardize the name of the journal and the title of the article, then I would present less information. It's too hard to keep track of all those things, although one indicator may be better than the other, it is not obvious. One thing I would avoid is to bias the subject toward journal he is closer to—that's why I would rather use fictitious names.

For me citations are important, but citations/year is more important discriminant on whether I should read the work. An old article with few citations is less important to read than an article that is new and has few citations. Reviewers will never gonna build on the former, while they could demand the knowledge of the latter.

In your example, I chose the paper on big data in economics because the topic is of much more interest to me than the other papers and because I know that *Management Science* is a good journal. I don't need any bibliometrics data to know what the good journals are for my research. More important than the journals and the articles data are the authors' data.

Isn't bibliometric information more important for selecting a journal in which to publish (and hence, for planning one's own career) than for selecting articles to read?

Journal rankings are always political in some way (the construction of the metrics employed in the rankings or the ranking process itself is usually biased, not necessarily intentionally by the source of the ranking). Journal quality is thus somewhat subjective and a function of the community of scholars to which one belongs (as I have published in two distinct business disciplines, I am conscious of the challenges of cross such community boundaries). Top journals do publish bad papers (bad in the sense that they are either uninteresting and make only trivial but rigorous contributions, or bad in the sense that they are flawed at the level of the paradigm in which they operate). Citation counts are measures of popularity. For example, my most cited articles on my own CV are not my best academic work. Rather, they were good pieces that were highly topical and timely, or provided a contribution that could be sufficiently broadly applied to generate lots of cites (e.g., framework/method papers tend to have this outcome). There is no substitute for reading a paper. Personally, I am opposed to rule-based ranking approaches and slavish following of citation counts—they do not necessarily reflect true quality. Most of what is valuable in a paper is not easily measurable, and attempts to measure impact, etc. only lead people to try to game the metrics for their own purposes (hence the politicization of journal rankings).

Key issue for me is the topic of the article, and also the authors. Journal title, independent of formal metrics, is also important.

N/A

N/A

N/A

No

No

No, I selected the article because it has the most relevant title.

None

Not the number of citations/readings is important! What matters is the content. All the scores are bad for science, because more papers are produced to get higher scores for the authors. Most of them are not read (but only clicked, what is counted as "read"). I would prefer much less papers with much better results.

Please include the title and the abstract in order to investigate how they compare with metrics.
Salting hit scores is easy and such indices constitute noise only.
See my previous response ("what other info would you use?"). I believe the survey task should be expanded to specify something like "Assume that all articles are equally relevant for the research project you are currently working on."
Sie arbeiten an einer deutschen Forschungeinrichtung und fragen deutsche Hochschullehrer - warum in einer Fremdsprache?
Some of these information items are more relevant when you decide where to publish rather than what to read (which is more about themes, key words, and the abstract).
Strange that you haven't mentioned Google Scholar's measurements. Are you looking at organization and country rankings? Virtually all of these measures are irrelevant if your management has a tight list of approved journals. (A seriously flawed approach in rapidly developing disciplines.)
The main criteria I use to select which article to read first are: relevance of the topic, reputation of the authors, and reputation of the journal.
The reason I choke the article I did was that it was in a journal that focuses on surveys, which the other don't. It would have been better if all journals focused on original contributions.
The survey should be wider. Do not consider only altmetric and Big Data, but many other sources of bibliographic data, for example, Google Scholar or Scopus and Web of Science. Also ResearchGate, which is the larger source of data, is never mentioned.
The topic of the article is most important in the decision, thereafter reading it will be the basis of deciding if I can refer to it or not.
The vignette asked me to imagine that I am part of the economics department (not management), yet the articles seemed to have been from management journals. Was this intentional?
The wording of some questions needed to be improved. The job position list is for the United States and Europe only, I am in Australia. For example, my job position is senior lecturer which is not in the list. Most of other job titles in Australia were not included. Another question was the discipline area—I work in the marketing discipline—is this part of business studies or "Other." You needed to provide a list of discipline areas that was comprehensive and mutually exclusive. Good luck with your research!
This is quite a strange survey, I think. I have never thought to read a paper based on stuff like this? I know the journals/authors in my area, so I would read the good journals/authors first. Perhaps this type of thing is more useful if you send me a paper about something/an area I know nothing about and then, I would need to go blind into it, and may use this type of stuff.
Title—implied audience—personal knowledge of journal profile.
To me, the title of the paper and the journal are most important in selecting what to look at. Thus, indicators of highly respected journals (in my area?) have an effect even if I do not consider them directly. Next, I would look at the abstract to see if I want to read more. Often I do not.

There are other ways to find out about papers but I am not sure that they are systematic enough to represent a search strategy to complete a literature review.

To pick up articles, I typically do not use bibliometric information at the article level. My selection at the beginning of the survey is entirely guided by the article's content and by the journal. I am interested in the specific content and prefer journals from my personal experience. I know they publish good stuff. Probably this is correlated with bibliometric indicators but very broadly and indirectly. I am skeptical about the assumption that people pick up article looking at very detailed bibliometric characteristics.

Very nice technical implementation! Other researchers could learn from this.

Very nicely designed.

Was quite complex having all those numbers.

What also got my attention is the title—seems more potentially relevant as many papers really tell me little that I can apply.

When I choose which article to read, my indicators are primarily: the topic of the article, the name of the journal it was published in (with time, one knows what type/quality/level of articles to expect in the common journals in one's field), the names and provenance of the authors, and their expertise in the topic. None of these appear in the information you have selected. The impact factor of the journal is useful only so far that it is correlated with the "good" journals in one's field. The rest of the information you provide is not very useful for me and I would not in general base my decision to read an article on that information.

When I was at the beginning of my career, I used citation as a source for reference. Now I go to the homepage of the researcher and I surf on the net.

When not knowing the Altmetric score, one doesn't have a reference whether such a score of 16 is large or not. For this reason, the last question cannot really be answered.

You might test people's knowledge and understanding of some of the sources, like altmetrics and Mendeley saves, prior to asking their decision. On the other hand, I skipped forward to find out and the info was there on the same page so I'm not sure it makes much difference. Depends on whether people are linear in their strategy, I bounced back and forth from info to decision. Having said that, a reminder of the relevance of these might be helpful. I'm assuming altmetrics is media and social media. Maybe I'm cynical but I don't really care how many Twitter mentions an article gets. What gets picked up as click bait is not always sound or meaningful science. God help us if we all end up investigating gender and ideology and social effects on watching cute kitten films while at work.

Your question on specifying "Country" can be misleading for international global citizens. For example, you could have "country of birth," "country (or countries) of citizenship," "country of educational attainment," "country currently employed." That would give you a better picture of the demographics of academics.

Also, often, none of the metrics are useful in choosing something to read/study. Journal reputation plays a huge role here. Also, academics read papers in prepublication format, for example, conference papers and discussion papers.

All in all I have enjoyed participating; a subject worth pursuing.